The Charlton Standard Catalogue of Canadian Coins

51ST EDITION 1997

W. K. CROSS
Publisher

The Charlton Press

TORONTO, ONTARIO
BIRMINGHAM, MICHIGAN

The National Library of Canada has catalogued this title as follows:

Main entry under title:
Charlton's standard catalogue of Canadian coins

29th ed. (winter 1980) -
Issues for winter 1981- have title: Charlton
standard catalogue of Canadian coins.
Continues: Standard catalogue of Canadian coins.
ISSN 0714-6701
ISBN 0-88968-169-4 (51st ed.)

1. Coins, Canadian - Periodicals.
2. Coins - Prices - Periodicals.

CJ1864.S82   737.4971   C82-031158-8

**Printed in Canada
in the Province of Quebec**

The Charlton Press

2040 Yonge Street, Suite 208
Toronto, Ontario, M4S 1Z9
Telephone: (800) 442-6042 Fax: (800) 442-1542

EDITORIAL

Editor	W. K. Cross
Editorial Assistant	Nicola E. Leedham
Editorial Assistant	Davina Rowan

SPECIAL MENTION

We wish to thank the American Numismatic Association and David Q. Bowers, the author of the "Official Grading Standards For U.S. Coins," for allowing us to use parts of their work in our introduction.

PANEL OF CONTRIBUTORS FOR THE 51ST EDITION

The publisher would like to thank the following individuals and institutions for all their assistance and work that made the 51st edition possible:

Individuals:

Ed Agopian
Bob Armstrong
Geoff Bell
Brian Cornwell
Peter Degraaf
Ron Fritz
Terry Frost
Nick Gerbinski
Jeffrey Hoare

Joe Iorio
Sean Issacs
Keith Kwallek
Ian Laing
James Lawson
Guy Lestrade
Tony Ma
Peter MacDonald
Charles Moore

Bill Popynick
Ken Potter
Hugh Powell
Michael Rogozinsky
Marc Verret
Michael Walsh
Verrol Whitmore
Randy Weir

Institutions:

Royal Canadian Mint - Ago Aarand and Pierre L. Morin
Bank of Canada, National Currency Collection - Hillel Kaslove and Graham Esler

TABLE OF CONTENTS

INTRODUCTION

The Charlton Standard Catalogue of Canadian Coins is an illustrated, descriptive price catalogue for the principal types of commercial and commemorative coins used in Canada over the years, including pre-Confederation regions. As a standard catalogue, it provides an accurate overview and introduction to Canadian numismatics and current market values. Each major variety of all issues of Canadian coins is listed, illustrated and priced. Several minor varieties that have a wide appeal to collectors, such as Arnprior dollars, are also included. Historical introductions provide important background information for each series, and relevant technical information is provided wherever available.

The new reader should find in this catalogue all the basic information needed to identify and evaluate individual coins as he or she embarks upon an old and widely enjoyed hobby. Continuing and expanding upon the completely revised and enlarged text introduced in the 32nd edition, readers will find herein more historical information, technical data and statistics than has ever before been compiled for a Canadian coin catalogue. A summary of the principal foreign coins used during the French and British regimes is included, as well as local, pre-decimal issues. The decimal series is complete for the provinces of British North America and Canada from its inception to the present, and also includes patterns, essais and test tokens.

This edition is just the latest in our continuing efforts to bring readers the best possible reference book for one of Canada's most popular and profitable pastimes. Welcome then to this new edition of the Charlton Standard Catalogue of Canadian Coins and the exciting field of Canadian numismatics.

THE COLLECTING OF CANADIAN DECIMAL COINS
PAST AND PRESENT

Today, the majority of those collecting Canadian numismatic material specialize in the decimal coin series. The collecting popularity of decimal coins is a relatively recent phenomenon, however. When Canada's first coin club was formed in Montreal in 1862, there was little interest in either coins or paper money. Eighty years later this was still the case. Most collectors specialized in Canadian tokens, the private coppers that served for so long as a medium of exchange in the absence of official coins. Decimal coins were mostly collected by type. One or two examples of each design were sufficient, and there was little concern regarding the relative scarcity of the various dates and varieties.

The current preoccupation with collecting decimal coins by date and variety arose in the 1940's, under the influence of U.S. dealer Wayte Raymond. Shortly after World War II and on into the 1950's, Canadian pioneers J. Douglas Ferguson, Fred Bowman, Sheldon Carroll and Leslie Hill attempted to establish the relative rarities of the decimal coins issued up to that time.

In 1950 collectors in the Ottawa area joined with scattered groups and individuals to form the Canadian Numismatic Association. Its official publication, and annual conventions beginning in 1954, served to bridge the miles and facilitate the exchange of information and ideas.

Two years after the C.N.A. was formed, the Charlton Standard Catalogue made its appearance. Early editions were modest paperback pamphlets with line drawings, but they were a serious attempt to list and price Canadian coins, tokens, paper money and some medals. The first hard-cover edition of 128 pages appeared in 1960. By 1971 it had grown to 200 pages, and by 1978 so much additional numismatic information was available that it was decided the needs of collectors could best be met by splitting the catalogue into separate, specialized works.

The 27th (1979) Edition became the *Standard Catalogue of Canadian Coins*, now issued yearly. This was followed by the annual edition of The Charlton Standard Catalogue of *Canadian Government Paper Money, The Standard Catalogue of Canadian Colonial Tokens*, and *The Charlton Standard Catalogue of Canadian Bank Notes*. A new title, "Canadian Commemorative Medals" is under development.

BUILDING A COLLECTION

Decimal coin collections can be formed in a variety of ways. Coins may come from pocket change, family hoards, the bank, the mint or from other collectors. In general, older coins no longer circulate and the excitement of searching through change for missing dates has been diminished by the withdrawal of most silver coins from circulation.

Collecting is a matter of individual taste. Some people collect by design type, others concentrate on one or two denominations or monarchs, while some brave souls try to collect the entire decimal series. Regardless of which path you choose, there is a variety of coin boards, envelopes and other supplies available to help house and organize your collection. For reasons of security many collectors keep their best coins in a bank vault.

Another decision that must be made when building a collection is the minimum state of preservation one will accept when buying coins. As a general rule, it is advisable to buy the best condition coins one can afford.

COMMEMORATIVE

A group of decimal coins that has attracted considerable international interest is the commemorative series. These coins have special designs to mark an event or the anniversary of an event.

The first commemoratives, beginning with the 1935 silver dollar, were issued for general circulation. However, in 1967 a new trend of producing commemoratives as collectors pieces only began, with no corresponding issue for general circulation. The two groups are listed separately below.

Commemorative Coins Struck for Collectors and for General Circulation

Date	Denomination	Composition	Event
1935	$1	Silver	George V Silver Jubilee
1939	$1	Silver	Royal Visit
1949	$1	Silver	Newfoundland
1951	5¢	Nickel	Discovery and Naming of Nickel
1958	$1	Silver	British Columbia as a Crown Colony
1964	$1	Silver	Confederation Conferences
1967	1¢	Copper	Confederation
1967	5¢	Nickel	Confederation
1967	10¢-$1	Silver	Confederation
1970	$1	Nickel	Manitoba
1971	$1	Nickel	British Columbia
1973	25¢	Nickel	Royal Canadian Mounted Police
1973	$1	Nickel	P.E.I. Centennial
1974	$1	Nickel	Winnipeg
1982	$1	Nickel	Constitution
1984	$1	Nickel	Cartier's Landing
1992	25¢ (12 pieces)	Nickel	125th Anniversary of Confederation
1992	$1	Nickel Plated Bronze	125th Anniversary of Canada
1994	$1	Nickel Plated Bronze	War Memorial

Commemorative Coins Struck for Collectors Only

Date	Denomination	Composition	Event
1967	$20	Gold	Confederation
1971	$1	Silver	British Columbia
1973	$1	Silver	Royal Canadian Mounted Police
1973-1976	$5 & $10	Silver	Olympics

Cont'd. ....

Date	Denom.	Comp.	Event	Date	Denom.	Comp.	Event
1974	$1	Silver	Winnipeg	1990	$200	Gold	Canada Flag Sil. Jub.
1975	$1	Silver	Calgary	1990	$30	Platinum	Polar Bear
1976	$1	Silver	Library of Parliament	1990	$75	Platinum	Polar Bear
1976	$100	Gold	Olympics	1990	$150	Platinum	Polar Bear
1977	$1	Silver	Elizabeth II Silver Jubilee	1990	$300	Platinum	Polar Bear
1977	$100	Gold	Elizabeth II Silver Jubilee	1991	$1	Silver	Frontenac
1978	$1	Silver	Commonwealth Games	1991	$20	Silver	A.E.A. Silver Dart
1978	$100	Gold	Canadian Unity	1991	$20	Silver	de Havilland Beaver
1979	$1	Silver	The Griffon	1991	$100	Gold	Empress of India
1979	$100	Gold	Year of the Child	1991	$200	Gold	A National Passion
1980	$1	Silver	Arctic Territories	1991	$30	Platinum	Snowy Owl
1980	$100	Gold	Arctic Territories	1991	$75	Platinum	Snowy Owl
1981	$1	Silver	Trans-Canada Railway	1991	$150	Platinum	Snowy Owl
1981	$100	Gold	"O Canada"	1991	$300	Platinum	Snowy Owl
1982	$1	Silver	Regina Centenary	1992	$1	Silver	Stagecoach
1982	$100	Gold	Cdn. Constitution	1992	$20	Silver	Curtis JN-4
1983	$1	Silver	World Univ. Games	1992	$20	Siilver	DeHavilland G. Moth
1983	$100	Gold	Sir Humphrey Gilbert	1992	$100	Gold	City of Montreal
1984	$1	Silver	150th Toronto Anniv.	1992	$175	Gold	The Olympic Vision
1984	$100	Gold	450th Cartier Anniv.	1992	$200	Gold	Niagara Falls
1985	$1	Silver	National Parks	1992	$30	Platinum	Cougar
1985	$20	Silver	Winter Olympics	1992	$75	Platinum	Cougar
1985	$100	Gold	National Parks	1992	$150	Platinum	Cougar
1986	$1	Silver	Vancouver	1992	$350	Platinum	Cougar
1986	$20	Silver	Winter Olympics	1993	$1	Silver	Stanley Cup
1986	$100	Gold	Year of Peace	1993	$20	Silver	Fairchild
1987	$1	Silver	Davis Strait	1993	$20	Silver	Lockheed
1987	$20	Silver	Winter Olympics	1993	$100	Gold	Horseless Carriage
1987	$100	Gold	Winter Olympics	1993	$200	Gold	R.C.M.P.
1988	$1	Silver	St. Maurice	1993	$30	Platinum	Arctic Fox
1988	$20	Silver	Winter Olympics	1993	$75	Platinum	Arctic Fox
1988	$100	Gold	Bowhead Whale	1993	$150	Platinum	Arctic Fox
1989	$1	Silver	MacKenzie River	1993	$300	Platinum	Arctic Fox
1989	$100	Gold	Ste. Marie	1994	$1	Silver	R.C.M.P.
1990	$1	Silver	Henry Kelsey	1994	$20	Silver	Curtis HS-2L
1990	$20	Silver	Anson and Harvard	1994	$20	Silver	Vickers Vedette
1990	$20	Silver	Lancaster	1994	$100	Gold	Home Front
1990	$100	Gold	Literacy Year	1994	$200	Gold	Anne of Green Gables

AGE - RARITY - DEMAND - CONDITION - VALUE

The value of a coin on the numismatic market is dictated by a complex mixture of factors. One feature that those unfamiliar with coins often mistakenly believe to be of great importance is age. That age is a minor contributor to value is illustrated by the fact that the 1969 Large Date variety 10 cents is worth far more than the 1870 10-cent piece, a coin nearly 100 years older!

Basically, a coin's value is determined by a combination of supply and demand. The 1870 50-cent piece does not command as high a premium as the 1921 coin of the same denomination because there are many more 1870s than 1921s available. On the other hand, the variety of the 1872H 50-cents with an "A" punched over the "V" in "VICTORIA" on the obverse sells for about the same as the variety with a normal "V" even though the coins from the blundered die are much rarer. The modest price difference reflects the slight difference in demand.

Finally, the state of preservation of a coin markedly influences its value. It is not unusual for an uncirculated (brand new) George V silver coin, for example, to sell for 50 times what a coin of the same date and denomination would bring in well-worn condition.

GRADING CANADIAN COINS

Canadian coins, as with coins of any other country, can be distinguished from each other by a simple comparison of their coin type, denomination, and date of issue. Coins of the same type, denomination and date can be further identified from each other by each coin's "condition" or state of preservation.

Coin conditions vary considerably. They range from the poorest state where the date and other details can barely be determined to the best states where details are as sharp and clear as the moment the coin was minted. Generally coin conditions are dvided into one or two categories, namely, circulated condition or uncirculated condition. Examples of circulated coins are those that you might find in pocket change. These coins have varying degrees of surface wear as a result of human handling or use as "money" in our world of commerce. Uncirculated coins (also called mint state coins) differ from circulated coins in that they must have absolutely no visible signs of wear on any part of the coin's surface. However uncirculated coins are not necessarily flawless. The majority will still have small marks, as opposed to wear, which are a result of contact with other coins received when they were distributed by the mint to our banking system in large bags.

Once a coin's condition is understood it can be assigned one of a number of circulated or uncirculated "grades" according to grading standards accepted by the coin industry in Canada. Early standards for grading Canadian coins that appeared in the first Charlton catalogue in 1952 used terms like Very Good and Extremely Fine to describe some of these grades. Since that time coin grading has been considerably refined. Today there are ten offically recognized grades for circulated coins and a further ten to designate all of the uncirculated grades, although only five of the latter are generally in use.

Since 1979 the Charlton Standard Catalogue has utilized a grading system similar to that accepted by the American Numismatic Association for United States coinage in 1977. Some of the following general text has been reproduced from "The Official ANA Grading Standards for United States Coins". We wish to express our appreciation to the American Numismatic Association for allowing us to do so.

ADJECTIVAL AND NUMERICAL GRADING SYSTEMS

New coin collectors and investors are often confused when they read or hear about an adjectival grading scheme on the one hand and a numerical system on the other. There is no need for this confusion. Both systems use the same grade definitions. They simply refer to them by different labels.

Adjectival grading, as the name implies, uses adjectives to describe coin grades. This scheme has been in use since the earliest days of Canadian numismatics and is therefore the traditional grading nomenclature. The following adjectives represent most of the officially accepted grades (from poorest quality to best) in use today: About Good (AG), Good (G), Very Good (VG), Fine (F), Very Fine (VF), Choice Very Fine (Choice VF), Extremely Fine (EF), Choice Extremely Fine (Choice EF), About Uncirculated (AU), Choice About Uncirculated (Choice AU)), Typical Uncirculated (Unc. or BU), Select Uncirculated (Select Unc.), Choice Uncirculated (Choice Unc.), Gem Uncirculated (Gem Unc.) and Perfect Uncirculated (Perfect Unc.).

The numerical grading system is a modern day development by comparison. It was devised by Dr. William Sheldon in the late 1940's. Sheldon's numerical grading scale used numbers ranging from one to seventy. All circulated grades were assigned in the range of 1 to 59 while the numbers from 60 to 70 were reserved for the uncirculated grades. His intent was to have a grading scheme that would inter-relate both coin grades and coin prices for each grade. He accomplished this by assigning specific numbers from these ranges to each of the traditionally used adjectival grades. A summary of these adjectival grades with his numerical designation follows:

About Good-3, Good-4, Very-Good 8, Fine-12, Very Fine-20, Choice Very Fine-30, Extremely Fine-40, Choice Extremely Fine-45, About Uncirculated-50, Choice About Uncirculated-55, Typical Uncirculated-60, Select Uncirculated-63, Choice Uncirculated-65, Gem Uncirculated-67, Perfect Uncirculated-70.

The basis of his actual number selection was the relative prices of early American copper coins in each of the various grades. For example, in the late 1940's, a typical uncirculated coin (MS-60) was determined to be about 7 1/2 times the price of a typical Very Good (VG-8) example of the same kind and so on.

The numerical system has now been extended beyond early American copper coins to include most areas of North American numismatics. Sheldon's number assignments no longer have any relevance to current coin pricing as they once did. Today a typical MS-60 coin might easily be priced 50 to 100 times more than a typical VG-8 coin of the same kind! Unfortunately this only adds to the confusion of those graders who expect his number assignments to have some special pricing or other scientific meaning.

ABOUT THE PRICING IN THIS CATALOGUE

The purpose of this catalogue is to give the most accurate, up-to-date retail prices for all Canadian coinage. To this end, we have from the very inception of this catalogue, used a pricing panel of established experts who submit the most current market values from across Canada. These individual market results are drawn from both dealer and collector activity, recent auction results are averaged to reflect the current marketplace for Canadian coins.

A necessary word of caution. No catalogue can or should propose to be a fixed price list. Except in the case of newly minted coinage (where the published price is actually a manufacturers suggested retail price) collector interest, rarity factors and other vagaries of the hobby itself invariably dictate published retail values.

This catalogue then, should be considered as a guide, showing the most current retail prices possible for the collector and dealer alike.

COIN GRADING AND HUMAN NATURE

Before actually trying to understand all of the rules relating to coin grading, it is equally important to appreciate the human elements that often surround the act of grading a coin. Inexperienced coin graders are often dismayed by the seemingly large number of grading arguments, some very heated, that arise within this industry. Why are there differences of opinion in the field of grading coins? There are numerous reasons, but the most common are as follows:

Grading coins can never be completely scientific in all areas. A great deal of human judgement is also involved. One may weigh a coin and also obtain its specific gravity by mechanical devices and the result will be factual if accurate equipment is used carefully. There are no scientific means available to measure the surface condition — the amount of wear — of a coin.

In grading coins, considerations such as striking, surface of the planchet, the presence of heavy toning (which may obscure certain surface characteristics), the design, and other factors each lend an influence. A panel containing a dozen of the foremost numismatic industry leaders justifiably could have some **slight** difference of opinion on the precise grade of some coins.

However, it is not **slight** differences which concern us here; it is serious or major differences. The term "overgrading" refers to describing a coin as a grade higher than it actually is. For example, if a coin in AU (About Uncirculated) grade is called Uncirculated, it is overgraded. If a coin in Very Fine grade is called Extremely Fine, it is overgraded.

What induces overgrading? Here are some of the factors:

Buyers Seeking Bargains. The desire to get a bargain is part of human nature. If a given Uncirculated coin actively traded at $100 is offered at $70, it will attract a lot of bargain seekers. These same buyers would reject an offering such as: "I am offering this stock which trades on the New York Stock Exchange for $100 for just $70 cash," or "I am offering $100 bills for $70 each."

In coins, as in any other walk of life, you get what you pay for. If a coin which has a standard value of $100 is offered for $70 there may be nothing wrong, but chances are that the piece is overgraded.

False Assumptions. Buyers often assume falsely that any advertisement which appears in a numismatic publication has been approved by that publication. Actually, publishers cannot be expected to examine coins and approve of all listings offered. A person who has no numismatic knowledge or experience whatsoever can have letterheads and business cards printed and, assuming he has good financial and character references (but not necessarily numismatic expertise), run large and flashy advertisements. Months or years later it is often too late for the deceived buyer to get his money back. The solution to this is to learn how to grade coins and think for yourself. Examine the credentials of the seller. Is he truly an expert in his field? How do you know? What do collectors with more experience think of this seller? To what professional organizations does this dealer belong? It is usually foolish to rush and spend your hard-earned money with a coin seller who has no professional credentials and whose only attraction is that he is offering "bargains." Think for yourself!

The Profit Motive. Sellers seeking an unfair markup may overgrade. For purposes of illustration, let us assume that a given variety of coin is worth the following prices in these grades: AU $75, and Uncirculated $150. A legitimate dealer in the course of business would buy, for example, an AU coin at $50 or $60 and sell it retail for $75, thus making a profit of $15 to $25. However, there are sellers who are not satisfied with the normal way of doing business. They take shortcuts. They pay $50 or $60 for the same AU coin which is worth $75 retail, but rather than calling it AU they call it "Uncirculated" and sell it for $150. So, instead of making $15 to $25 they may make $90 to $100!

Inexperience or error on the part of the seller may lead to incorrect grading — both overgrading and undergrading.

GRADING CIRCULATED COINS

Once a coin enters circulation it begins to show signs of wear. As time goes on the coin becomes more and more worn until, after a period of many decades, only a few of the coin's original detailed features may be left. Some coins that have not entered circulation may still show signs of wear, usually through mishandling and poor storage. These too must be graded as circulated coins, as long as there is some visible sign of wear to the naked eye.

While numbers from 1 through 59 are continuous, it has been found practical to restrict their use to the limited number that follow. Hence, this text uses the following descriptions and their numerical equivalents.

Choice About Uncirculated-55. Abbreviation: AU-55. Only a small trace of wear is visible on the highest points of the coin. As is the case with other grades here, specific information is listed in the following text under the various types, for wear often occurs in different spots on different designs.

About Uncirculated-50. Abbreviation: AU-50. With traces of wear on nearly all of the highest areas. At least half of the original mint lustre is present.

Choice Extremely Fine-45. Abbreviation: EF-45. With light overall wear on the coin's highest points. All design details are very sharp. Mint lustre is usually seen only in protected areas of the coin's surface.

Extremely Fine-40. Abbreviation: EF-40. With only slight wear but more extensive than the preceeding, still with excellent overall sharpness. Traces of mint lustre may still show.

Choice Very Fine-30. Abbreviation: VF-30. With light even wear on the surface; design details on the highest points lightly worn, but with all lettering and major features sharp.

Very Fine-20. Abbreviation: VF-20. As preceeding but with moderate wear on highest parts.

Fine-12. Abbreviation: F-12. Moderate to considerable even wear. Entire design is bold. All lettering visible, but with some weaknesses.

Very Good-8. Abbreviation: VG-8. Well worn. Most fine details such as hair strands, leaf details, and so on are worn nearly smooth.

Good-4. Abbreviation: G-4. Heavily worn. Major designs visible, but with faintness in areas. Other major features visible in outline form without centre detail.

About Good-3. Abbreviation: AG-3. Very heavily worn with portions of the lettering, date and legends being worn smooth. The date is barely readable.

Note: The exact descriptions of circulated grades vary widely from issue to issue, so the preceeding commentary is only of a very general nature. It is essential to refer to a detailed grading guide when grading any coin.

HELPFUL TIPS WHEN GRADING CIRCULATED COINS

While circulated coins are graded primarily by the amount of wear shown on the coin's surfaces, it is sometimes difficult for beginner graders to appreciate just how much wear is allowable at each grade level. Several grading aids can help the beginner achieve a reasonable degree of grading accuracy and consistency from coin to coin:

(a) Standard photographs of coins of each coin type and grade are helpful for comparison grading. They indicate the approximate wear you can expect on a typical coin of that series and grade.
(b) Familiarize yourself with all of a coin's highest points of relief before trying to decide if the coin shows signs of wear or is strictly uncirculated.
(c) Circulated coins are more abundant in the commercial marketplace than uncirculated coins. This offers the novice grader ample opportunity to visually check with many graders for their interpretation of what constitutes each of the circulated grades. This is a more detailed form of comparison grading than (a).

Ask a recognized grading authority to criticize your grading ability and technique. Listen and learn from the professionals if you want to grade well.

GRADING UNCIRCULATED COINS

As the name implies, an uncirculated coin is one that has never been in circulation. Such coins must show absolutely no signs of wear to the naked eye. However the actual grade of the coin is determined by assessing three specific factors (none involving surface wear as with circulated coins) and furthermore can be influenced by still other considerations. Uncirculated coins are more difficult to grade than circulated coins. Some of the reasons are:

(a) **Three primary grading factors -** the grade of an uncirculated coin is determined by assessing the qualities of each of the coin's lustre, surface condition and fullness of strike. Furthermore these factors are inter-dependent. That is, if one factor is of truly exceptional quality it can "make-up" for a deficiency in the quality of another factor.
(b) **Toning is not a grading factor -** unlike popular belief, the toning that might be present on a coin and which might add considerably to the coin's overall eye appeal is not to be considered one of the grading elements. Toning is an enhancing feature that might affect the coins final price but not its grade. Coins that are toned are best graded as if they were fully brilliant. Toning, if present, is described separately from the grade with such adjectives as "attractive rainbow toning" and so on.
(c) **Understand typical mintstate characteristics -** it is not possible to accurately grade an uncirculated coin unless the grader understands what qualities to expect for each of the factors of lustre, surfaces, and strike for a coin of that type. This is the main reason why graders of another country's coins can find so much difficulty in properly grading Canadian coins.
(d) **Understand the coinage metal -** the strike and surface quality of an uncirculated coin is partially dependent on the base metal used in the manufacture of a coin. Coin graders must understand that each of the metals of nickel, copper, gold and silver vary dramatically in the damage they will sustain when they come in contact with other hard objects. Gold coins are relatively soft and heavy. They damage easily. Nickel coins are very hard and often display mushy strikes.
(e) **Expect marks on normal uncirculated coins -** with the exception of certain special mint sets made in recent years for collectors. Uncirculated or normal production struck coins were produced on high speed presses, stored in bags together with other coins, run through counting machines, and in other ways handled without regard to numismatic posterity. As a result, it is the rule and not the exception for an Uncirculated coin to have bag marks and evidence of coin-to-coin contact, although the coin might not have had actual commercial circulation. The number of such marks will depend upon the coin's actual size and metal composition.

(f) **Striking and minting peculiarities -** certain early coins have mint-caused planchet or adjustment marks, a series of parallel striations. If these are visible to the naked eye they should be described adjectively in addition to the numerical or regular descriptive grade. For example: "MS-60 with adjustment marks," or "MS-65 with adjustment marks," or "Perfect Uncirculated with very light adjustment marks," or something similar.

If an Uncirculated coin exhibits weakness due to striking or die wear, or unusual (for the variety) die wear, this must be adjectively mentioned in addition to the grade. Examples are: "MS-60, lightly struck," or "Choice Uncirculated, lightly struck," and MS-70, lightly struck."

DEFINITIONS FOR UNCIRCULATED COINS

Uncirculated coins may be assigned one of a possible five grades that are officially in use within the numismatic industry. These are (with their numerical grade in brackets): Uncirculated (Mintstate-60), Select Uncirculated (MS-63), Choice Uncirculated (MS-65), Gem Uncirculated (MS-67) and Perfect Uncirculated (MS-70). The use of the remaining numbers in the range from 60 to 70 is not recommended. To do so might suggest or attach a degree of grading accuracy that is either unwarranted or unrecognizeable to all but the most expert of graders. The definitions for each of the uncirculated grades are:

Perfect Uncirculated (MS-70). MS-70 is the finest quality available. Such a coin under 4X magnification will show no marks, lines or other evidence of handling or contact with other coins. The strike will be full and show all of the detail as intended by the engraver. The coin's lustre will be of the highest imagineable quality for a coin of that particular series or type.

A brilliant coin may be described as "MS-70, Brilliant" or "Perfect Brilliant Uncirculated." A lightly toned coin may be described as "MS-70, Toned" or "Perfect Toned Uncirculated." In the case of particularly attractive or unusual toning, additional adjectives may be used such as "Perfect Uncirculated with attractive irridescent peripheral toning."

Note for copper coins: To qualify as MS-70 or Perfect Uncirculated, a copper coin must have its full lustre and original natural surface colour, and may not be toned brown, olive or any other colour. Copper coins with toned surfaces which are otherwise perfect should be described as MS-67 as the following text indicates.

Gem Uncirculated (MS-67). MS-67 coins will appear as perfect coins to all but the most expert of graders. They are exceptional in all respects: superb surfaces, superb lustre and full strike or nearly so. If there are any negatives they will not be obvious at first glance but discovered only after extensive study and with 4X magnification.

Choice Uncirculated (MS-65). An MS-65 coin is easily distinguished from lower grades of uncirculated coins by its distinctive "quality" look. To the normal naked eye an MS-65 coin will appear "almost" perfect at first glance. Only under more detailed examination will minor flaws be discovered. The coin's lustre will usually be better than typically seen for uncirculated coins of this type. The strike will be at least typical for the series if not better. The surfaces will show only slight marks that will not at all be distracting to the overall appeal of the coin. Occasionally one of these factors may be of such high quality as to make-up for another factor which is less than desirable; ie. superb lustre accommodating one extra slight bagmark.

Select Uncirculated (MS-63). An MS-63 coin is basically a nice example of an MS-60 which does not meet the strict "quality" requirements of an MS-65. Many of the MS-63 coin's features will be attractive and at least typical of what you would expect of a new coin of this particular type. The surface marks generally are noticeable but their number and size are such that they are not major or bothersome distractions to the viewer. The lustre is generally attractive but may have a slight dullness or dull areas. The strike is most likely typical for the series. Often MS-63 coins are MS-65 coins that have slight "problems" such as "one mark too many" and so on. Very often one grading factor, with exceptional qualities not normally expected at this grade, will make up for weaker factors (eg. flawless surface makes up for dulled, less than typical lustre).

Typical Uncirculated (MS-60). An MS-60 coin will have a moderate number of bag marks of varying sizes depending on the softness of the coin's metal. The surfaces may have what is typically described as a "baggy" look. Also present may be minor edge nicks but none of a major concern. Unusually deep marks, however caused, must be described separately. The lustre may be impaired by dullness from cleaning and the like and consequently be considered less than typical for a new coin of this type. The strike may show clear evidence of weaknesses in one or more areas. Many of the coins "problems" will be distracting to anyone who thinks a "new" coin is in near-perfect condition.

SELECTION OF AN UNCIRCULATED GRADE

The definitions of the uncirculated grades at each end of the grading range (ie. MS-60 and MS-70) are straightforward. The MS-60 coin must show no signs of wear. The MS-70 coin must be perfect as defined earlier. Most graders have difficulty with the in-between uncirculated grades of MS-63, MS-65 and MS-67. This also seems to be the area where most grading conflicts exist. These difficulties arise because graders (a) are unfamiliar with a particular coin's typical mintstate characteristics which serve as a reference point, and (b) do not really appreciate that the factors of lustre, surfaces and strike can inter-relate with each other, ie. that trade-offs can exist at each grade level. Graders of uncirculated coins must appreciate the following:

(a) **Lustre qualities -** An uncirculated coin with excellent lustre can make an otherwise undesirable uncirculated coin desirable. That's because lustre, especially that which is 'alive' or 'blazing' can add considerably to a coin's overall eye appeal and divert attention away from other distracting problems with the coin. On the other hand, lustre that is dull or lifeless can have the opposite effect on the coin viewer and make the coin a very undesirable object.

(b) **Surface condition -** An uncirculated coin is judged for the number, size and location of marks (as opposed to wear) on its surfaces. Coins that have fewer marks are more desirable that those that have many and look "baggy". Smaller marks are preferred to those that are large and very distracting. Marks, if they are to be present at all, are preferred to be hidden in unnoticeable places such as in the coin's detail rather than in open areas where they can be very distracting. Marks that are awkwardly located, such as on the nose of the monarch, are undesirable because they lower the aesthetic appeal of the coin.

(c) **Strike qualities -** All uncirculated coins are judged for the quality of their strike relative to that typically seen on a mintstate coin of that particular series. Generally the fuller a coin's strike, the more desirable the coin. Strike qualities can vary considerably within the Canadian decimal series and even from date to date within a specific type series.

(d) **Inter-relationship of grading factors -** Particularly for the in-between grades of MS-63, MS-65 and MS-67, the three factors of lustre, surfaces and strike can occur in many combinations to still yield the same overall grade selection. The coin grader must therefore develop a "feel" for how one factor that might be of exceptional quality can make up for another that is slightly deficient from that typicaly expected.

HELPFUL HINTS FOR GRADING UNCIRCULATED COINS

Grading uncirculated coins is a more complex and demanding task than that required by circulated coins. To help achieve a reasonable degree of grading accuracy and grading consistency from uncirculated coin to uncirculated coin, graders should develop the following grading habits:

(a) Always follow a fixed grading routine. Grading an uncirculated coin requires mental preparation, having the right equipment, studying the coin, analyzing the observed data, selecting a grade and checking your decision for reasonableness.

(b) Study heavily toned coins carefully. Use good lighting and a strong magnifier. Toning can hide marks and other serious coin problems.

(c) Examine coins under a wide range of lighting sources and angles at which the light strikes the coin's surfaces. Lighting can be very deceptive.

(d) Do not attempt to grade too many coins at one sitting. For best results your eyes must be relaxed. Allow ample time to consider all factors.

(e) Clearly understand the typical mintstate characteristics of the coin type that you are about to grade. This is your reference point to tell you what to expect so that you can then accurately select a grade.

SPLIT AND INTERMEDIATE GRADES

It is often the case that because of the peculiarities of striking or a coin's design, one side of the coin will grade differently from the other. In this situation, a diagonal mark is used to separate the two. For example, a coin with an AU-50 obverse and a Choice Extremely Fine-45 reverse can be described as AU-EF or alternatively 50/45. If, in the preceeding example, the grader chooses to select only one overall or composite grade to describe the coin, then the lower of the two grades must be chosen, ie. Choice Extremely Fine-45.

Most advanced collectors and dealers find the official grade designations to be sufficient to fairly describe the majority of coins that appear in the marketplace. However, some coins might more than meet the minimum requirements of one grade but not quite those of the next higher grade. The use of intermediate grades such as EF-42 or EF-43 to describe a nice example of an EF coin is not encouraged. Grading is not that precise and such finely split intermediate grades suggests a degree of accuracy that probably can not be verified by other numismatists. In this situation the best policy is to stick with the official designation of EF-40 and append adjectives to the grade such as in "a nice example of EF-40" and so on.

LIGHTING AND MAGNIFICATION

The same coin can have a different appearance depending upon the lighting conditions and also the amount of magnification used to examine it. For purposes of standardization, we recommend that a magnifying glass of four to eight power be used. This is sufficient to reveal all the differences and peculiarities necessary to grade the coin accurately. At the same time it is not too much magnification. Under extensive magnification — 10 power or more — even the finest coin may show many marks and imperfections in an exaggerated fashion. You may wish to keep a stronger magnifying glass on hand, however, for examination of minute die details.

It is also desirable to use a magnifying glass of sufficient width so that a fairly large amount of the coin's surface can be studied at one time.

Recommended for grading is a 100 watt incandescent light bulb approximately three feet (one metre) from the coin (or a 50 watt bulb at about half the distance, or other equivalents). Incandescent light furnishes a pinpoint light source and enables surface characteristics to be studied in more detail. Fluorescent light, which spreads illumination from a diffused origin, is apt to conceal minute differences. "Tensor" type lamps, popular at coin conventions, furnish a high intensity pinpoint light source and are satisfactory for grading.

To grade a coin, hold it between your fingertips (over a soft surface to prevent damage in the event of dropping) at an angle so that light from the bulb reflects from the coin's surface into your eye. Turn or rotate the coin horizontally so that different characteristics can be observed in better detail. You will want to examine the edge also.

Lamp wattages and magnifying intensities are less critical with circulated grades. They are very important, however, for Uncirculated and Proof coins where judgment is dependant upon relatively small differences in surface appearance.

NATURAL COLOURATION OF COINS

Knowledge of the natural colour which coinage metals acquire over a period of years is useful to the collector. To an extent, a coin's value is determined by the attractiveness of its colouration. Also, certain types of unnatural colour might indicate that a coin has been cleaned or otherwise treated.

The basic coinage metals used in Canada are alloys of copper, nickel, silver and gold. Copper tends to tone the most rapidly. Gold is the least chemically active and will tone only slightly and then only over a long period of years.

Copper. Copper is among the most chemically active of all coinage metals. When a copper coin is first struck, it emerges from the dies with a brilliant pale orange surface.

Once a freshly minted copper coin enters the atmosphere it immediately begins to oxidize. Over a period of years, especially if exposed to actively circulating air of if placed in contact with sulphites, the coin will acquire a glossy brown surface. In between the brilliant glossy brown stages it will be part red and part brown.

An Uncirculated coin with full original mint brilliance, usually slightly subdued in colouration, is typically described as Brilliant Uncirculated (our example here is for a typical Uncirculated or MS-60 coin); a Choice piece would be called Choice Brilliant Uncirculated, and so on. One which is part way between the brilliant and brown surface hues would be called Red and Brown Uncirculated. Specimens with brownish surfaces can be called Brown Uncirculated. Particularly valuable coins can have the colouration described in more detail. Generally, in any category of grading, the more explanation given, the more accurate the description.

Early copper coins with full original mint brilliance are more valuable than Red and Brown Uncirculated or Brown Uncirculated pieces. The more original mint brilliance present, the more valuable a coin will be. The same is true of Proofs.

Circulated copper coins are never fully brilliant, but are toned varying shades of brown.

Nickel. Uncirculated nickel coins when first minted are silver/gray in appearance, not as bright as silver but still with much brilliance. Over a period of time nickel coins tend to tone a hazy gray. Circulated nickel coins have a gray appearance.

Silver. When first minted, silver coins have a bright silvery-white surface. Over a period of time silver, a chemically active metal, tends to tone deep brown or black. Uncirculated and Proof silver pieces often exhibit very beautiful multi-coloured iridescent hues after a few years. The presence of attractive toning often increases a silver coin's value. Advanced collectors will often prefer attractive toned coins. Beginners sometimes think that "brilliant is best." Circulated silver coins will often have a dull gray appearance, sometimes with deep gray or black areas.

Gold. When first struck, gold coins are a bright yellow-orange colour. As gold coins are not pure gold but are alloyed with copper and traces of other substances, they do tend to tone over a period of time. Over a period of decades, a gold coin will normally acquire a deep orange colouration, sometimes with light brown or orange-brown toning "stains" or streaks in certain areas (resulting from improperly mixed copper traces in the alloy). Light toning does not affect the value of a gold coin.

Very old gold coins, particularly those in circulated grades, will sometimes show a red oxidation. Gold coins which have been recovered from treasure wrecks after centuries at the sea bottom will sometimes have a minutely porous surface because of the corrosive action of sea water. Such pieces sell for less than specimens which have not been so affected. Care must be taken to distinguish these from cast copies which often have a similar surface.

HANDLING AND STORAGE OF COINS

As a coin collector you are commissioned by posterity to handle each coin in your possession carefully and to preserve it in the condition in which it was received.

When examining a coin you should hold it by its edges and over a cloth pad or other soft surface. In this way if it accidentally falls no harm will be done. A coin should never be touched on either of its faces, obverse or reverse, for the oil and acid in one's skin will eventually leave fingerprints - if not soon, then years later. Also, one should avoid holding a coin near one's mouth while talking as small drops of moisture may land on the coin's surface and later cause what are commonly referred to as "flyspecks" - tiny pinpoints of oxidation.

Coins should be sorted in a dry location free of harmful fumes. The presence of sulphur in the atmosphere, a situation caused by certain types of coal combustion and also by industrial processes, sometimes will impart to silver coins in particular a yellowish or blackish toning. Dampness will result in oxidation or, in extreme instances, surface corrosion. Dampness can be best solved by moving coins to a drier location. If this is not possible, then a packet of silica gel (available in drugstores or photography supply stores) put in with the coins will serve to absorb moisture and may alleviate the problem. Also, the storage of coins in airtight containers will help.

The more a coin is exposed to freely circulating air, the more tendency it has to change colour or tone. Storage of coins in protective envelopes and hard plastic holders will usually help prevent this.

CLEANING COINS

Experienced numismatists will usually say that a coin is best left alone and not cleaned. However, most beginning collectors have the idea that "brilliant is best" and somehow feel that cleaning a coin will "improve" it. As the penchant for cleaning seems to be universal, and also because there are some instances in which cleaning can actually be beneficial, some important aspects are presented here.

All types of cleaning, "good" and "bad," result in the coin's surface being changed, even if only slightly. Even the most careful "dipping" of a coin will, if repeated time and time again, result in the coin acquiring a dullish and microscopically etched surface. It is probably true to state that no matter what one's intentions are, for every single coin actually improved in some way by cleaning, a dozen or more have been decreased in value. Generally, experienced numismatists agree that a coin should not be cleaned unless there are spots of oxidation, pitting which might worsen in time, or unsightly streaking or discolouration.

PROCESSING, POLISHING AND OTHER MISTREATMENT OF COINS

There have been many attempts to give a coin the appearance of being in a higher grade than it actually is. Numismatists refer to such treatments as "processing." Being different from cleaning (which can be "good" or "bad"), processing is never beneficial.

Types of processing include polishing and abrasion which removes metal from a coin's surface, etching and acid treatment, and "whizzing," the latter usually referring to abrading the surface of the coin with a stiff wire brush, often in a circular motion, to produce a series of minute tiny parallel scratches which to the unaided eye or under low magnification often appear to be like mint lustre. Under high magnification (in this instance a very strong magnifying glass should be used) the surface of a whizzed coin will show countless tiny scratches. Also, the artificial "mint lustre" will usually be in a uniform pattern throughout the coin's surfaces, whereas on an Uncirculated coin with true mint lustre the sheen of the lustre will be different on the higher parts than on the field. Some whizzed coins can be extremely deceptive. Comparing a whizzed coin with an untreated coin is the best way to gain experience in this regard.

Often one or more methods of treating a coin are combined. Sometimes a coin will be cleaned or polished and then by means of heat, fumes, or other treatment, an artificial toning will be applied. There are many variations.

When a coin has been polished, whizzed, artificially retoned, or in any other way changed from its original natural appearance and surface, it must be so stated in a description. For example, a coin which was Extremely Fine but whizzed to give it the artificial appearance of Uncirculated should be described as "Extremely Fine, whizzed." An AU coin, which has been recoloured should be described as "AU, recoloured." The simple "dipping" (without abrasion) of an already Uncirculated or Proof coin to brighten the surface does not have to be mentioned unless such dipping alters the appearance from when the coin was first struck (for example, in the instance of a copper or bronze coin in which dipping always produces an unnatural colour completely unlike the coin when it was first struck.)

COIN CERTIFICATION SERVICE

In recent years there has been an increase in the number of North American companies that offer third party professional coin grading services. Another service offered is that of an opinion as to whether a particular coin is genuine or counterfeit. Most of these companies operate along similar lines, that is, a coin is submitted by its owner for an independent grading and/or authentification assessment, an opinion is offered along with a certificate and a fee is charged on a per coin basis. These services are widely used by collectors and investors who recognize their grading skills are not at an expert's level. Many dealers in the United States also make use of such services because their clients often demand that the coins they buy have an official certificate with them. To date the most popular U.S. coin grading services appear to be: The Professional Coin Grading Service (PCGS) located in California, and The Numismatic Guaranty Corporation (NGC) located in New Jersey. All of these services specialize in U.S. coinage. In Canada the only such service is that offered by International Coin Certification Service (ICCS) in Toronto. ICCS specializes in all aspects of Canadian numismatics and includes amongst its senior consulting staff Bill Cross, Ingrid Smith, Jeffrey Hoare, Bob Armstrong, Randy Weir and Brian Cornwell. Further information can be obtained from: International Coin Certification Service, 2010 Yonge Street, Suite 202, Toronto, Ontario, M4S 1Z9.

OBVERSE DESCRIPTIONS FOR VARIOUS SERIES

Victoria Laureated Head
G-4 - Braid worn through near ear.
VG-8 - No detail in braid around ear.
F-12 - Segments of braid beginning to merge into one another.
VF-20 - Braid is clear but not sharp.
EF-40 - Braid is slightly worn but generally sharp and clear.
AU-50 - Slight traces of wear on high points. Degree of mint lustre still present.
MS-60 - No traces of wear. High degree of lustre.
MS-63 - No traces of wear. Attractive lustre. Typical strike with minor surface marks.

Edward VII All Denominations
G-4 - Band of crown worn through.
VG-8 - Band of crown worn through at the highest point.
F-12 - Jewels in the band of crown blurred.
VF-20 - Band of the crown is still clear but no longer sharp.
EF-40 - Band of crown slightly worn but generally sharp and clear, including jewels.
AU-50 - Slight traces of wear on high points. Degree of mint lustre still present.
MS-60 - No traces of wear. High degree of lustre.
MS-63 - No traces of wear. Attractive lustre. Typical strike with minor surface marks.

George VI All Denominations
VG-8 - No details in hair above ear.
F-12 - Only slight detail in hair above the ear.
VF-20 - Where not worn, the hair is clear but not sharp.
EF-40 - Slight wear in hair over ear.
AU-50 - Slight traces of wear on high points. Degree of mint lustre still present.
MS-60 - No traces of wear. High degree of lustre.
MS-63 - No traces of wear. Attractive lustre. Typical strike with minor surface marks.

Victoria Crowned Head
G-4 - Hair over ear worn through.
VG-8 - No details in the hair over ear.
F-12 - Strands of hair over ear beginning to run together.
VF-20 - Hair and jewels clear, but not sharp.
EF-40 - Hair over ear is sharp and clear. Jewels in diadem show sharply and clearly.
AU-50 - Slight traces of wear on high points. Degree of mint lustre still present.
MS-60 - No traces of wear. High degree of lustre.
MS-63 - No traces of wear. Attractive lustre. Typical strike with minor surface marks.

George V All Denominations
G-4 - Band of crown worn through.
VG-8 - Band of crown worn through at the highest point.
F-12 - Jewels in the band of crown blurred.
VF-20 - Band of the crown is still clear but no longer sharp.
EF-40 - Band of crown slightly worn but generally sharp and clear, including jewels.
AU-50 - Slight traces of wear on high points. Degree of mint lustre still present.
MS-60 - No traces of wear. High degree of lustre.
MS-63 - No traces of wear. Attractive lustre. Typical strike with minor surface marks.

Elizabeth II Young Head
F-12 - Leaves worn almost through. Shoulder fold indistinct.
VF-20 - Leaves are considerably worn; shoulder fold clear.
EF-40 - Laurel leaves on the band are somewhat worn.
AU-50 - Traces of wear on hair. Degree of mint lustre still present.
MS-60 - No traces of wear. High degree of lustre.
MS-63 - No traces of wear. Attractive lustre. Typical strike with minor surface marks.

UNCIRCULATED, MS-60 OBVERSE - There can be absolutely no wear of any kind on the hair and diadem. There may be a nick, a few bag marks or some discolouration but a high degree of lustre or frost should remain.
REVERSE - All detail in the wreath, crown and bow must be sharp and maple boughs clearly defined.

ABOUT UNCIRCULATED, AU-50 OBVERSE - Very slight traces of wear on diadem and in hairlines but details still sharp. Half of mint lustre remaining.
REVERSE - Slight trace of wear on high points: knot in wreath, crown and lower leaves.

EXTREMELY FINE, EF-40 OBVERSE - Trace of wear on eyebrow, four jewels in rim of diadem, strands of hair over the ear, knot at back and hairlines on top of head.
REVERSE - Trace of wear around the outer edges of lower leaves, knot in wreath and crown.

VERY FINE, VF-20 OBVERSE - Slight wear on eyebrow, cheek, nose, ear lobe and all of the jewels. Ribbon end and neck beginning to merge. Hair over the ear and knot slightly worn.
REVERSE - All leaves show wear on outer edges. Knot in wreath and centre part of crown worn.

FINE, F-12 OBVERSE - Considerable wear on all facial features, also hair and jewels. Ribbon end fused with cheek. Strands of hair over the ear beginning to merge together. Ear lobe barely showing.
REVERSE - All leaves considerably worn over entire area, also crown. Pearls in crown and beads of border beginning to merge.

VERY GOOD, VG-8 OBVERSE - Ear lobe fused with cheek. Hairlines separating face from hair obliterated. Practically no detail in hair over ear and knot at back. Jewels mostly worn away.
REVERSE - Very little detail in the leaves and crown remaining. Border beads blurred. Value and date worn.

GOOD, G-4 OBVERSE - Details of jewels, diadem and hair worn off. Little but outline of portrait remaining. Legend is weak.
REVERSE - Leaves and crown badly worn, with little but outlines remaining. Value and date are weak. Border beads are blurred.

EDWARD VII GRADING SYSTEM

UNCIRCULATED, MS-60 OBVERSE - Robe, shoulder bow, crown, ear and side whiskers all show sharp detail. All jewels in the crown including eight pearls clear and distinct. A high degree of lustre or frost must remain.
REVERSE - All details in the wreath, crown and bow are sharp and maple boughs clearly defined.

ABOUT UNCIRCULATED, AU-50 OBVERSE - Very slight wear on shoulder bow, ear and crown. Half of mint lustre remaining.
REVERSE - Slight trace of wear on high points: knot in wreath, crown and lower leaves.

EXTREMELY FINE, EF-40 OBVERSE - Eyebrow worn. Slight wear on ear, moustache and side whiskers. Band of crown slightly worn but all jewels, including eight pearls showing.
REVERSE - Trace of wear around the outer edges of lower leaves and centre arch of crown.

VERY FINE, VF-20 OBVERSE - Eyebrow, moustache and side whiskers considerably worn, also robe, shoulder bow and ornamental chain. Band of crown worn, but four to six pearls remain.
REVERSE - Wear on outer edges of leaves consists of about one-third their area. Central arch of crown shows slight wear.

FINE, F-12 OBVERSE - Robe, shoulder bow, jewels on chain and band of crown considerably worn. At least half of band remains. Top of ear merges with hair.
REVERSE - Wear on leaves increased to about one-half their area. Pearls in the arches of crown beginning to merge.

VERY GOOD, VG-8 OBVERSE - Band of crown worn through in the centre. Only weak outline of robe, shoulder bow and chain remaining. Outline of ear is indistinct and moustache and beard are blurred.
REVERSE - Very little detail remaining in the leaves. Pearls in crown are blurred and the centre often worn through.

GOOD, G-4 OBVERSE - Band of the crown and ear are worn away, also detail of robe, chain, beard and moustache. Legend is weak.
REVERSE - Leaves and crown badly worn with little but outlines remaining. Lettering and numerals are weak. Border heads blurred.

GEORGE V GRADING SYSTEM

UNCIRCULATED, MS-60 OBVERSE - Robe, shoulder bow, crown and moustache all clearly defined. Ornamental chain detail sharp and clear. A high degree of lustre remaining.
REVERSE - No trace of wear showing on wreath, crown or bow. All detail on maple boughs sharp and clear.

ABOUT UNCIRCULATED, AU-50 OBVERSE - Very slight wear on moustache, crown, ear and hairlines. Half of mint lustre remaining.
REVERSE - Slight trace of wear on high points: knot in wreath, crown and lower leaves.

EXTREMELY FINE, EF-40 OBVERSE - Eyebrow worn. Band of crown slightly worn near centre but all eight pearls showing. Trace of wear on tip of moustache and side whiskers. All six pearls down centre of crown clearly defined.
REVERSE - Trace of wear around outer edges of most leaves and centre arch of crown.

VERY FINE, VF-20 OBVERSE - Eyebrow, moustache, beard and side whiskers are considerably worn, also robe, shoulder bow and ornamental chain. Band of crown is worn but four to six pearls remain, also at least two pearls at top of crown.
REVERSE - Wear on outer edges of leaves consists of about one-third their area. Slight wear on centre arch of crown.

FINE, F-12 OBVERSE - Jewels in the band of crown blurred, but four pearls and one-half to three-quarters of band remains. Eyebrow indistinct. Beard and moustache worn together. Details of robe, shoulder bow and chain beginning to blur. Top of ear merging with hair.
REVERSE - Wear on leaves about one-half their area. Pearls in centre arch of crown beginning to merge.

VERY GOOD, VG-8 OBVERSE - Band of crown is worn through in centre with only front and rear portions remaining. Eyebrow worn off. Little detail remaining in robe, bow and chain.
REVERSE - Very little detail remaining in the leaves. Considerable wear on the centre arch of crown.

GOOD, G-4 OBVERSE - Band of crown worn away, also most of ear and other details. Legend is weak.
REVERSE - Leaves and crown badly worn with little but outlines remaining. Lettering and numerals are weak.

GEORGE VI GRADING SYSTEM

UNCIRCULATED, MS-60 OBVERSE - Hairlines, ear, eyebrow all sharp and distinct. Possible nick or bag marks but a high degree of lustre remains.
REVERSE - No wear on lion or unicorn. All details in shield and crown sharp and clear.

ABOUT UNCIRCULATED, AU-50 OBVERSE - Only a slight trace of wear showing on cheek, ear and hairlines. Half of mint lustre remaining
REVERSE - Very slight wear showing on shield. All details still sharp.

Many of the 50-cent pieces, particularly the 1947, 1947ML and 1948 were weakly struck in the area at the top left corner of shield and base of crown. The weakness should not be mistaken for wear on strictly uncirculated coins.

EXTREMELY FINE, EF-40 OBVERSE - Slight wear at eyebrow, ear lobe and hair above ear. Sideburn in front of ear clearly showing.
REVERSE - Slight wear on thighs and forelegs of lion and unicorn. Trace of wear on details of crown and shield.

VERY FINE, VF-20 OBVERSE - Eyebrow indistinct. Hairlines above the ear and side of head are blurred. Exposed portions of ear and cheek-bone show wear. Sideburn barely showing.
REVERSE - Some overall wear on bodies of lion and unicorn. Slight wear at bottom of crown and top of shield.

FINE, F-12 OBVERSE - Eyebrow worn off. Only slight detail in hair between the ear and part in hair. Considerable wear on ear, facial features and back of neck.
REVERSE - Considerable wear on lion and unicorn, bottom of crown and upper portion of shield. Border beads beginning to merge.

VERY GOOD, VG-8 OBVERSE - No detail in hair above ear. Outer rim of ear is worn flat and merges with hair. Much wear on nose and other facial features.
REVERSE - Lion and unicorn worn. Crown and shield somewhat worn but most details remain.

ELIZABETH II GRADING SYSTEM

YOUNG HEAD 1953 - 1964

UNCIRCULATED, MS-60 OBVERSE - All 11 leaves of laurel wreath, hairlines and shoulder fold sharply defined. High degree of lustre.
REVERSE - No wear showing on lion or unicorn. All details in shield and crown sharp and clear.

ABOUT UNCIRCULATED, AU-50 OBVERSE - Very slight wear on hairlines, shoulder and laurel wreath. Half of mint lustre remaining.
REVERSE - Trace of wear on lion, unicorn and crown.

EXTREMELY FINE, EF-40 OBVERSE - Slight wear at eyebrow, cheek, shoulder and laurel wreath. All 11 leaves showing.
REVERSE - Slight wear on thighs and forelegs of lion and unicorn, and at base of crown and top of shield.

VERY FINE, VF-20 OBVERSE - Considerable wear at eyebrow, bottom of ear and hair between ear and forehead. Laurel wreath is worn but eight to ten leaves showing. Shoulder is worn but shoulder fold visible on that variety.
REVERSE - Slight wear on lion and unicorn and at base of crown and upper panels of shield.

YOUNG HEAD 1953 - 1964

FINE, F-12 OBVERSE - Much wear over entire portrait with few hairlines visible. Only faint outlines of the bottom of ear, nose and mouth remaining. Outlines of four to seven leaves showing.
REVERSE - Lion and unicorn considerably worn. Crown and shield slightly worn but most of details remain.

MATURE HEAD 1965 - 1989

UNCIRCULATED, MS-60 OBVERSE - No evidence of wear at eyebrow, the hair over the ear, temple and forehead. Drapery over the shoulder and band of the diadem sharply defined.
REVERSE - No signs of wear on lion or unicorn. All details in shield and crown are sharp and clear.

ABOUT UNCIRCULATED, AU-50 OBVERSE - Slight trace of wear on cheek, hairlines, tiara and drapery on shoulder. Half of mint lustre remaining.
REVERSE - Very slight wear on lion, unicorn and crown.

EXTREMELY FINE, EF-40 OBVERSE - Slight wear at eyebrow and hair over the ear. Also hair at temple and forehead. Drapery over the shoulder showing slight wear, particularly the line at top of queen's gown.
REVERSE - Slight wear on crown, front of helmet and the forelegs of the lion and unicorn.

THE MANUFACTURE OF CANADIAN COINS

The steps involved in the production of Canadian coins can be divided into the following: 1) production of a large three-dimensional model (for a new design); 2) the engraving of the dies and collar; 3) production of the blanks (planchets); and 4) the coining of them.

THE LARGE THREE-DIMENSIONAL MODEL

The design for a new coinage usually begins as a sketch. After the theme for the design is chosen, a suitable sketch is obtained in one of three ways. The most direct way is to generate the sketch "in house." This was done, for example, in the case of the 1977 Queen's Silver Jubilee silver dollar when Royal Canadian Mint engraver Walter Ott made an ink drawing of the throne of the senate. On other occasions, such as for the 1937 coinage, a select group of outside artists is invited to submit designs. To date, this has been the method most frequently used by the Royal Canadian Mint. The final method is to have an open competition that any Canadian can enter. The designs for the 1951 commemorative 5-cent piece, the 1964 silver dollar, the twelve 1992 twenty-five cent pieces and the 125th Anniversary Dollar were the results of open competitions.

Once a suitable sketch is at hand, a three-dimensional plaster model of the design about 8 inches in diameter is made. This is sometimes produced by the original artist, but more often the modelling is done in the mint. Such models are usually made as a positive (i.e. the design elements are raised as on the final coin). A plastic, negative mould made from this model serves as the starting point for the next series of operations.

DIE PRODUCTION

The plastic, negative mould (design elements sunken) is placed in a device called a reducing machine. This machine works on the principle of the pantograph, reproducing on a reduced scale in three dimensions the design of the plastic model in metal. Generally the reduction proceeds in two steps. The first is to reproduce the plastic model as a brass block, making the design about 3 inches in diameter. This brass intermediate model then serves as the pattern for the machine during the reduction to coin scale. In the second reduction the design is engraved into a soft steel block. After the beads are added and other finishing touches applied, the steel block is hardened to become a reduction matrix.

From the reduction matrix one or more punches are made by placing it in a powerful press and impressing its design into soft steel blocks, which are later hardened. A punch has its design elements raised just as on the coins. The next step is to make the dies. Dies are made in the same way as punches, except it is a punch that is used to sink the design into soft steel blocks in the press. A single punch can produce thousands of dies before it must be retired.

The collar (the piece of metal that restrains the sideways expansion of the blank during striking and gives the coin its shape and edge design) is made at the Ottawa mint. For plain edge coins a hole is simply drilled in the centre of an appropriate piece of steel. If the collar is to be for a reeded edge coin, a smooth-edge hole is first drilled. Then the hole is given a serrated edge by the use of a small, hardened steel wheel.

If the design for the reverse is to be used for more than one year, the final digit or digits of the date are ground from a punch and a new matrix made from the modified punch. The missing digit(s) is then punched into the blank space in the matrix. From this matrix new punches are made.

Since 1945 dies for Canadian coinages have, with rare exceptions, been chromium plated. This extends the die-life and gives the coins a superior finish.

THE PREPARATION OF THE BLANKS

At the present time Canadian coins are struck in bronze, nickel, silver, gold and platinum. The blanks for gold coins are obtained from an outside source. When blanks are produced in the Ottawa mint, as is the case with bronze and silver, the components of the metal alloys are mixed together in the melting pot and cast into bars. The bars are annealed (softened by heat treatment) and rolled to an exact thickness. The rolled metal is bent into the form of a large coil, which is then sent to the cutting room. In the cutting room the coils are fed into blanking presses, which punch blanks out of them. Following passage over a vibrating screen to remove defective (undersize) blanks, the good blanks are put through a machine which compresses their edges so as to produce raised rims. This facilitates coining by reducing the amount of metal that has to be displaced in the blank during striking. The rimmed blanks are next fed through a special furnace in which they are annealed. Finally, the cooled blanks are cleaned and dried, ready for the coining press.

Nickel is a difficult metal to work with, so both the Ottawa and the Winnipeg mints obtain this metal in strip or coil form. Winnipeg also obtains its blank bronze in this form.

COINING

Blanks are fed into the coining chamber of the press through a feed tube attached to a vibrating hopper of blanks contained above. A metal fork pushes a fresh blank over the hole in the collar and at the same time pushes away the coin just struck. The blank, being slightly smaller than the diameter of the hole in the collar, drops in and comes to rest on the bottom (obverse) die. The top die then descends and makes contact with the blank. This causes the blank to expand, filling the crevices of the dies and the collar to become a coin. Both dies rise, forcing the coin out of the collar so that it can be pushed away by the next blank being positioned. Struck coins are collected, examined, counted and bagged for issue.

TECHNICAL INFORMATION

This catalogue presents the most complete set of technical statistics ever assembled for the Canadian decimal series.

It is important to note that the artistic talent that goes into the production of a new coinage design does not end with the individual who did the original drawing. The designing, modelling and engraving of the master tools for a modern coinage also require great skill and, in some cases, each step may be the work of a different person. As far as possible, they are all listed.

Compositions are given as decimal fractions, adding up to 1.00; they can be converted to percentages by multiplying by 100. Weights are given in grams and can be converted into troy ounces by dividing by 31.1035. Diameters are given in millimetres and can be converted into inches by multiplying by .03937.

Canadian coins have been struck with both major die axis arrangements. In the medal arrangement (designated ↑↑) a coin held vertically between one's fingers with its obverse design right side up finishes with it reverse design right side up when it is rotated on its vertical axis. Dies in the coinage arrangement (↑↓) will result in the reverse being upside down when the coin is turned as previously described.

THE TREATMENT OF VARIETIES

A variety can be described as "any alteration in the design of a coin." A major variety is a coin of the same date, mint mark and denomination as another, but struck from a different set of dies, the finished coin having at least one major device added, removed or redesigned. In other words, a major variety is the result of an intentional change by the mint. A minor variety is one with all major devices the same as another, but with some easily recognizable variation. Minor varieties are thus the result of unintentional mint errors or other deviations.

Since this is a standard catalogue designed for general collectors, it is not possible to list minor varieties, nor to remark upon all the nuances of interest to the specialist. Following the format established in the 31st edition, the Charlton Standard Catalogue includes every major variety and several minor varieties that have a wide appeal to collectors. More specialized treatments will be available in the forthcoming *The Charlton-Zoell Variety Catalogue*.

MINTS, MINT MARKS AND OTHER LETTERS

Until 1908, all Canadian coins were produced in England. Most were coined at the Royal Mint in London and have no identifying mint mark. From time to time, however, the Royal Mint was so busy with other coinages that Canadian authorities were allowed to have their coins struck by a private mint in Birmingham. This mint, called Heaton's Mint until 1889 and The Mint, Birmingham thereafter, used a small "H" mint mark on all its Canadian issues except for the Prince Edward Island cent of 1871.

January 2, 1908 saw the opening of a mint in Ottawa, authorized under the Imperial Coinage Act of 1870. Until 1931 it was the Ottawa Branch of the Royal Mint. Its issues for the Dominion of Canada bear no mint mark, but those for elsewhere (British sovereigns and Newfoundland and Jamaica coinages) have a small "C" on the reverse. In 1931 the name of the Ottawa mint was changed to the Royal Canadian Mint and it came under the full control of the Canadian government as a branch of the Department of Finance. The status of the mint was altered in March, 1969 by the Government Organization Act, and it became a Crown Corporation effective April 1, 1969.

Today, Canada has three mints: the Ottawa mint, the Hull mint (established in 1965 for striking collectors coins) and the Winnipeg mint (opened in 1975). None of these mints employ mint marks.

The only recent occasion when Canadian coins were produced outside the country was in 1968. In that year part of the 10-cents issue was coined at the Philadelphia Mint in the United States. The Philadelphia Mint did not place a mint mark on these coins, but the Canadian and U.S. strikings can be distinguished by the shape of the grooves in the edge (see ten-cent section).

Other identifying letters refer to designers, modellers or engravers. They include the following:

B	Patrick Brindley	WO or WO monogram . . .	Walter Ott
RRC	Robert R. Carmichael	H.P.	T. Humphrey Paget
PC	Paul Cedarberg	DDP	Donald D. Paterson
DJC	David J. Craig	PP	Paul Pederson
DES	George W. DeSaulles	FP	Friedrich Peter
M.G.	Mrs. Mary Gillick	B.P.	Benedetto Pistrucci
EH or H	Emanuel Hahn	WWP	William Weseley Pole
DH	Dora de Pedery-Hunt	TS or T.S.	Thomas Shingles
K.G. or KG	George E. Kruger-Gray	RT	Raymond Taylor
B.M	Sir E. Bertram MacKennal	ST or ST monogram .	Stephan Trenka
TM	Terry Manning	D.V.	Dinko Vodanovic
JM	John Mardon	L.C.W.	Leonard C. Wyon
P.M.	Percy Metcalfe		

The location of all mint marks and other initials is indicated in the listings of each series.

FRATERNAL AFFILIATION

Over the years, coin clubs have sprung up in many Canadian communities. In addition, both Canada and the United States have national organizations which hold annual conventions.

Coin clubs constitute one of the most attractive features of present-day collecting. They offer beginning collectors the opportunity for good fellowship and the encouragement and knowledge of more experienced collectors. The larger groups maintain lending libraries and publish a journal or newsletter on a regular basis. Memberships and other information can be obtained from:

The Canadian Numismatic Association
Post Office Box 226
Barrie, Ontario,
Canada L4M 4T2

The American Numismatic Association
818 N. Cascade Avenue
Colorado Springs, Colorado,
U.S.A. 80903-3279

Ontario Numismatic Association
Post Office Box 33
Waterloo, Ontario,
Canada N2J 3Z6.

FOREIGN COINS IN CANADA

Strictly speaking, Canada (rather, the areas that now form Canada) did not have a coinage struck for its specific use until the mid-19th century. After 1820, some provincial governments issued their own coppers, but this was without imperial government sanction until the 1850s. Thus, for some two centuries Canada relied on foreign coins to provide the lifeblood for her commerce.

The importance of foreign coins in our currency history has not been given the emphasis it deserves in Canadian catalogues. Certainly it is difficult to deal with this subject. None of the foreign coins that were once so important here can strictly be called Canadian. This includes the coins of the French regime, some of which have been listed in past catalogues. To simply list some French issues is both misleading and illogical. The Spanish-American dollar, for example, was a more important coin in our overall currency history than any French (or British) coin ever was. A more realistic listing must include coins of France, Great Britain, Spain and Spanish America, Portugal and the United States.

It has been decided to attempt to list the most important foreign coins that circulated in Canada, regardless of their country of origin. In order to qualify for listing a coin must have been specifically imported and in reasonable quantity. The many coins that filtered into North America in small quantities through trade cannot be listed.

NOTE: The prices listed below for broad types of coins, which may encompass several separate types and a span of many years, are for the most commonly encountered form of the coin only. Readers are advised to see specialized foreign catalogues for specific varieties, dates and prices.

COINS OF FRANCE

During the French regime (c. 1600-1760), French imperial coins were intermittently shipped to New France by the king or were imported by local merchants. Occasionally these were supplemented by general colonial coinages intended for circulation in France. But, as New France was just one of the recipients of the colonial issues, they cannot be considered to have been specifically for Canada. French coins became less important in Canada after 1760. The silver ecus and 1/2 ecus, however, remained in commercial use well into the next century.

Between 1680 and the early 1720's, French coins were subject to considerable variations in the rate at which they were to be officially current. We will not attempt to detail these changes or "reformations" for each coin. A single example is sufficient to make the point. One of the few French coins with its original value actually stated on it is the "mousquetaire" or 30-denier piece minted between 1710 and 1713. Its initial rate of 30 deniers was lowered to 27 deniers in 1714 and to 22 deniers the next year. It remained at that level until the wild inflation of John Law (1720-1721), when it soared to 60 deniers and quickly fell back to 45 deniers. In 1724 its rate was returned to 27 deniers and in 1732 it was lowered to 24 deniers. It continued at that level in New France until the Conquest.

By 1726 the French government realized the folly of frequent changes in the value of coins and generally the currency was stabilized.

MINT MARKS ON FRENCH COINS. Numerous mints produced French coins. Only for issues produced by a small number of mints will the listings by mint be separated. The following mint marks were employed on coins that circulated in quantity in New France and British Canada:

A - Paris	K - Bordeaux	S - Reims	& - Aix
B - Rouen	L - Bayonne	T - Nantes	AA - Metz
C - Caen	M - Toulouse	V - Troyes	BB - Strasbourg
D - Lyon	N - Montpellier	W - Lille	)(- Besancon
E - Tours	O - Riom	X - Amiens	a cow - Pau
G - Poitiers	P - Dijon	Y - Bourges	
H - LaRochelle	O - Perpignan	Z - Grenoble	
I - Limoges	R - Orleans	9 - Rennes	

COPPER COINS

DENIER. Along with the copper double and liard, the denier was one of the predominant coins in circulation in New France up to the early 1660's. The denier, although rated at 1 denier in France, circulated as a 2-denier piece in New France. The merchants saw a chance for a quick profit and imported these coins in large quantities. This resulted in an oversupply prompting the government at Quebec to ban the denier altogether in 1664.

Type and Denomination	VG	VF	EF	AU
Louis XIII or XIV Denier	10.00	20.00	45.00	150.00

DOUBLE. In 1664 the Order of the Sovereign Council which demonetized the denier allowed the double to remain in circulation but reduced its value to 1 denier to curb its excessive importation. It had formerly circulated at 4 deniers in New France.

Type and Denomination	VG	VF	EF	AU
Louis XIII or XIV Double	10.00	20.00	45.00	150.00

LIARD. Until the Order of Sovereign Council of 1664, the liard passed in New France as a 6-denier piece. After 1664 its value was reduced to 2 deniers to discourage its excessive importation.

Type and Denomination	VF	EF	AU
Louis XIV or XV Liard	20.00	50.00	175.00

1/2 SOL COINAGE OF 1710-1712. The first coinage of this denomination in copper took place in 1710-1712. When first issued it was rated at 6 deniers.

Type and Denomination	F	VF	EF	AU
1710-1712 1/2 Sol	10.00	20.00	100.00	250.00

COPPER COINAGE OF 1719-1724. This coinage consisted of a liard, a 1/2 sol and a double sol. The middle denomination (the half sou) was shipped to New France in large amounts in 1720.

Type and Denomination	VG	VF	EF	AU
1719-1724 1/2 Sol	8.00	25.00	80.00	275.00

Type and Denomination	F	VF	EF	AU
1719-1724 Sol	12.00	35.00	130.00	400.00

COLONIAL 9 DENIER COINAGE 1721-1722. This was a special colonial issue imported by a private trading company, the Company of the Indies. Following difficulties in circulating their new coins, the company attempted to have them transferred to the government of New France. This was not successful, so most of the coinage was returned to France in 1726. These coins were also sent to other French colonies.

Type and Denomination	VG	F	VF	EF	AU
1721B 9 Deniers	200.00	300.00	400.00	700.00	-
1721H 9 Deniers	20.00	40.00	65.00	225.00	450.00
1722H 2 over 1	20.00	40.00	65.00	225.00	400.00
1722H Normal Date	20.00	40.00	65.00	225.00	400.00

BILLON SOLS MARQUES COINAGES

The most important coinages in circulation during the French regime were a group of billon (low-grade silver) pieces collectively called sols (or sous) marques. They often constituted the smallest denomination coins because copper was generally unpopular with the colonists. There were no less than six coinages of sols marques; the coinages of 1709-1713 and 1738-1764 also had double sol denominations.

COUNTERSTAMPED DOUZAINS (1640). During the Middle Ages a new French coin called a gros tournois made its appearance. It was about the size of a 25-cent piece and made of good silver. By the first part of the 17th century this coin had become a billon piece called a douzain. The douzain or sol was rated at 12 deniers. In 1640 the French government called in all douzains and counterstamped them with a small fleur-de-lis in an oval to change their rating to 15 deniers. The term sol marque (marked sol) came from the fact that these coins were counterstamped. It later came to apply to all sols.

Type and Denomination	F	VF	EF	AU
Counterstamped Douzain (1640)	40.00	80.00	-	-

COINAGE OF 1641. The next billon coin in the series was a new design dated 1641. It was initially rated at 15 deniers and supplemented the douzains counterstamped the year before. Its relation to these coins is clearly shown by its design (both obverse and reverse) containing a fleur-de-lis in an oval, in imitation of the counterstamp on the earlier issue.

Type and Denomination	F	VF	EF	AU
1641 15 Deniers	125.00	200.00	500.00	1,000.00

COINAGE OF 1658. The douzain of 1658 was rated at 12 deniers in France but was given a rating of 20 deniers when it made its first appearance in New France in 1662. A 6-denier piece was also struck, but there is no reason to believe that denomination circulated in quantity in the colony.

Type and Denomination	F	VF	EF	AU
1658 Douzain	125.00	200.00	500.00	1,000.00

COINAGE OF 1692-1698. Beginning in 1692 and continuing through 1698, a new issue of sols marques was made. The designs were new, but instead of being struck on fresh blanks, many were struck over previous issues of sols. It is sometimes possible to detect parts of the undertypes on the overstruck coins. The new issue was rated at 15 deniers when it first came out.

Type and Denomination	F	VF	EF	AU
1692-1698 15 Deniers	10.00	15.00	50.00	100.00

"Mousquetaire" Issues of 1709-1713

This issue consisted of a 15-denier piece and a 30-denier piece. The name mousquetaire is believed to have come from the cross on the reverse of the coins, which resembled the crosses on the cloaks of the legendary musketeers.

Type and Denomination	F	VF	EF	AU
1709-1713 15 Deniers	100.00	200.00	350.00	700.00

Type and Denomination	F	VF	EF	AU
1709-1713 30 Deniers	30.00	75.00	200.00	500.00

Coinage of 1738-1764

The final billon coinage used in New France was that of 1738-1764, consisting of a sol and double sol. The double sol has often been mistakenly referred to as "the" sou marque. First, there is no single sol marque; some six coinages are involved. Second, the sol or sou was by 1738 a coin about the size of our present small cent. The larger coin so often called a sou marque is in fact a double sol.

SOL (SOU) 1738-1754. This coin was rated at 12 deniers in both France and New France.

Type and Denomination	F	VF	EF	AU
1738-1754 Sol	40.00	80.00	200.00	400.00

DOUBLE SOL (2 SOUS) 1738-1764. Although this type was struck until 1764, it is unlikely that any dated later than 1760 circulated in New France. This coin was rated at 24 deniers.

Large quantities of contemporary counterfeits were made of the double sol, particularly of the dates 1740, 1741, 1742, 1750, 1751, 1755 and 1760. Differences in the rendition of the crown are the easiest way to tell the genuine from the counterfeit.

Original

Typical Counterfeit

Type and Denomination	F	VF	EF	AU
1738-1760 Double sol, genuine	10.00	25.00	60.00	250.00
1740-1760 Double sol, counterfeit	8.00	20.00	40.00	100.00

SILVER COINS

1/2 ECU. The 1/2 ecu was not routinely imported into French America; nevertheless, it did circulate in some quantity during the British regime in the first third of the 19th century. It is assumed that these coins came primarily from issues of Louis XIV and XV.

Type and Denomination	F	VF	EF	AU
Louis XIV and XV 1/2 Ecu	60.00	135.00	225.00	450.00

ECU. The ecu, a large silver coin about the size of the Canadian silver dollar, was imported into French America in significant quantities. The ecu continued in use after the fall of New France, when it was called the French crown. Most types of ecu minted between 1640 and the 1750s probably circulated in Canada.

Type and Denomination	F	VF	EF	AU
Louis XIII, XIV, or XV Ecu	100.00	275.00	450.00	700.00

Colonial Coinage of 1670

In 1670 a special coinage of silver 5-sol and 15-sol pieces was produced for circulation in the French colonies in the New World. On the reverse was "GLORIAM REGNI TVI DICENT" meaning "They shall speak of the glory of Thy kingdom" and taken from the 145th Psalm of the Bible. Despite their fame, these coins barely qualify as "Canadian." Period documents suggest that they probably were intended for the West Indies rather than New France. Authorities in the West Indies were anxious to obtain a subsidiary silver coinage for payment of day labourers and artisans, who were being paid in goods. In New France these coins were not particularly wanted because they could not be used for buying goods in France; they were not legal tender there. In any case it is quite clear that these coins had a very limited circulation in French America.

Date and Denomination	Quantity Minted	VG	F	VF	EF	AU
1650A 5 Sols	200,000	350.00	500.00	1,000.00	1,500.00	-

Date and Denomination	Quantity Minted	VG	F	VF	EF	AU
1670A 15 Sols	40,000	1 2,000.	16,000.	30,000.	-	-

Reduced Silver Coinages of 1674 - 1709

In the late 17th and early 18th centuries the French government was in a rather precarious financial condition. As a money-raising scheme it struck seven coinages with reduced silver content (approximately .800 fine) at the same time as the regular .917 fine silver types were being produced. Most of the reduced fineness types were sent to New France in quantity.

4 SOLS ISSUES OF 1674-1677. By 1679 there were so many of these coins in circulation in New France that they were being used in payment by the bagfull. An ordinance passed in that year lowered their value to 3 sols 6 deniers and placed strict limits on the quantity that could be used for any one payment.

Date and Denomination	F	VF	EF	AU
1674-1677 4 Sols	15.00	35.00	90.00	200.00

4 SOLS ISSUES OF 1691-1700. This coin was the successor to the previous reduced silver 4-sol piece and was struck over it.

Date and Denomination	F	VF	EF	AU
1691-1700 4 Sols	20.00	40.00	100.00	225.00

5 SOLS OF 1702-1709. The next reduced silver coinage used in New France was a piece of approximately the same weight as the old 4-sol pieces, but which was called a 5-sol piece instead.

Date and Denomination	F	VF	EF	AU
1702-1709 5 Sols	15.00	30.00	75.00	150.00

10 SOLS OF 1702-1708. This 10-sol piece is from the same series as the 5-sols.

Date and Denomination	F	VF	EF	AU
1702-1708 10 Sols	20.00	40.00	80.00	275.00

LIVRE OF 1720. In 1720, during the wild inflation brought about by the schemes of John Law, a special coin was produced in pure silver and issued at the over-valued rating of one livre. The Company of the Indies imported a quantity of these coins into French America in 1722.

Date and Denomination	Quantity Minted	F	VF	EF	AU
1720A Livre	6,918,583	80.00	175.00	300.00	-

SMALL SILVER LOUIS OF 1720. In 1720 a new coin called a small silver louis (petit louis d'argent) was brought into Canada. Its initial rating was 60 sols, but this was soon reduced to 40 sols.

Date and Denomination	F	VF	EF	AU
1720 Small Silver Louis	25.00	70.00	200.00	400.00

GOLD COINS

THE GOLD LOUIS. The only French gold coin to see significant circulation in French North America was the gold louis (louis d'or). Louis d'or were regularly sent over and saw use even after the Conquest. Any of the types struck between the 1640s and the 1750s potentially circulated here in quantity.

| Type of 1680 | Type of 1723-1725 |

Type and Denomination	VG	F	VF	EF	AU
Louis XIV, Commom	225.00	400.00	600.00	1,000.00	1,750.00
Louis XV, 1723-1725	225.00	550.00	800.00	1,350.00	1,850.00
Louis XV, 1726-1739	225.00	375.00	500.00	750.00	1,250.00

COINS OF GREAT BRITAIN

For most of the British colonial period (c. 1760-1870) the British government was hardly better than the French government had been at supplying Imperial coins for use in Canada. British coinage was stuck infrequently during the last half of the 18th century, and England and her colonies alike suffered from the lack of coin.

A major alteration took place in the British coinage in 1816. The silver coinage was reduced to a subsidiary status (along with the coppers) by lowering the amount of silver it contained to bring the bullion value of the coins below the face value. This left gold as the sole standard coinage and marks the beginning of the British gold standard. The coinage of silver was begun on a large scale and British coins gradually became more available. In 1825-1826 a serious attempt was made to establish Imperial coins as the principal coinage of the colonies and to drive out the Spanish-American coins. This attempt largely failed in British North America. Nevertheless, at various times some British coins did achieve a significant circulation here, particularly in Nova Scotia. That province came the closest to adopting sterling coinage; when it was decided to institute a decimal currency in 1859, the dollar was rated so as to allow the continued circulation of British coins. The 2-shilling piece (florin) became a 50-cent piece, the shilling became a 25-cent piece and so on. The halfpenny and shilling also saw much use in Upper and Lower Canada and later in the united Province of Canada.

COPPER COINS

Halfpenny

GEORGE II ISSUES OF 1740-1754. These coins, along with the George III halfpenny listed below, formed the most important part of the British North American copper currency until the War of 1812. After that time they were supplemented by the tokens issued by local merchants and others. But, until the first bank tokens, they were the only copper sanctioned by the British government.

Date and Denomination	VG	F	VF	EF	AU	UNC
1740-1754 1/2d	4.00	10.00	35.00	150.00	250.00	400.00

GEORGE III ISSUES OF 1770-1775. The majority of the coins of this issue that circulated in both Great Britain and America were contemporary counterfeits. Issues of halfpennies during later reigns seem not to have circulated in quantity in British North America.

Genuine Issue

Typical Counterfeit

Date and Denomination	VG	F	VF	EF	AU	UNC
1770-1775 1/2d, genuine	3.00	7.00	15.00	40.00	200.00	350.00
1770-1775 1/2d, counterfeit		15.00	25.00			

Penny

The penny was not a frequently used denomination in British North America. In 1832, however, a special shipment was made to Upper Canada. This is known to have consisted of coins dated 1831.

Date and Denomination	VG	F	VF	EF	AU	UNC
William IV, 1831 Penny	4.00	10.00	45.00	150.00	300.00	600.00

SILVER COINS

British silver coins became more important in circulation in some parts of British North America after about 1830. The intermediate denominations were the most common.

Six Pence

Type and Denomination	VG	F	VF	EF	AU	UNC
William IV, Six Pence	2.00	7.00	30.00	70.00	140.00	200.00
Victoria (Young Head) 1838-1866 Six Pence	1.00	4.00	15.00	75.00	110.00	160.00

Shilling

Type and Denomination	VG	F	VF	EF	AU	UNC
William IV, Shilling	3.00	7.00	30.00	130.00	190.00	300.00
Victoria (Young Head) 1838-1863 Shilling	3.00	7.00	25.00	75.00	110.00	200.00

13

Florin

This denomination probably saw use in Nova Scotia during the 1850s and 1860s. In 1861 the florin, shilling and sixpence were imported into British Columbia.

Type and Denomination	VG	F	VF	EF	AU	UNC
Victoria (Gothic Head) 1851-1887 Florin*	5.00	15.00	40.00	150.00	250.00	400.00

*On these coins the date is on the obverse in the form of a Roman numeral.

Halfcrown

Type and Denomination	VG	F	VF	EF	AU	UNC
George IV, Halfcrown	6.00	15.00	35.00	160.00	240.00	350.00
William IV, Halfcrown	9.00	18.00	50.00	175.00	275.00	400.00
Victoria (Young Head), Halfcrown	4.00	10.00	30.00	95.00	150.00	275.00

GOLD COINS

GEORGE III 1/2 GUINEA. The 1/2 guinea was usually rated at 10 shillings 6 pence in Great Britain.

Type and Denomination	VG	F	VF	EF	AU	UNC
George III, 1/2 Guinea, 1787-1800	50.00	100.00	150.00	250.00	375.00	550.00

GEORGE III GUINEA 1761-1813. The guinea or 21-shilling piece was one of the principal gold coins to circulate in British North America.

Type of 1765-1773

Type and Denomination	VG	F	VF	EF	AU	UNC
George III, Guinea	150.00	200.00	300.00	600.00	900.00	1400.00

1/2 SOVEREIGN. The 1/2 sovereign was the successor to the 1/2 guinea and probably saw enough circulation in British North America and the Dominion of Canada to warrant its inclusion in this listing.

Type and Denomination	F	VF	EF	AU	UNC
George III, 1/2 Sovereign	75.00	150.00	450.00	550.00	750.00
George IV, 1/2 Sovereign	100.00	200.00	550.00	750.00	1,100.00
William IV, 1/2 Sovereign	110.00	250.00	800.00	1,000.00	1,500.00
Victoria (Young Head), 1/2 Sovereign	70.00	90.00	150.00	250.00	400.00

SOVEREIGN. The sovereign was perhaps the most widely used gold coin in Canada. It was used extensively by banks and the government for redeeming paper money right up to the 20th century.

Type and Denomination	F	VF	EF	AU	UNC
George III, Sovereign	175.00	275.00	750.00	950.00	1,500.00
George IV, Sovereign	175.00	275.00	750.00	950.00	1,350.00
William IV, Sovereign	150.00	250.00	750.00	950.00	1,450.00
Victoria (Shield), Sovereign	100.00	125.00	175.00	250.00	550.00

COINS OF PORTUGAL

During the 18th and early 19th centuries, several types of gold coins issued by Portugal found their way into British North America and were used extensively here.

MOIDORE. This coin had a denomination of 4,000 reis in Portugal and bore on its reverse the Cross of Jerusalem. It was struck from the reign of Alfonso VI (1656-1683) to the reign of John V (1706-1750).

Type and Denomination	VG	F	VF	EF
Alfonso VI to John V, Moidore	250.00	325.00	500.00	700.00

6,400 REIS (1/2 JOE). This coin, with a formal denomination of 6,400 reis, was introduced in the 1720's, along with a 12,800 reis coin of similar design. The king of Portugal at the time was John (Joao) V and from his name on the coins, Johannes V, came the nickname "Joe" for the 12,800 reis coin and "1/2 Joe" for the 6,400 reis coin. The "1/2 Joe" was also applied to the 6,400 reis coins issued in subsequent reigns. The larger coin was not issued in later reigns and "Joe" was eventually used for the 6,400 reis denomination.

Type and Denomination	VG	F	VF	EF
John V to John VI 1706 - 1826 "1/2 Joe" (6,400 reis)	300.00	375.00	550.00	900.00

12,800 REIS (JOE). This was a coin of 12,800 reis issued during the reign of John V (see above).

Type and Denomination	VG	F	VF	EF
John V, "Joe" 1724 - 1732 (12,800 reis)	750.00	1,350.00	2,750.00	4,000.00

COINS OF SPAIN, SPANISH AMERICA AND FORMER SPANISH COLONIES

This group of coins was more important in the currency history of what is now Canada for a longer period of time than any other foreign coinage. It was the Spanish-American dollar that served as the basis for the United States dollar, upon which in turn was based the decimal dollar of the Province of Canada in 1858.

COINS OF SPAIN

The Spanish metropolitan coinage is relatively unimportant compared to that of her New World colonies, with one exception: the pistareen. This was the nickname for a reduced standard 2-real piece minted only in Spain and which enjoyed wide circulation in British North America in the first half of the 19th century.

Type and Denomination	VG	F	VF	EF	AU
18th Century, Spanish Pistareen	10.00	20.00	35.00	50.00	100.00

COINS OF SPANISH AMERICA

The coinage of Spain's colonies emanated from the following principal mints: Potosi in Bolivia, Santiago in Chile, Sante Fe do Bogota and Popayan in Colombia (Nueva Granada). Guatemala in Guatemala, Mexico City in Mexico and Lima and Cuzco in Peru. Minting of Spanish-American coins began in the early 16th century with the coins being of conventional round appearance. These were replaced about 1580 by the "cob" series: crude-appearing coins hand-struck on irregular blanks hewn from bars of refined bullion.

The cob series was finally superseded by round coins in 1732. The first round gold issues bore the portrait of the reigning Spanish monarch from the first; however, the silver did not carry portraits until 1772. In the intervening 40 years the obverses featured the "two world" or "pillar" design, consisting of two crowned hemisphere between the crowned pillars of Hercules.

The Spanish-American series came to an end in the 1820's as Spain's colonies successfully revolted and became independent. Nevertheless, the Spanish-American coins had been minted in such great quantities that they continued to exert an important influence for decades. Probably the most important coinages for Canada are those struck under the rulers Charles III (1760-1788), Charles IV (1788-1808) and Ferdinand VII (1808-1821).

1 REAL

Type and Denomination	VG	F	VF	EF	AU
Philip V to Charles III, 1 Real, Pillar Type	10.00	20.00	40.00	80.00	200.00
Charles III to Ferdinand VII, 1 Real, Bust Type	4.00	10.00	20.00	75.00	150.00

2 REALES

Type and Denomination	VG	F	VF	EF	AU
Philip V to Charles III, 2 Reales, Pillar Type	11.00	20.00	40.00	80.00	200.00
Charles III to Ferdinand VII, 2 Reales, Bust Type	7.00	14.00	20.00	135.00	250.00

4 REALES

Type and Denomination	VG	F	VF	EF	AU
Philip V to Charles III, 4 Reales, Pillar Type	100.00	135.00	200.00	600.00	—
Charles III to Ferdinand VII, 4 Reales, Bust Type	30.00	50.00	100.00	500.00	—

8 REALES. This is by far the most important foreign coin to circulate in Canada. It was known and appreciated all over the civilized world and was the principal end product of the vast amounts of silver mined in the New World. The 8-real piece had the nickname dollar (even though it was not a decimal coin) due to its similarity in size to the European thalers and dalders. It is the famous "piece-of-eight" of pirate lore. The first 8-real pieces were produced in 1556 at the Mexico City mint.

Type and Denomination	VG	F	VF	EF	AU
Philip V to Charles III, 8 Reales (Dollar), Pillar Type	65.00	100.00	140.00	275.00	600.00
Charles III to Ferdinand VII, * Reales, Bust Type	25.00	60.00	80.00	135.00	275.00

GOLD COINS

2 ESCUDOS. This gold coin was popularly known as the Spanish pistole and, next to the doubloon (see below), was the most widely used Spanish-American gold coin in Canada.

Type and Denomination	VG	F	VF	EF	AU
Charles III to Ferdinand VII, 2 Escudos	150.00	300.00	425.00	725.00	—

4 ESCUDOS

Type and Denomination	VG	F	VF	EF	AU
Charles III to Ferdinand VII, 4 Escudos	375.00	600.00	900.00	1,650.00	—

8 ESCUDOS (DOUBLOON). The most important gold coin in Canada was the 8-escudo piece or doubloon. It circulated widely, but was especially popular in the Atlantic provinces. After the Spanish colonies gained their independence, these coins were called "Royal" doubloons (as opposed to "Patriot" doubloons discussed below).

Type and Denomination	VG	F	VF	EF	AU
Charles III to Ferdinand VII, 8 Escudos (Doubloon)	500.00	700.00	1,200.00	1,800.00	—

COINS OF FORMER SPANISH COLONIES

By 1826 Spain had lost all her colonies in the New World. This ushered in new coinages on the existing standards by each of the former colonies. They were accepted and circulated alongside the coins of the Spanish-American series. Probably only two denominations are necessary in this listing — the silver dollar and the gold doubloon.

8 REALES (DOLLAR). The most important dollars of former Spanish colonies to circulate in Canada are undoubtedly those of Mexico.

Type and Denomination	VG	F	VF	EF	AU	UNC
1820s to 1840s, Mexican 8 Reales (Dollar)	25.00	45.00	65.00	110.00	225.00	—

8 ESCUDOS (DOUBLOON). In the case of the doubloon it is more difficult to single out any one former colony's coinage as being the most important for Canada. Therefore a general listing is given. Contemporary sources refer to such doubloons as "Patriot" doubloons to distinguish them for the "Royal" doubloons of the Spanish-American series. It is known that "Patriot" doubloons were specifically imported into such provinces as Nova Scotia.

Typical "Patriot" Doubloon from Chile

Type and Denomination	VG	F	VF	EF	AU	UNC
1817 to 1830s, "Patriot" 8 Escudos (Doubloon)	B.V.	475.00	550.00	1,000.00	—	—

Note: B.V. is the abbreviation for bullion value

COINS OF THE UNITED STATES

It is to the United States coinage that we owe our present decimal currency system. By the 1850s trade links between British North America and the U.S. were so strong and her coinage so commonplace here that the proponents of a currency akin to that of the U.S. instead of Great Britain won out.

The U.S. coinage on a decimal basis began in the 1790s and it has circulated here to varying degrees ever since. A great influx of U.S. silver coins took place during the 1850s and 1860s, after the proportion of silver contained in the 5-, 10-, 25- and 50-cent pieces was reduced. Previous to that time, U.S. large cents came across the border in quantity and large numbers of half dollars were imported to help pay for work on such projects as the Rideau Canal. The larger denominations of U.S. gold coins were important in Canada almost up to the beginning of this century because they were widely imported by banks and the government for use in backing and redeeming paper money.

COPPER COINS

1 CENT

Type and Denomination	VG	F	VF	EF	AU	UNC
1816-1836 Coronet Head	18.00	30.00	70.00	140.00	200.00	350.00
1837-1857 Braided Hair	15.00	18.00	25.00	65.00	100.00	225.00

SILVER COINS

HALF DIME

Type and Denomination	VG	F	VF	EF	AU	UNC
1837-1838 Seated Liberty Half Dime 4 Varieties	45.00	60.00	115.00	225.00	400.00	700.00
1839-1859	10.00	13.00	25.00	65.00	125.00	250.00
1860-1873	10.00	13.00	18.00	40.00	80.00	200.00

DIME

Type and Denomination	VG	F	VF	EF	AU	UNC
1837-1838 Seated Liberty Dime 5 Varieties	50.00	80.00	300.0	650.00	900.00	1,350.00
1839-1873	10.00	13.00	24.00	55.00	175.00	400.00
1873-1891	6.00	10.00	16.00	35.00	90.00	200.00

QUARTER DOLLAR

Type and Denomination	VG	F	VF	EF	AU	UNC
1838-1853 Seated Liberty Quarter 5 Varieties	15.00	30.00	60.00	100.00	300.00	600.00
1854-1875	14.00	25.00	40.00	110.00	250.00	700.00
1875-1891	13.00	22.00	35.00	60.00	125.00	375.00

HALF DOLLAR

Type and Denomination	VG	F	VF	EF	AU	UNC
1807-1839 Capped Bust Half Dollar 3 Varieties	40.00	45.00	70.00	135.00	335.00	950.00
1839-1853 Seated Liberty Half Dollar 5 Varieties	30.00	40.00	60.00	100.00	200.00	650.00
1854-1865	25.00	45.00	60.00	125.00	350.00	1,000.00
1866-1891	25.00	45.00	55.00	100.00	200.00	600.00

GOLD COINS

HALF EAGLE (FIVE DOLLARS)

Type and Denomination	F	VF	EF	AU	UNC
1834-1838 Classic Head	325.00	400.00	650.00	1,200.00	3,500.00
1839-1866 Coronet Head	175.00	200.00	275.00	375.00	2,000.00
1866-1908	150.00	180.00	200.00	225.00	275.00

EAGLE (TEN DOLLARS)

Type and Denomination	F	VF	EF	AU	UNC
1838-1865 Coronet Head 2 Varieties	250.00	300.00	400.00	750.00	5,000.00
1866-1907	B.V.	260.00	285.00	325.00	400.00

DOUBLE EAGLE (TWENTY DOLLARS)

Type and Denomination	F	VF	EF	AU	UNC
1849-1866 Coronet Head 3 Varieties	B.V.	575.00	650.00	850.00	2,700.00
1866-1876	B.V.	575.00	625.00	750.00	1,000.00
1877-1907	B.V.	560.00	575.00	600.00	675.00

LOCAL PRE-DECIMAL COINS

Although it is sometimes stated that the first coins produced for local use in Canada were the 1858-1859 decimal coins for the Province of Canada, this is not the case. A small but important group of local coinages was produced prior to the adoption of decimal currency. These coinages were at first specially modified Spanish-American silver coins, but coppers were added to this group in the 1850s.

NEW FRANCE (FRENCH REGIME)

COUNTERSTAMPED SPANISH-AMERICAN COINS

During the last part of the 17th century, the quantity of Spanish-American silver coins in circulation in New France increased. This increase was due primarily to the illegal trade in furs which the colonists were carrying on with the Dutch and English. At that time such coins circulated at a value that depended upon their weight; the more worn the coin was, the lower it was valued compared to unworn pieces. Since many Spanish-American coins in New France had varying amounts of wear, their use in commerce was difficult. Colonial authorities were not anxious to see these coins used in preference to French coins, but the latter were so scarce that they relented. In the early 1680s treasury officials weighed a quantity of these coins and counterstamped each with a fleur-de-lis. Underweight coins also received a Roman numeral counterstamp (from I to IV) to indicate the amount by which the weight was deficient. The coins could then be compared to a table to determine the exact value at which they were current.

Unfortunately for collectors, no surviving examples of this interesting local issue are known.

NOVA SCOTIA, NEW BRUNSWICK, PRINCE EDWARD ISLAND

For the pre-decimal coinage of Colonial New Brunswick, Nova Scotia and Prince Edward Island, see *The Charlton Standard Catalogue of Canadian Colonial Tokens.*

HISTORY OF CANADIAN DECIMAL COINS

The decimal coins which we take so much for granted today have a history that stretches back into the last century and beyond. During the 1700s, the single most important coin in North America was the Spanish-American dollar, a large silver coin produced in great quantities by mints in Mexico, Peru and other parts of the New World. The Spanish-American dollar was not a decimal coin; its formal denomination was 8 reales. It was nicknamed dollar in deference to its resemblance in size to German thalers and other large European coins of similar name. This Spanish-American coin was so important in the United States that when the U.S. adopted a decimal system of dollars and cents in the 1790s, their silver was made with the same amount of silver as the Spanish-American dollar.

In British North America in the first half of the 19th century each colony used a system of accounting which consisted of pounds, shillings and pence. However, the coins actually in circulation were mostly Spanish-American and U.S. As trade with the United States increased in the 1840s and 1850s, the British North American colonies (provinces) were naturally drawn closer toward the adoption of a currency system more like that of the U.S. than Great Britain.

All through the 1850s British North America struggled with the problem of currency standards. The Province of Canada, under Francis Hincks, took the lead in fighting for a decimal system. Acts passed in 1851 and 1853 stipulated that public accounts be kept in dollars and cents, but no coins were issued under their provisions. An 1857 act provided a broader base for a decimal currency system. It directed that both government and private accounts be kept in dollars, cents and mils. A decimal coinage followed in 1858-1859, based upon a dollar equal to the U.S. gold dollar.

Other British North American provinces soon followed the Province of Canada's lead. New Brunswick and Nova Scotia adopted decimal systems in 1859-1860, Newfoundland followed suit in 1864 and Prince Edward Island went decimal in 1871. Thus, even before Confederation the use of decimal coins was firmly established.

NOVA SCOTIA

In the years immediately preceding the adoption of a decimal currency system in Nova Scotia in 1859, British coins formed an important part of the circulating currency, much more so than in the other British North American provinces. Consequently, the Nova Scotia government chose a decimal dollar equal to one-fifth of a pound sterling (i.e. $5 * £1), allowing British silver coins to conveniently fit into the new system and continue circulating. The British 2-shilling piece (florin) became a 50-cent piece, the shilling became a 25-cent piece and the sixpence became a 12 1/2-cent piece. The only coins the province needed to have specially produced were a cent, and to make change for the sixpence and half crown, a half cent.

HALF CENT
Victoria 1861 - 1864

The half cent was coined the same diameter as the British farthing and utilized the same obverse. Pattern pieces incorporated the royal crown and a wreath of roses (see NS-1 to NS-3 and NS-5 in the chapter on Patterns). However, a local campaign in favour of the provincial flower, the mayflower, resulted in the adoption of a design using the royal crown surrounded by a wreath of both roses and mayflowers.

Designer and Modeller:
Obverse — Leonard C. Wyon
Reverse — Leonard C. Wyon
from a model by C. Hill
Composition: .95 copper, .04 tin, .01 zinc
Weight: 2.84 grams
Diameter: 20.65 mm
Edge: Plain
Die Axis: ↑↑

Date and Mint Mark	Quantity Minted	VG-8	F-12	VF-20	EF-40	AU-50	MS-60	MS-63
1861	400,000	7.00	10.00	15.00	25.00	60.00	125.00	225.00
1864	400,000	7.00	10.00	15.00	25.00	60.00	110.00	200.00

ONE CENT
Victoria 1861 - 1864

The cent was minted the same diameter as the British halfpenny and used the same obverse. The reverse designs are similar to those used for the half cent, including pattern pieces with a wreath of roses (see NS-4 and NS-6 in the chapter on Patterns).

The circulation issues of this denomination have two distinct reverses. The first (1861) has much detail in the crown and a large rosebud at the lower right part of the wreath. On the second reverse (1861-1864) the crown has a narrower headband and generally less detail, the rosebud at the lower right is smaller, and the rosebud and certain other parts of the design come closer to the lettering and the raised line just inside the rim denticles.

MINTAGE FIGURES 1861-1862. The mintage figures of 800,000 for 1861 and 1,000,000 for 1862 have puzzled collectors for many years since the 1862-dated coins are scarcer. The probable explanation is that some, perhaps most, cents struck in 1862 were from dies dated 1861. Therefore, the mintages for the two years have been combined.

Designer and Modeller:
  Obverse — Leonard C. Wyon
  Reverse — Leonard C. Wyon
  from a model by C. Hill
Engraver: Leonard C. Wyon
Composition: .95 copper, .04 tin, .01 zinc
Weight: 5.67 grams
Diameter: 25.53 mm
Edge: Plain
Die Axis: ↑↑

| | Large Rosebud | | | | | | Small Rosebud |

Date and Mint Mark	Quantity Minted	VG-8	F-12	VF-20	EF-40	AU-50	MS-60	MS-63
1861 Large Bud	1,800,000	6.00	10.00	13.00	25.00	60.00	190.00	375.00
1861 Small Bud	Incl. above	5.00	8.00	12.00	22.00	50.00	165.00	325.00
1862	Incl. above*	35.00	45.00	85.00	165.00	300.00	550.00	1,250.00
1864	800,000	6.00	10.00	13.00	22.00	50.00	165.00	375.00

*Most of the cents issued in 1862 were dated 1861.

NEW BRUNSWICK

When New Brunswick adopted a decimal dollar in 1860, it chose the same rating for its dollar and ordered the same denominations as the Province of Canada: cents in bronze and 5-, 10- and 20-cent pieces in silver. The effective date for the decimal currency act was November 1, 1860 but, like Nova Scotia, New Brunswick had to wait until early 1862 before the first coins arrived from England. In the meantime, the government introduced other decimal coins as a temporary expedient. Thus, in late 1861 and early 1862 some 500,000 Province of Canada cents and a quantity of United States small denomination silver coins were put into circulation in the province.

HALF CENT
Victoria 1861

This denomination was not required by the province since its dollar and hence British coins went at a different rating than in the sister province of Nova Scotia. Nevertheless, the Royal Mint became confused and struck a half cent for New Brunswick. Over 200,000 of these coins came off the presses before the error was discovered. Most of the mintage was returned to the melting pot. The circulation strikes that survived are thought to have become mixed with the Nova Scotia half cents and sent to Halifax.

The obverse is that of the British farthing and the reverse is a royal crown and a rose/mayflower wreath very similar to that used for Nova Scotia.

Designer and Modeller:
Obverse — Leonard C. Wyon
Reverse — Leonard C. Wyon
from a model by C. Hill
Engraver: Leonard C. Wyon
Composition: .95 copper, .04 tin, .01 zinc
Weight: 2.84 grams
Diameter: 20.65 mm
Edge: Plain
Die Axis: ↑↑

Date and Mint Mark	Quantity Minted	G-4	VG-8	F-12	VF-20	EF-40	AU-50	MS-60	MS-63
1861	222,800*	65.00	110.00	165.00	250.00	325.00	525.00	750.00	1,250.00

*most were melted prior to issue.

ONE CENT
Victoria 1861 - 1864

The New Brunswick 1-cent pieces have the British halfpenny obverse and a reverse similar to that used for the Nova Scotia cent.

For the 1864 issue two styles of 6 were used in the date: a figure with a round centre in its loop and a short top, and a figure with a more oval centre and a longer top.

Designer and Modeller:
Obverse — Leonard C. Wyon
Reverse — Leonard C. Wyon
from a model by C. Hill
Engraver: Leonard C. Wyon
Composition: .95 copper, .04 tin, .01 zinc
Weight: 5.67 grams
Diameter: 25.53 mm
Edge: Plain
Die Axis: ↑↑

Short 6   Tall 6

Date and Mint Mark	Quantity Minted	G-4	VG-8	F-12	VF-20	EF-40	AU-50	MS-60	MS-63
1861	1,000,000	3.00	6.00	10.00	15.00	25.00	55.00	200.00	350.00
1864 Short 6	1,000,000	3.00	6.00	10.00	15.00	25.00	55.00	225.00	375.00
1864 Tall 6	Incl. above	3.00	6.00	10.00	15.00	25.00	55.00	225.00	375.00

FIVE CENTS
Victoria 1862 - 1864

The production of New Brunswick's first silver decimal coinage had to await the completion of the bronze coinage. Consequently, it could not commence until 1862. The 5-cent piece designs were basically those of the Province of Canada with an appropriately modified obverse legend.

Two styles of 6 were employed in dating the 1864 issue: a small 6 and a large 6.

Engraver: Obverse — Leonard C. Wyon
Composition: .925 silver, .075 copper
Weight: 1.16 grams
Diameter: 15.49 mm
Edge: Reeded
Die Axis: ↑↓

Small 6   Large 6

Date and Mint Mark	Quantity Minted	G-4	VG-8	F-12	VF-20	EF-40	AU-50	MS-60	MS-63
1862	100,000	30.00	65.00	110.00	250.00	500.00	1,500.00	2,750.00	6,000.00
1864 Small 6	100,000	30.00	65.00	110.00	250.00	500.00	1,750.00	3,250.00	7,000.00
1864 Large 6	Incl. above	30.00	65.00	110.00	250.00	500.00	1,750.00	3,250.00	7,000.00

TEN CENTS
Victoria 1862 - 1864

The designs for the New Brunswick 10-cent piece were adapted from existing Province of Canada designs. The reverse was used without modification and the obverse involved changing the legend only.

The 1862 issue is usually collected as two varieties. One has a normal date and the other has an obviously double-punched 2.

Engraver: Obverse — Leonard C. Wyon
Composition: .925 silver, .075 copper
Weight: 2.32 grams
Diameter: 17.91 mm
Edge: Reeded
Die Axis: ↑↓

1 8 6 2   1 8 6 2

Normal Date   Double-punched 2

Date and Mint Mark	Quantity Minted	G-4	VG-8	F-12	VF-20	EF-40	AU-50	MS-60	MS-63
1862	150,000	33.00	50.00	90.00	225.00	450.00	900.00	2,000.00	5,000.00
1862 D-P 2	Incl. above	50.00	70.00	135.00	350.00	750.00	1,500.00	3,000.00	—
1864	150,000	33.00	50.00	90.00	225.00	500.00	1,100.00	2,500.00	6,000.00

TWENTY CENTS
Victoria 1862 - 1864

The New Brunswick 20-cent piece has an unusual reverse design once rejected for the Province of Canada (see PC-4 in the chapter on Patterns). The reverse adopted by the Province of Canada differs in style, although uses the same elements, from the reverse chosen by New Brunswick. This stylistic difference, plus the fact a die for the New Brunswick 20-cent piece of 1862 was used to strike one side of George W. Wyon's obituary medalet, suggests that it was George Wyon and not Leonard Wyon who engraved this reverse. The obverse utilizes the Province of Canada 20 cents portrait with a special legend for New Brunswick.

Designer and Modeller:
Reverse — possibly Geo. W. Wyon
Engraver: Obverse — Leonard C. Wyon
Composition: .925 silver, .075 copper
Weight: 4.65 grams
Diameter: 23.27 mm
Edge: Reeded
Die Axis: ↑↓

Date and Mint Mark	Quantity Minted	G-4	VG-8	F-12	VF-20	EF-40	AU-50	MS-60	MS-63
1862	150,000	20.00	25.00	40.00	100.00	275.00	700.00	1,750.00	5,000.00
1864	150,000	20.00	25.00	40.00	100.00	275.00	700.00	1,750.00	4,500.00

PRINCE EDWARD ISLAND

ONE CENT
Victoria 1871

Prince Edward Island adopted a decimal currency system in 1871. Its dollar was given the same rating as those of the provinces of Canada and New Brunswick. The only coinage in the new system was bronze cents in 1871. The island entered Confederation two years later. The provincial government experienced considerable difficulty placing its cents in circulation. It took almost ten years to deplete the stock and the last of it was sold at a 10 percent discount.

The reverse was prepared specifically for the Prince Edward Island government, incorporating the seal of the island and a Latin phrase, "PARVA SUB INGENTI," meaning "The small beneath the great." The seal shows a large oak tree, representing England, sheltering three young oak trees, representing the three counties on the island.

Because of pressure to produce domestic coin, the Royal Mint in London made arrangements with Heaton's Mint in Birmingham to strike P.E.I. cents. For some unknown reason Heaton's familiar "H" mint mark is absent from the coins.

Designer and Modeller:
Obverse — Leonard C. Wyon,
from a portrait model by William Theed
Reverse — Leonard C. Wyon
Composition: .95 copper, .04 tin,
.01 zinc
Weight: 5.67 grams
Diameter: 25.40 mm
Edge: Plain
Die Axis: ↑↑

Date and Mint Mark	Quantity Minted	G-4	VG-8	F-12	VF-20	EF-40	AU-50	MS-60	MS-63
1871	2,000,000	1.50	3.00	5.00	10.00	20.00	45.00	135.00	200.00

NEWFOUNDLAND

Since Newfoundland remained separate from Canada until 1949, it has a much larger decimal coin series than the other pre-Confederation British colonies. The island adopted decimal currency in 1863, hoping to have coins on the new standard in circulation in 1864. The most important coin in Newfoundland had been the Spanish-American dollar or 8-real piece, so the government set its dollar equal in value to this coin. This made the new decimal cent equal to the British halfpenny and $4.80 equal to £1 sterling.

ONE CENT
Victoria 1865 - 1896

Beginning in 1864, several designs were considered for the Newfoundland cent. The first tendency was to use the same designs as New Brunswick. Pattern dies are known for an 1864 Newfoundland cent with the royal crown, rose/mayflower design (see NF-1 in the chapter on Patterns). This design was rejected in favour of a royal crown and wreath of pitcher plant (the provincial flower) and oak, with unusual broad, bold lettering and date. The obverse incorporated the British halfpenny portrait with the legend "VICTORIA QUEEN," also in the same bold type (see NF-6 in the chapter on Patterns). However, it was decided that this legend was inappropriate and the cents struck for circulation in 1865 use the British halfpenny obverse legend - "VICTORIA D:G:BRITT:REG:F:D:."

An interesting variation in die axes occurs on this denomination. For all dates except 1872 the dies are in the medal arrangement (↑↑) but on the 1872s they are coinage arrangement (↑↓). The most reasonable explanation for this difference is that the Heaton Mint, which struck the 1872 cents, did not receive specific instructions regarding which die arrangement to use and chose the same arrangement as for the silver. The error was corrected in 1876 when Heaton's next coined cents for Newfoundland.

Designer:
    Reverse — Horace Morehen
Engraver: Thomas J. Minton
Composition: .95 copper, .04 tin,
                .01 zinc
Weight: 5.67 grams
Diameter: 25.53 mm
Edge: Plain
Die Axis:↑↑ (1865, 1873-1896);
              ↑↓ (1872)

Heaton Mint issues have an "H" mint mark at the bottom of the wreath (1872-1876). London Mint strikings have no letter.

Date and Mint Mark	Quantity Minted	VG-8	F-12	VF-20	EF-40	AU-50	MS-60	MS-63
1865	240,000	5.00	7.00	12.00	30.00	100.00	225.00	600.00
1872H	200,000	5.00	7.00	12.00	30.00	75.00	100.00	225.00
1873	200,000	6.00	11.00	25.00	60.00	200.00	450.00	1,750.00
1876H	200,000	5.00	7.00	12.00	45.00	135.00	300.00	600.00

VARIETIES 1880. Three date varieties exist for 1880. The first has a narrow 0 in the date, while the second and third have a wide 0, in different positions. The positional differences between the second and third varieties are not felt to be important, so they are combined into one variety, the Wide 0.

1880 Narrow O   1880 Wide O

Date and Mint Mark	Quantity Minted	VG-8	F-12	VF-20	EF-40	AU-50	MS-60	MS-63
1880 Narrow 0	400,000	150.00	200.00	300.00	500.00	800.00	1,250.00	2,500.00
1880 Wide 0	Incl. above	5.00	7.00	17.00	35.00	110.00	225.00	500.00
1885	40,000	35.00	60.00	85.00	175.00	300.00	700.00	2,500.00
1888	50,000	30.00	55.00	75.00	150.00	275.00	750.00	3,000.00
1890	200,000	5.00	7.00	12.00	25.00	100.00	250.00	900.00
1894	200,000	5.00	7.00	12.00	25.00	100.00	225.00	600.00
1896	200,000	5.00	7.00	12.00	25.00	100.00	200.00	500.00

ONE CENT
Edward VII 1904 - 1909

The reverse design is a modification of the Victorian reverse, substituting the Imperial State crown for the St. Edward's crown. The obverses of most Edward VII denominations were those of the corresponding Dominion of Canada coinage; however, the Newfoundland cent has a distinctive design. The bust is very large and the letter size in the legend correspondingly small.

Designer and Modeller:
   Portrait — G. W. DeSaulles,
   (DES below bust)
Engraver: Reverse — W. H. J. Blakemore,
           modifying existing coinage tools
Composition: .95 copper, .04 tin,
           .01 zinc
Weight: 5.67 grams
Diameter: 25.53 mm
Edge: Plain
Die Axis: ↑↑

The Mint, Birmingham issue (1904 only) has an "H" mint mark at the bottom of the wreath. Royal Mint strikings have no letter.

Date and Mint Mark	Quantity Minted	VG-8	F-12	VF-20	EF-40	AU-50	MS-60	MS-63
1904H	100,000	9.00	17.00	35.00	60.00	150.00	500.00	1,000.00
1907	200,000	3.00	6.00	10.00	25.00	100.00	200.00	500.00
1909	200,000	3.00	6.00	10.00	22.00	90.00	175.00	275.00

ONE CENT
George V 1913 - 1936

The reverse for the cents of this reign is that established for the Edward VII series and the obverse is that of the Dominion of Canada cents.

Designer and Modeller:
   Portrait — Sir E.B. MacKennal,
   (B.M. on the truncation)
Composition: .95 copper, .04 tin,
          .01 zinc (1913-1920);
          .955 copper; .030 tin,
          .015 zinc (1926-1936)
Diameter: 25.53 mm (1913, 1929-1936);
         25.40 mm (1917-1920)
Edge: Plain
Die Axis: ↑↑

Ottawa Mint issues (1917-1920) have a "C" mint mark at the bottom of the wreath, Royal Mint strikings have no letter.

Date and Mint Mark	Quantity Minted	VG-8	F-12	VF-20	EF-40	AU-50	MS-60	MS-63
1913	400,000	1.00	2.00	4.00	8.00	35.00	70.00	100.00
1917C	702,350	1.00	2.00	4.00	8.00	35.00	125.00	225.00
1919C	300,000	1.00	2.00	5.00	10.00	60.00	200.00	500.00
1920C	302,184	1.00	2.00	7.00	20.00	100.00	300.00	1,500.00
1929	300,000	1.00	2.00	4.00	8.00	35.00	100.00	175.00
1936	300,000	1.00	2.00	3.00	6.00	20.00	50.00	100.00

ONE CENT
George VI 1938 - 1947

In 1937 the Newfoundland government reviewed the question of converting to a small cent, similar to those used in Canada and the United States. The smaller coin was less expensive to produce and Newfoundlanders objected to the reverse design of the large cent, in which their provincial flower was forced into an unnatural configuration.

The reverse design adopted for the new coins was a very life-like rendition of the pitcher plant in bloom. The plant is native to Newfoundland, and is one of the insectivores of the plant kingdom. The large leaves are pitcher-like receptacles, the inner surfaces being covered with downward-sloping bristles. Insects are attracted onto their leaves by a sweet sticky syrup at the bottom and the bristles help prevent their escape. The digestible portions of the insects are then absorbed by the plant.

During World War II, Newfoundland cents were coined at Ottawa rather than in England to avoid the risks of transatlantic shipping. In 1940 and 1942 the "C" mint mark was omitted in error.

Designer and Modeller:
  Portrait — Percy Metcalfe
  (P.M. below bust)
  Reverse — Walter J. Newman
Composition: .955 copper, .030 tin,
  .015 zinc
Weight: 3.24 grams
Diameter: 19.05 mm
Edge: Plain
Die Axis: ↑↑

Royal Canadian Mint issues (1940-47) have a "C" mint mark to the right of CENT on the reverse (except for the 1940 and 1942 issues, which have none). The Royal Mint issue (1938) has no mint mark.

Date and Mint Mark	Quantity Minted	VG-8	F-12	VF-20	EF-40	AU-50	MS-60	MS-63
1938	500,000	1.50	2.00	3.00	5.00	10.00	25.00	40.00
1940	300,000	2.50	3.50	5.00	11.00	30.00	60.00	250.00
1941C	827,662	.75	1.25	2.00	3.00	10.00	25.00	125.00
1942	1,996,889	.75	1.25	2.00	3.00	10.00	25.00	75.00
1943C	1,239,732	.75	1.25	2.00	3.00	10.00	25.00	75.00
1944C	1,328,776	1.50	2.50	5.00	12.00	35.00	85.00	400.00
1947C	313,772	1.50	2.50	5.00	13.00	40.00	100.00	400.00

FIVE CENTS

Victoria 1865 - 1896

Work on the coinage tools for the silver began later than for the cent, so there are no legend wording varieties for this denomination. The first pattern is a bronze striking of the adopted obverse (derived from the New Brunswick obverse by substitution of "NEWFOUNDLAND" for "NEW BRUNSWICK") and the Canada/New Brunswick reverse with a maple wreath and royal crown (see NF-2 in the chapter on Patterns). A later pattern, in silver, has an arabesque design similar to the adopted design, except the arches are thinner (see NF-8 in the chapter on Patterns).

Designer and Modeller:
Reverse — Leonard C. Wyon
Engraver: Obverse — Leonard C. Wyon
Composition: .925 silver, .075 copper
Weight: 1.18 grams
Diameter: 15.49 mm
Edge: Reeded
Die Axis: ↑↓

Heaton Mint issues have an "H" mint mark either on the obverse under the bust (1872-1876) or on the reverse under the date (1882). London Mint strikings have no letter.

Date and Mint Mark	Quantity Minted	G-4	VG-8	F-12	VF-20	EF-40	AU-50	MS-60	MS-63
1865	80,000	22.00	40.00	60.00	110.00	275.00	550.00	1,600.00	3,250.00
1870	40,000	40.00	70.00	110.00	175.00	350.00	800.00	2,000.00	3,750.00
1872H	40,000	28.00	50.00	65.00	135.00	275.00	550.00	1,250.00	2,250.00
1873	40,000	45.00	100.00	130.00	275.00	500.00	1,000.00	2,500.00	5,000.00
1873H	Incl. above	700.00	1,300.00	2,000.00	3,000.00	4,000.00	6,000.00	-	-
1876H	20,000	65.00	150.00	225.00	350.00	500.00	900.00	2,000.00	3,000.00
1880	40,000	33.00	60.00	85.00	175.00	325.00	850.00	2,000.00	4,000.00
1881	40,000	17.00	35.00	65.00	100.00	250.00	550.00	2,000.00	4,000.00
1882H	60,000	17.00	30.00	60.00	100.00	225.00	550.00	1,750.00	3,500.00
1885	16,000	100.00	175.00	300.00	425.00	700.00	1,750.00	3,500.00	7,500.00
1888	40,000	22.00	50.00	70.00	125.00	275.00	600.00	2,250.00	4,000.00
1890	160,000	6.00	12.00	25.00	60.00	135.00	500.00	1,750.00	4,000.00
1894	160,000	6.00	12.00	25.00	60.00	135.00	500.00	1,750.00	3,500.00
1896	400,000	4.00	8.00	16.00	35.00	90.00	450.00	1,500.00	3,500.00

FIVE CENTS
Edward VII 1903 - 1908

The obverse for this denomination is that of the Dominion of Canada issues. The reverse, a new design by G.W. DeSaulles, is one of the last coinage designs he did before his death.

Designer and Modeller:
George W. DeSaulles,
(DES. below bust)
Composition: .925 silver, .075 copper
Weight: 1.18 grams
Diameter: 15.49 mm
Edge: Reeded
Die Axis: ↑↓

The Mint, Birmingham issue of 1904 has an "H" mint mark below the oval at the bottom on the reverse. Royal Mint issues have no letter.

Date and Mint Mark	Quantity Minted	VG-8	F-12	VF-20	EF-40	AU-50	MS-60	MS-63
1903	100,000	6.00	12.00	35.00	85.00	325.00	850.00	2,500.00
1904H	100,000	4.00	8.00	25.00	60.00	175.00	300.00	400.00
1908	400,000	3.00	6.00	20.00	50.00	150.00	400.00	900.00

FIVE CENTS
George V 1912 - 1929

The obverse is the same as for the Dominion of Canada issue and the reverse is the same as the Newfoundland Edward VII issue.

Designer and Modeller:
  Portrait — Sir E.B. MacKennal,
  (B.M. on the truncation)
Composition: .925 silver, .075 copper
Weight: 1.18 grams (1912);
  1.17 grams (1917-1929)
Diameter: 15.49 mm (1912-1919);
  15.69 mm (1929)
Edge: Reeded
Die Axis: ↑↑

The Ottawa Mint issues (1917-1919) have a "C" mint mark below the oval at the bottom on the reverse. Royal Mint strikings have no letter.

Date and Mint Mark	Quantity Minted	VG-8	F-12	VF-20	EF-40	AU-50	MS-60	MS-63
1912	300,000	1.25	2.50	7.00	30.00	80.00	200.00	400.00
1917C	300,319	1.25	2.50	6.00	25.00	90.00	375.00	800.00
1919C	100,844	2.50	5.00	13.00	60.00	300.00	1,500.00	3,500.00
1929	300,000	1.25	2.50	5.00	20.00	80.00	300.00	600.00

FIVE CENTS
George VI 1938 - 1947

While considering the replacement of the large cent, the Newfoundland government also contemplated dropping its "fish scale" silver 5-cent piece in favour of a nickel coin similar to Canada's. At that time, because of a strong conservative element, it was decided to change only the cent. The reverse design was continued from the previous reign and the obverse used the standard portrait for British colonial coinages.

Designer and Modeller:
  Portrait — Percy Metcalfe,
  (P.M. below bust)
Composition: .925 silver,
  .075 copper (1938-1944)
  .800 silver, .200 copper
  (1945-1947)
Weight: 1.17 grams
Diameter: 15.69 mm (1938);
  15.49 mm (1940-1947)
Edge: Reeded
Die Axis: ↑↑

Royal Canadian Mint issues (1940-47) have a "C" mint mark below the oval at the bottom on the reverse. The Royal Mint issue (1938) has no letter.

Date and Mint Mark	Quantity Minted	VG-8	F-12	VF-20	EF-40	AU-50	MS-60	MS-63
1938	100,000	1.00	2.00	3.50	7.00	35.00	125.00	350.00
1940C	200,000	1.00	2.00	3.50	6.00	25.00	125.00	400.00
1941C	612,641	1.00	2.00	3.50	4.50	12.00	25.00	50.00
1942C	298,348	1.00	2.00	3.50	5.00	15.00	30.00	60.00
1943C	351,666	1.00	2.00	3.50	5.00	12.00	25.00	50.00
1944C	286,504	1.00	2.00	3.50	5.00	18.00	45.00	150.00
1945C	203,828	1.00	2.00	3.50	5.00	12.00	25.00	50.00

1946C - 1947C ISSUES. The 1946C issue is an anomaly. Published official mint reports, as well as unpublished mint accounting records, do not indicate any mintage of this denomination during 1946. It appears that this scarce issue was actually coined during 1947. The mintage figures given for the years 1946 and 1947 must be considered unofficial although they are believed to have come from a mint officer many years ago.

Date and Mint Mark	Quantity Minted	VG-8	F-12	VF-20	EF-40	AU-50	MS-60	MS-63
1946C	2,041	250.00	375.00	500.00	700.00	1,000.00	1,750.00	2,750.00
1947C	38,400	3.00	6.00	10.00	20.00	50.00	90.00	225.00

TEN CENTS
Victoria 1865 - 1896

Like the 5 cents, the 10 cents has a bronze pattern with the adopted obverse (derived from the New Brunswick obverse by substituting "NEWFOUNDLAND" for "NEW BRUNSWICK") and the Canada/New Brunswick reverse (see NF-3 in the chapter on Patterns). As well there is a silver pattern with very thin arches in the arabesque design on the reverse (see NF-9 in the chapter on Patterns).

Designer and Modeller:
Reverse — Leonard C. Wyon
Engraver: Obverse — Leonard C. Wyon
Composition: .925 silver, .075 copper
Weight: 2.36 grams
Diameter: 17.98 mm
Edge: Reeded
Die Axis: ↑↓

Heaton Mint issues have an "H" mint mark either on the obverse under the bust (1872-1876) or on the reverse under the date (1882). London Mint strikings have no letter.

Date and Mint Mark	Quantity Minted	G-4	VG-8	F-12	VF-20	EF-40	AU-50	MS-60	MS-63
1865	80,000	11.00	25.00	45.00	110.00	325.00	750.00	2,000.00	3,750.00
1870	30,000	135.00	250.00	350.00	700.00	1,400.00	2,250.00	4,500.00	8,000.00

1871H NEWFOUNDLAND/CANADA MULE. A rare variety exists because an 1871H Dominion of Canada reverse die was muled, apparently accidentally, with an "H" Newfoundland obverse die. All known examples are in well-worn condition.

1871H Newfoundland/Canada Mule

Date and Mint Mark	Quantity Minted	G-4	VG-8	F-12	VF-20	EF-40	AU-50	MS-60	MS-63
1871H Mule	40,000				VERY RARE				
1872H	Incl. above	11.00	22.00	40.00	90.00	225.00	600.00	1,500.00	3,000.00
1873	20,000	17.00	35.00	75.00	200.00	750.00	2,000.00	3,500.00	7,500.00
1876H	10,000	20.00	40.00	75.00	160.00	450.00	1,100.00	2,250.00	3,500.00

All examples of the 1880 issue are from dies in which the second 8 of the date is punched over a 7.

1880 Second 8 over 7

Date and Mint Mark	Quantity Minted	G-4	VG-8	F-12	VF-20	EF-40	AU-50	MS-60	MS-63
1880	10,000	22.00	50.00	95.00	225.00	500.00	1,200.00	2,750.00	4,500.00
1882H	20,000	17.00	30.00	70.00	200.00	750.00	1,500.00	-	-
1885	8,000	55.00	100.00	200.00	400.00	900.00	1,750.00	4,000.00	8,000.00
1888	30,000	17.00	30.00	60.00	150.00	750.00	2,000.00	-	-
1890	100,000	5.00	11.00	20.00	45.00	150.00	500.00	2,000.00	5,000.00
1894	100,000	5.00	11.00	20.00	45.00	150.00	500.00	1,750.00	3,500.00
1896	230,000	5.00	11.00	20.00	45.00	150.00	500.00	2,000.00	4,500.00

TEN CENTS
Edward VII 1903 - 1904

The obverse is that used for the Dominion of Canada issues. The reverse is a new design by G.W. DeSaulles.

Designer and Modeller:
G.W. DeSaulles,
(DES. below bust)
Composition: .925 silver, .075 copper
Weight: 2.36 grams
Diameter: 17.96 mm
Edge: Reeded
Die Axis: ↑↓

The Mint, Birmingham issue of 1904 has an "H" mint mark below the oval at the bottom on the reverse. The Royal Mint issue (1903) has no letter.

Date and Mint Mark	Quantity Minted	G-4	VG-8	F-12	VF-20	EF-40	AU-50	MS-60	MS-63
1903	100,000	3.50	9.00	20.00	60.00	200.00	400.00	1,750.00	5,000.00
1904H	100,000	2.50	5.00	12.00	35.00	100.00	200.00	300.00	650.00

TEN CENTS
George V 1912 - 1919

The obverse is the same as for the Dominion of Canada issues. The reverse is a continuation of the Newfoundland Edward VII designs.

Designer and Modeller:
Portrait — Sir E.B. MacKennal,
(B.M. on the truncation)
Composition: .925 silver, .075 copper
Weight: 2.36 grams (1912-1917)
2.33 grams (1919)
Diameter: 17.96 mm (1912)
18.03 mm (1917-1919)
Edge: Reeded
Die Axis: ↑↑

Ottawa Mint issues (1917-1919) have a "C" mint mark below the oval at the bottom on the reverse. The Royal Mint issue (1912) has no letter.

Date and Mint Mark	Quantity Minted	G-4	VG-8	F-12	VF-20	EF-40	AU-50	MS-60	MS-63
1912	150,000	1.00	2.50	5.00	16.00	55.00	200.00	350.00	550.00
1917C	250,805	1.00	2.00	4.00	15.00	50.00	175.00	650.00	2,750.00
1919C	54,342	2.00	3.00	6.00	16.00	50.00	175.00	350.00	550.00

TEN CENTS
George VI 1938-1947

The obverse for this denomination used Percy Metcalfe's standard portrait of George VI for British colonial coinages and the existing Edward VII/George V reverse. The 1946C issue was probably coined in 1947 (see preceding comments on the 1946C 5 cents); the mintage figures for 1946 and 1947 must be considered unofficial.

Designer and Modeller:
Portrait — Percy Metcalfe,
(P.M. below bust)
Composition: .925 silver, .075 copper
(1938-1944);
.800 silver, .200 copper
(1945-1947)
Weight: 2.33 grams
Diameter: 18.03 mm
Edge: Reeded
Die Axis: ↑↑

Royal Canadian Mint issues of 1941-47 have a "C" mint mark below the oval at the bottom on the reverse. The Royal Mint issue (1938) and the Royal Canadian Mint issue of 1940 have no letter.

Date and Mint Mark	Quantity Minted	VG-8	F-12	VF-20	EF-40	AU-50	MS-60	MS-63
1938	100,000	1.25	2.00	4.50	12.00	40.00	175.00	375.00
1940	100,000	.75	1.50	3.50	10.00	35.00	150.00	375.00
1941C	483,630	.75	1.50	3.50	7.00	20.00	60.00	150.00
1942C	292,736	.75	1.50	3.50	7.00	20.00	60.00	150.00
1943C	104,706	.75	1.50	3.50	9.00	25.00	90.00	300.00
1944C	151,471	1.25	2.00	4.00	15.00	50.00	150.00	500.00
1945C	175,833	.75	1.50	3.50	7.00	20.00	60.00	150.00
1946C	38,400	3.00	7.00	13.00	30.00	70.00	125.00	325.00
1947C	61,988	1.50	3.00	6.00	20.00	50.00	100.00	275.00

TWENTY CENTS
Victoria 1865 - 1900

The first pattern known for the Newfoundland 20-cent piece is a bronze striking with the adopted obverse (derived from the New Brunswick obverse) and a reverse from a die for the 1864 New Brunswick 20 cents (see NF-4 in the chapter on Patterns). Later patterns in silver have an arabesque design similar to that finally adopted. The first (see NF-10 in the chapter on Patterns) has very thin arches and corresponds to similar 5-cent and 10-cent patterns. The second stands alone and has arches more like the adopted design and a raised line just inside the denticles (see NF-13 in the chapter on Patterns).

This denomination proved popular with Newfoundlanders and was minted on a regular basis throughout the remainder of Victoria's reign. With the passing years, however, it became increasingly unpopular with Canadians (due to its similarity to their 25-cent piece) and was replaced with a 25-cent coin during World War I.

Designer: Reverse — Horace Morehen
Modeller: Reverse — Leonard C. Wyon
Engraver: Obverse — Leonard C. Wyon
Composition: .925 silver, .075 copper
Weight: 4.71 grams
Diameter: 23.19 mm
Edge: Reeded
Die Axis: ↑↓

Heaton Mint issues have an "H" mint mark on the obverse under the bust (1872-1876) or on the reverse under the date (1882). London Mint strikings have no letter.

Date and Mint Mark	Quantity Minted	G-4	VG-8	F-12	VF-20	EF-40	AU-50	MS-60	MS-63
1865	100,000	9.00	20.00	35.00	90.00	275.00	650.00	1,750.00	3,750.00
1870	50,000	12.00	25.00	50.00	125.00	325.00	750.00	2,250.00	4,000.00
1872H	90,000	8.00	15.00	30.00	75.00	225.00	600.00	1,500.00	2,750.00
1873	40,000	10.00	20.00	40.00	110.00	450.00	1,250.00	3,000.00	-
1876H	50,000	11.00	22.00	40.00	125.00	300.00	750.00	2,250.00	4,000.00
1880	30,000	13.00	27.00	60.00	150.00	350.00	800.00	2,500.00	5,000.00
1881	60,000	6.00	10.00	25.00	60.00	200.00	700.00	2,000.00	5,000.00
1882H	100,000	6.00	9.00	22.00	60.00	200.00	700.00	2,000.00	5,500.00
1885	40,000	8.00	13.00	30.00	70.00	225.00	1,250.00	2,750.00	-
1888	75,000	6.00	10.00	22.00	65.00	225.00	550.00	2,000.00	5,000.00
1890	100,000	5.00	8.00	16.00	50.00	135.00	650.00	1,500.00	-
1894	100,000	5.00	8.00	16.00	50.00	135.00	550.00	1,500.00	4,000.00

1896 Small 96   1896 Large 96   1899 Small 99   1899 Large 99

Date and Mint Mark	Quantity Minted	G-4	VG-8	F-12	VF-20	EF-40	AU-50	MS-60	MS-63
1896 Small 96	125,000	4.00	7.00	13.00	45.00	125.00	550.00	2,000.00	-
1896 Large 96	Incl. above	5.00	8.00	22.00	55.00	300.00	750.00	2,250.00	-
1899 Small 99	125,000	15.00	30.00	60.00	110.00	350.00	800.00	2,000.00	5,000.00
1899 Large 99	Incl. above	4.00	7.00	15.00	45.00	125.00	450.00	2,000.00	5,000.00
1900	125,000	4.00	7.00	13.00	40.00	110.00	450.00	2,000.00	5,000.00

TWENTY CENTS
Edward VII 1904

Coins of this denomination were required on only one occasion during Edward's short reign, making the 1904 issue a one-year type.

Designer and Modeller:
Portrait — G.W. DeSaulles,
(DES. below bust)
Reverse — W.H.J. Blakemore,
copying DeSaulles design for
the reverse of 5¢ and 10¢ pieces
Composition: .925 silver, .075 copper
Weight: 4.71 grams
Diameter: 23.19 mm
Edge: Reeded
Die Axis: ↑↓

This issue was coined by The Mint, Birmingham and bears an "H" mint mark below the oval at the bottom on the reverse.

Date and Mint Mark	Quantity Minted	G-4	VG-8	F-12	VF-20	EF-40	AU-50	MS-60	MS-63
1904H	75,000	7.00	15.00	35.00	100.00	350.00	1,250.00	3,500.00	7,500.00

TWENTY CENTS
George V 1912

Like its Edwardian predecessor, the George V 20 cents is a one-year type. The reverse established for the previous reign was reused.

Designer and Modeller:
Portrait — Sir E.B. MacKennal,
(B.M. on truncation)
Composition: .925 silver, .075 copper
Weight: 4.71 grams
Diameter: 23.19 mm
Edge: Reeded
Die Axis: ↑↑

Date and Mint Mark	Quantity Minted	VG-8	F-12	VF-20	EF-40	AU-50	MS-60	MS-63
1912	350,000	2.50	5.00	15.00	60.00	225.00	600.00	1,250.00

TWENTY-FIVE CENTS
George V 1917 - 1919

The second time 20-cent pieces were required during George V's reign was toward the end of World War I. By that time, however, arrangements had been made for the Ottawa Mint to produce Newfoundland's coins. Canada took a dim view of the 20 cents because it circulated in Canada as well, and was confused with the Canadian 25 cents. The Canadian government convinced the Newfoundland government to drop the 20 cents and adopt a 25 cents, struck on the same standard as the corresponding Canadian coin. Indeed, the obverse of the new coin was identical to that for the Canadian 25 cents.

Designer and Modeller:
   Portrait — Sir E.B. MacKennal,
   (B.M. on truncation)
Engraver: Reverse — W.H.J. Blackmore,
   modifying the 20¢ reverse
Composition: .925 silver, .075 copper
Weight: 5.83 grams
Diameter: 23.62 mm
Edge: Reeded
Die Axis: ↑↑

This denomination was coined by the Ottawa Mint and bears a "C" mint mark below the oval at the bottom on the reverse.

Date and Mint Mark	Quantity Minted	VG-8	F-12	VF-20	EF-40	AU-50	MS-60	MS-63
1917C	464,779	2.00	3.50	6.00	15.00	60.00	225.00	450.00
1919C	163,939	2.00	4.00	7.00	20.00	100.00	400.00	1,750.00

FIFTY CENTS
Victoria 1870 -1900

The 50-cent piece was the last denomination to be added to the Victoria coinage, coming in 1870. Its laureate portrait is stylistically unlike anything used for the rest of the British North America series. This denomination became popular on the island and assumed even greater importance after the failure of the Commercial and Union Banks of Newfoundland during the financial period of 1894.

Designer and Modeller:
   Leonard C. Wyon
Composition: .925 silver, .075 copper
Weight: 11.78 grams
Diameter: 29.85 mm
Edge: Reeded
Die Axis: ↑↓

Heaton Mint issues have an "H" mint mark either on the obverse under the bust (1872-1876) or on the reverse under the date (1882). London Mint strikings have no letter.

Date and Mint Mark	Quantity Minted	G-4	VG-8	F-12	VF-20	EF-40	AU-50	MS-60	MS-63
1870	50,000	11.00	22.00	45.00	150.00	600.00	1,500.00	4,000.00	12,500.00
1872H	48,000	11.00	20.00	30.00	80.00	275.00	650.00	2,500.00	7,500.00
1873	32,000	35.00	65.00	135.00	350.00	1,250.00	2,500.00	7,500.00	-
1874	80,000	25.00	45.00	85.00	225.00	800.00	2,250.00	6,000.00	-
1876H	28,000	17.00	35.00	65.00	175.00	550.00	1,400.00	3,500.00	10,000.00

All examples of the 1880 issue are from dies in which the second 8 of the date is punched over a 7.

Date and Mint Mark	Quantity Minted	G-4	VG-8	F-12	VF-20	EF-40	AU-50	MS-60	MS-63
1880	24,000	17.00	35.00	65.00	200.00	700.00	1,750.00	4,500.00	-
1881	50,000	12.00	25.00	45.00	175.00	600.00	1,250.00	4,500.00	12,500.00
1882H	100,000	9.00	17.00	25.00	80.00	350.00	1,000.00	4,000.00	12,500.00
1885	40,000	11.00	25.00	45.00	150.00	550.00	1,250.00	5,000.00	15,000.00
1888	20,000	17.00	35.00	65.00	175.00	600.00	1,750.00	4,500.00	-
1894	40,000	8.00	11.00	25.00	100.00	400.00	1,000.00	4,000.00	12,500.00
1896	60,000	8.00	11.00	20.00	75.00	300.00	900.00	3,500.00	10,000.00
1898	79,607	8.00	11.00	20.00	75.00	300.00	1,000.00	4,500.00	10,000.00

Narrow 9s with
thick sides and oval centres

Wide 9s with
thin sides and round centres

Date and Mint Mark	Quantity Minted	G-4	VG-8	F-12	VF-20	EF-40	AU-50	MS-60	MS-63
1899 Narrow 9's	150,000	8.00	11.00	20.00	60.00	250.00	900.00	4,000.00	10,000.00
1899 Wide 9's Incl. above		8.00	11.00	20.00	65.00	275.00	1,000.00	4,500.00	10,000.00
1900	150,000	8.00	11.00	20.00	60.00	250.00	1,000.00	4,500.00	10,000.00

FIFTY CENTS
Edward VII 1904 - 1909

The obverse for this denomination is that of the Dominion of Canada issues.

Designer and Modeller:
Portrait — G.W. DeSaulles,
(DES. below bust)
Reverse — W.H.J. Blakemore,
copying DeSaulle's design for
5¢ and 10¢ pieces
Composition: .925 silver, .075 copper
Weight: 11.78 grams
Diameter: 29.85 mm
Edge: Reeded
Die Axis: ↑↓, ↑↑

The Mint, Birmingham issue (1904) has and "H" mint mark below the oval at the bottom on the reverse. Royal Mint issues have no letter.

Date and Mint Mark	Quantity Minted	VG-8	F-12	VF-20	EF-40	AU-50	MS-60	MS-63
1904H	140,000	5.00	10.00	27.00	70.00	175.00	425.00	1,250.00
1907	100,000	6.00	12.00	33.00	80.00	250.00	450.00	1,500.00
1908	160,000	5.00	10.00	22.00	65.00	150.00	325.00	1,000.00
1909	200,000	5.00	10.00	22.00	65.00	150.00	375.00	1,250.00

FIFTY CENTS
George V 1911 - 1919

The obverse for the Newfoundland 50-cent piece is the same as that for the 1912-1936 Dominion of Canada coins. That legend contains "DEI GRA" (see Dominion of Canada George V one-cent section) indicating that the modification of the Canadian obverses was made during 1911, prior to commencing the production of the Newfoundland issue for the year. The reverse continued the Edwardian design.

In 1917-1919 nearly 1,000,000 50 cents were struck and many were used to replace the discontinued government "cash notes" for making relief payments to the poor. The need for silver for this purpose diminished in 1920, when a new issue of government paper money was made.

Designer: Portrait — Sir E.B. MacKennal, (B.M. on truncation)
Composition: .925 silver, .075 copper
Weight: 11.78 grams (1911);
11.66 grams (1917-1919)
Diameter: 29.85 mm (1911)
29.72 mm (1917-1919)
Edge: Reeded
Die Axis: ↑↑

Ottawa Mint issues (1917-1919) have a "C" mint mark below the oval at the bottom on the reverse. The Royal Mint issue has no letter.

Date and Mint Mark	Quantity Minted	VG-8	F-12	VF-20	EF-40	AU-50	MS-60	MS-63
1911	200,000	4.00	6.00	15.00	45.00	150.00	425.00	800.00
1917C	375,560	4.00	6.00	12.00	35.00	90.00	250.00	400.00
1918C	294,824	4.00	6.00	12.00	35.00	90.00	275.00	400.00
1919C	306,267	4.00	6.00	12.00	35.00	90.00	325.00	900.00

TWO DOLLARS
Victoria 1865 - 1888

In the original planning for the Newfoundland coinage a gold dollar was considered. However, it was decided that such a coin would be so small it could be easily lost by the fishermen, so a 2-dollar denomination was chosen instead. The initial bronze pattern combines the adopted obverse (derived from the New Brunswick 10 cents obverse and identical to the Newfoundland 10 cents obverse with the crown and maple wreath of the Canada/New Brunswick 10 cents reverse (see NF-5 in the chapter on Patterns). The adopted reverse has more conventional letters and the unusual feature of expressing the denomination three ways: 2 dollars, 200 cents, 100 pence, the last being the equivalent value in sterling (British money). Newfoundland was the only British colony with its own gold issue.

Designer and Modeller:
Reverse — Leonard C. Wyon
Engraver: Obverse — Leonard C. Wyon
Composition: .917 gold, .083 copper
Weight: 3.33 grams
Diameter: 17.98 mm
Edge: Reeded
Die Axis: ↑↓

The Heaton Mint issue (1882) has an "H" mint mark below the date on the reverse. London Mint strikings have no letter.

Date and Mint Mark	Quantity Minted	VF-20	EF-40	AU-50	MS-60	MS-63
1865	10,000	250.00	375.00	650.00	2,000.00	8,500.00
1870	10,000	300.00	400.00	750.00	2,000.00	9,000.00
1870 Dot	(Incl. in above)	450.00	650.00	1,250.00	3,750.00	12,500.00
1872	6,000	375.00	550.00	1,250.00	3,250.00	12,500.00
1880	2,500	1,700.00	2,000.00	3,500.00	7,500.00	20,000.00
1881	10,000	200.00	300.00	550.00	1,750.00	8,000.00
1882H	25,000	190.00	225.00	300.00	600.00	2,750.00
1885	10,000	200.00	275.00	400.00	750.00	3,250.00
1888	25,000	190.00	225.00	300.00	600.00	3,250.00

PROVINCE OF CANADA

LARGE CENTS
Victoria 1858 - 1859

After the decision to adopt decimal coins was approved, a number of designs, sizes and compositions were considered for the cent. The first trials used a reverse design consisting of 19 maple leaves placed side by side, radiating from the centre (see PC-1 to PC-3 in the chapter on Patterns). However, a motif of 16 serpentine maple leaves was adopted and trial pieces were struck in a cupro-nickel alloy. Later, it was decided the new cents would be bronze.

The adopted obverse design shows a youthful, idealized bust of the queen wearing a laurel wreath in her hair. In fact, by the late 1850s the queen was quite pudgy and decidedly older looking than the coinage portraits suggested.

The government optimistically ordered approximately 10,000,000 1-cent pieces, which proved to be much more than the province could absorb. At the time both Canada East and Canada West were inundated with the copper tokens issued by banks and individuals. The bank tokens were heavier than the thin cents (which weighed 1/100 lb. avoirdupois) and slowed their public acceptance. The majority of the mintage remained unissued in the original boxes. In 1861 part of it was sent to the New Brunswick government to provide a temporary supply of decimal coins while the province awaited the arrival of its own issues, but the bulk of the stock went to the Bank of Upper Canada, the governments's bank. Until 1866, when it closed its doors, the Bank of Upper Canada experienced considerable difficulty in reducing its stock of cents, even when it offered to sell them at 20 percent below face value.

A stock of several million Province of Canada cents was inherited by the Dominion of Canada government in 1867 and it proceeded to issue them as Dominion currency.

Designer and Modeller:
Leonard C. Wyon
Composition: .95 copper, .04 tin, .01 zinc (except for the rare brass)
Weight: 4.54 grams
Diameter: 25.4 mm
Edge: Plain
Die Axis: ↑↑

Date and Mint Mark	Quantity Minted	G-4	VG-8	F-12	VF-20	EF-40	AU-50	MS-60	MS-63
1858	421,000	40.00	60.00	80.00	100.00	150.00	225.00	400.00	900.00

VARIETIES 1859. Since the coining of cents did not begin until the latter part of 1858, production continued throughout most of 1859, with most coins bearing an 1859 date. The first 1859s were undoubtedly overdates, on which a special wide 9 punch was employed to alter the second 8 to a 9, produced from several 1858-dated dies.

The majority of the 1859 dies were not overdates: they were dated with a narrow 9 punch. Many such dies were made and numerous re-punching varieties exist. Only those most widely collected are listed here.

Double-punched Narrow 9 #1: Resembles and often designated "narrow 9 over 8." Actually it is a double-punched narrow 9, confused by the presence of a die defect causing a small "tail" at the lower left of the 9.
Double-punched Narrow 9 #2: Traces of the original 9 at the left.

A very rare variety of the plain, narrow 9 exists in brass, which can be identified by its distinctive yellow colour.

Overdate:
Wide 9 over 8   Plain, Narrow 9

Date and Mint Mark	Quantity Minted	G-4	VG-8	F-12	VF-20	EF-40	AU-50	MS-60	MS-63
1859 W9/8	9,579,000	22.00	45.00	55.00	80.00	110.00	165.00	275.00	500.00
1859 N9, bronze	Incl. above	2.50	3.50	6.00	8.00	12.00	25.00	65.00	225.00
1859 N9, brass	Incl. above	850.00	1,750.00	2,250.00	2,750.00	-	-	-	-

Double-punched Narrow 9 #1   Double-punched Narrow 9 #2
Resembles narrow 9 over 8   Traces of original 9 at left

Date and Mint Mark	Quantity Minted	G-4	VG-8	F-12	VF-20	EF-40	AU-50	MS-60	MS-63
1859 D-P N9#1	Incl. above	190.00	325.00	450.00	600.00	1,000.00	1,500.00	2,250.00	3,000.00
1859 D-P N9#2	Incl. above	35.00	60.00	75.00	110.00	150.00	275.00	400.00	800.00

FIVE CENTS
Victoria 1858

The 5-cent piece chosen by the Province of Canada was a small silver coin, half the weight of the 10-cent piece and similar to the United States half dime. The obverse depicts an idealized, youthful laureated Victoria and the reverse features a maple wreath of 21 leaves surmounted by St. Edward's crown.

The first dies bore small, widely spaced digits in the date. Later strikings carried larger digits punched over the small figures, making the digits closer together.

Designer and Modeller:
   Leonard C. Wyon
Composition: .925 silver, .075 copper
Weight: 1.16 grams
Diameter: 15.5 mm
Edge: Reeded
Die Axis: ↑↓

1858 Small Date
Digits widely spaced

1858 Large Date over Small Date
Digits closely spaced

Date and Mint Mark	Quantity Minted	G-4	VG-8	F-12	VF-20	EF-40	AU-50	MS-60	MS-63
1858 SD	1,460,389	10.00	22.00	35.00	60.00	90.00	165.00	400.00	800.00
1858 LD/SD	Incl. above	100.00	175.00	300.00	500.00	700.00	1,100.00	2,250.00	5,000.00

TEN CENTS
Victoria 1858

   In design, the Province of Canada 10-cent pieces resemble the 5-cent pieces. An interesting variety occurred through a dating blunder in which a 5 punch was used to repair a defective first 8. The top of the 5 can be seen rising above the first 8, as these numbers were punched simultaneously.

Designer and Modeller:
   Leonard C. Wyon
Composition: .925 silver, .075 copper
Weight: 2.32 grams
Diameter: 18.0 mm
Edge: Reeded
Die Axis: ↑↓

1858
First 8 and 5 punched simultaneously

Date and Mint Mark	Quantity Minted	G-4	VG-8	F-12	VF-20	EF-40	AU-50	MS-60	MS-63
1858	1,216,402	15.00	25.00	50.00	100.00	165.00	275.00	450.00	1,500.00
1858 8 over 5	Incl. above			RARE - PRICE NOT ESTABLISHED					

TWENTY CENTS
Victoria 1858

This unusual denomination was chosen as a bridge between the two systems. It apparently deferred to the pounds, shillings, pence basis of the Halifax currency system while naming the new issue in the dollar, cents, mils system. The relationship between the two systems meant 20 cents was equivalent to a shilling in Halifax currency, and it was assumed that consequently the new coin would be found useful. This assumption proved unfounded because there had been no coin representing a shilling in the old system; the British shilling coin was worth just over 20 percent more than a shilling in Halifax currency. Furthermore, the size and weight of the 20-cent piece led to confusion with both British shillings and U.S. 25-cent pieces. As one would expect, the government had difficulty introducing the 20-cent piece and by 1860 it was decided to replace it with a 25-cent coin as the opportunity arose.

The replacement of the 20-cent piece with a 25-cent coin came after Confederation. The Dominion government actively withdrew the 20-cent pieces and at various times from 1885 onward sent them back to the Royal Mint in London for melting and recoining as 25-cent pieces.

Designer and Modeller:
Leonard C. Wyon
Composition: .925 silver, .075 copper
Weight: 4.65 grams
Diameter: 23.3 mm
Edge: Reeded
Die Axis: ↑↓

Date and Mint Mark	Quantity Minted	G-4	VG-8	F-12	VF-20	EF-40	AU-50	MS-60	MS-63
1858	730,392	50.00	75.00	110.00	160.00	300.00	600.00	1,200.00	3,500.00

DOMINION OF CANADA

ONE CENT CIRCULATING COINAGE
Victoria 1876 - 1901

The large cents produced in 1858-1859 for the Province of Canada were inherited by the Dominion of Canada government at the time of Confederation. It was decided to issue them as Dominion cents. Nearly ten years were required to use up the stock; the first cents struck for the Dominion came out in 1876. An 1876 pattern cent (see DC-1 in the chapter on Patterns) with the laureated obverse of 1858-1859 suggests that initially it was intended the Dominion cents be the same design as those of the Province of Canada. However, the obverse of the pieces actually issued bore a diademed head adapted from that used for the Jamaica halfpenny and the Prince Edward Island cent. The government also took the opportunity to increase the weight to 1/80th of an avoirdupois pound, the same as the British halfpenny.

Three varieties of the reverse, from independently engraved master tools, are known to exist: the Provincial Leaves reverse (1876-1882), the Large Leaves reverse (1884-1891), and the Small Leaves reverse (1891-1901). Only in 1891 are the two reverses employed for a single year's coinage (see below). Four varieties exist for the obverse; however, their detailed description and listing by year are not included in this standard catalogue.

Designer and Modeller:
Obverse — Leonard C. Wyon
Provincial and Large Leaves
Reverse — Leonard C. Wyon;
Small Leaves Reverse —
G.W. DeSaulles
Composition: .95 copper, .04 tin
.01 zinc
Weight: 5.67 grams
Diameter: 25.4 mm
Edge: Plain
Die Axis: ↑↑

Heaton Mint issues of 1876-1882 and The Mint, Birmingham issue of 1890 have an "H" mint mark on the reverse under the date. London Mint strikings have no letter.

Date and Mint Mark	Quantity Minted	G-4	VG-8	F-12	VF-20	EF-40	AU-50	MS-60	MS-63
1876H	4,000,000	2.50	3.50	5.00	8.00	14.00	35.00	85.00	175.00
1881H	2,000,000	3.50	5.00	8.00	11.00	22.00	50.00	110.00	250.00
1882H	4,000,000	2.50	3.50	5.00	7.00	13.00	25.00	65.00	150.00
1884	2,500,000	3.00	4.00	6.00	9.00	15.00	30.00	85.00	200.00
1886	1,500,000	3.50	6.00	9.00	15.00	22.00	55.00	120.00	300.00
1887	1,500,000	3.00	5.00	7.00	11.00	18.00	35.00	90.00	225.00
1888	4,000,000	2.50	3.50	5.00	7.00	11.00	25.00	65.00	135.00
1890H	1,000,000	5.00	8.00	14.00	22.00	40.00	80.00	175.00	375.00

Varieties 1891. Three major varieties of the 1891 cent are known. The first two have the Large Leaves reverse. The broad, flat leaves have very little detail and the bottom leaf runs into the rim denticles. The third variety has the Small Leaves reverse, which has slightly smaller leaves with much more detail. The bottom leaf ends well short of the rim denticles. The first variety has a large date; the second and third varieties have a small date.

Large Leaves, Large Date - leaves close to beads and vine; note broad figure "9."

Large Leaves, Small Date - leaves close to beads and vine; note narrow figure "9."

Small Leaves, Small Date - leaves far from beads and vine; note narrow figure "9."

Date and Mint Mark	Quantity Minted	G-4	VG-8	F-12	VF-20	EF-40	AU-50	MS-60	MS-63
1891 LL,LD	1,452,500	5.00	8.00	12.00	20.00	40.00	100.00	165.00	375.00
1891 LL,SD	Incl. above	45.00	80.00	100.00	150.00	200.00	350.00	550.00	1,100.00
1891 SL,SD	Incl. above	35.00	60.00	80.00	110.00	160.00	275.00	400.00	700.00
1892	1,200,000	4.00	6.00	9.00	14.00	22.00	45.00	95.00	175.00
1893	2,000,000	2.00	4.00	6.00	9.00	17.00	35.00	65.00	130.00
1894	1,000,000	6.00	9.00	15.00	22.00	40.00	90.00	150.00	275.00
1895	1,200,000	4.00	6.00	10.00	15.00	22.00	65.00	95.00	200.00
1896	2,000,000	2.00	4.00	5.00	7.00	11.00	28.00	65.00	125.00
1897	1,500,000	2.00	4.00	6.00	8.00	11.00	28.00	70.00	160.00

Note: MS-60 cents are brown in colour, while MS-63 cents are red/brown in colour. Higher mint state graded will require full red colour coins.

The Mint, Birmingham issues of 1898 and 1900 have an "H" mint mark on the reverse under the wreath at the bottom. London Mint strikings have no letter.

Date and Mint Mark	Quantity Minted	G-4	VG-8	F-12	VF-20	EF-40	AU-50	MS-60	MS-63
1898H	1,000,000	3.50	7.00	10.00	15.00	22.00	50.00	120.00	250.00
1899	2,400,000	2.00	3.50	5.00	7.00	10.00	22.00	65.00	110.00
1900	1,000,000	5.00	9.00	16.00	22.00	40.00	75.00	135.00	250.00
1900H	2,600,000	1.50	3.00	5.00	7.00	11.00	25.00	50.00	95.00
1901	4,100,000	1.50	3.00	5.00	7.00	11.00	25.00	50.00	100.00

ONE CENT
Edward VII 1902-1910

The reverse of this denomination is a continuation of the Victorian design.

Designer and Modeller:
Obverse — G.W. DeSalles
(DES. below bust)
Composition: .95 copper, .04 tin,
.01 zinc
Weight: 5.67 grams
Diameter: 25.4 mm
Edge: Plain
Die Axis: ↑↑

The Birmingham Mint issue of 1907 has an "H" mint mark on the reverse under the wreath at the bottom. London Mint strikings (1902-1907) and Ottawa Mint strikings (1908-1910) have no letter.

Date and Mint Mark	Quantity Minted	VG-8	F-12	VF-20	EF-40	AU-50	MS-60	MS-63
1902	3,000,000	2.50	4.00	5.50	10.00	15.00	35.00	55.00
1903	4,000,000	2.50	4.00	5.50	10.00	17.00	45.00	75.00
1904	2,500,000	3.00	5.00	8.00	12.00	22.00	55.00	100.00
1905	2,000,000	4.50	9.00	12.00	15.00	30.00	65.00	125.00
1906	4,100,000	2.50	4.00	5.50	10.00	17.00	50.00	110.00
1907	2,400,000	3.50	6.00	9.00	12.00	22.00	55.00	120.00
1907H	800,000	11.00	20.00	30.00	45.00	75.00	135.00	350.00
1908	2,401,506	3.50	6.00	9.00	12.00	22.00	50.00	110.00
1909	3,973,339	1.00	4.00	5.50	9.00	17.00	40.00	75.00
1910	5,146,487	2.00	3.50	4.50	8.00	17.00	40.00	75.00

ONE CENT - LARGE
George V 1911 - 1920

"GODLESS" OBVERSE 1911. The obverse introduced in 1911 broke a tradition set by the coins of the previous two reigns in which the Latin phrase "DEI GRATIA" (or an abbreviation for it) was included in the monarch's titles. Omission of the phrase aroused public criticism during which the coins were labeled "Godless." The coinage tools were modified during the year and cents with "DEI GRA:" in the legend appeared in 1912. The reverse also marked a departure from the previous reigns in the inclusion of "CANADA" in the legend. It had formerly been part of the obverse legend on this denomination.

Designer and Modeller:
Portrait — Sir E.B. MacKennal,
(B.M. on truncation)
Reverse — W.H.J. Blakemore
Composition: .95 copper, .04 tin,
.01 zinc
Weight: 5.67 grams
Diameter: 25.4 mm
Edge: Plain
Die Axis: ↑↑

Date and Mint Mark	Quantity Minted	VG-8	F-12	VF-20	EF-40	AU-50	MS-60	MS-63
1911	4,663,486	1.50	2.25	3.50	5.50	15.00	35.00	65.00

CANADA

MODIFIED OBVERSE LEGEND 1912 - 1936

Composition: .95 copper, .04 tin,
.01 zinc (1912-1919);
.955 copper, .030 tin, .015
zinc (1919-1920)

The physical specifications are as for the
1911 issue.

Date and Mint Mark	Quantity Minted	VG-8	F-12	VF-20	EF-40	AU-50	MS-60	MS-63
1912	5,107,642	1.25	1.75	2.75	4.50	13.00	35.00	70.00
1913	5,735,405	1.25	1.75	2.75	4.50	13.00	35.00	80.00
1914	3,405,958	1.50	2.00	3.00	5.00	18.00	45.00	125.00
1915	4,932,134	1.50	2.00	3.00	5.00	16.00	40.00	100.00
1916	11,022,367	.75	1.00	1.75	3.25	10.00	25.00	70.00
1917	11,899,254	.75	1.00	1.25	2.50	7.00	18.00	50.00
1918	12,970,798	.75	1.00	1.25	2.50	7.00	17.00	50.00
1919	11,279,634	.75	1.00	1.25	2.50	7.00	17.00	50.00
1920	6,762,247	1.00	1.25	1.50	2.75	8.00	20.00	65.00

ONE CENT - SMALL
George V 1920 - 1936

As a matter of economy the Canadian government introduced in 1920 a small cent similar in size and composition to that of the United States. The large cents were not immediately withdrawn, but were allowed to circulate until the late 1930s. The small coins lacked rim denticles, the first instance of this in the Canadian decimal series. The obverse design was retained while a new reverse design, featuring two maple leaves, was used.

Designer: Portrait — Sir E.B. MacKennal,
(B.M. on truncation)
Reverse — Fred Lewis
Modeller: Portrait — Sir E.B. MacKennal
Reverse — W.H.J. Blakemore
Composition: .955 copper, .030 tin,
.015 zinc
Weight: 3.24 grams
Diameter: 19.05 mm
Edge: Plain
Die Axis: ↑↑

Date and Mint Mark	Quantity Minted	G-4	VG-8	F-12	VF-20	EF-40	AU-50	MS-60	MS-63
1920	15,483,923	-	.30	.75	1.50	2.50	8.00	20.00	40.00
1921	7,601,627	-	1.00	1.50	3.00	7.00	12.00	30.00	75.00
1922	1,243,635	6.50	14.00	17.00	25.00	40.00	80.00	200.00	400.00
1923	1,019,002	11.00	25.00	30.00	40.00	60.00	140.00	350.00	1,000.00

Date and Mint Mark	Quantity Minted	G-4	VG-8	F-12	VF-20	EF-40	AU-50	MS-60	MS-63
1924	1,593,195	3.50	7.00	9.00	12.00	20.00	40.00	150.00	300.00
1925	1,000,622	10.00	20.00	25.00	35.00	50.00	90.00	250.00	500.00
1926	2,143,372	1.25	3.50	5.00	8.00	15.00	40.00	125.00	275.00
1927	3,553,928	-	2.00	3.00	5.00	8.00	20.00	60.00	100.00
1928	9,144,860	-	-	1.00	1.25	3.00	7.00	20.00	40.00
1929	12,159,840	-	-	1.00	1.25	3.00	7.00	20.00	40.00
1930	2,538,613	-	2.25	3.25	5.00	9.00	20.00	60.00	100.00
1931	3,842,776	-	1.00	1.25	2.50	5.50	15.00	50.00	100.00
1932	21,316,190	-	-	1.00	1.25	3.00	7.00	16.00	40.00
1933	12,079,310	-	-	1.00	1.25	3.00	7.00	16.00	40.00
1934	7,042,358	-	-	1.00	1.25	3.00	7.00	16.00	40.00
1935	7,526,400	-	-	1.00	1.25	3.00	7.00	16.00	40.00
1936	8,768,769	-	-	1.00	1.25	3.00	7.00	16.00	40.00

ONE CENT
George VI 1937 - 1952

COINAGE USING GEORGE V DIES 1936. In December,1936, the reigning British king, Edward VIII, abdicated in favour of his brother, who became George VI. This placed a great strain upon the Royal Mint in London. It was well along in the preparation of the tools for the British Commonwealth coinage obverses, including those for Canada. All this work had to be scrapped and new obverse tools made for George VI.

In 1937, during the delay involved in the preparation of new obverses in London, the Royal Canadian Mint was forced to strike from 1936 dies quantities of all denominations, except the 5-cent and 50-cent piece. The dies for the 1, 10, and 25 cent pieces are said to have been marked with a tiny dot on the reverse. This was to indicate that the coins were struck in a year different than that borne on the dies and with the bust of the preceding monarch.

The 1936 dot cent is an extreme rarity; only one business strike and three specimen strikes, all in mint state, are presently known. Numerous circulated examples of this rarity have come to light over the years; however, none has been satisfactorily authenticated. It seems unlikely that any genuine 1936 dot cents ever circulated, despite the supposedly official mintage of almost 700,000 pieces.

1936 with raised dot below date
struck in 1937

Date and Mint Mark	Quantity Minted		F-12	VF-20	EF-40	AU-50	MS-60	MS-63
1936 Dot	678,823		VERY RARE - PRICE NOT ESTABLISHED					

COINAGE OF GEORGE VI. In the early part of 1937 the Royal Mint in London decided to speed up the production of the new coinage tools for Canadian coinages by having some of the work done by the Paris Mint. Included in this work was the reverse for the cent. The model was sent to Paris for conversion into master coinage tools.

The reverse of the new cent continued the trend toward modernization of the Canadian coinage designs begun in 1935 with the voyageur silver dollar.

"ET IND:IMP:" IN OBVERSE LEGEND 1937 - 1947. The initial obverse (1937-1947) bore a legend containing the Latin abbreviation "ET IND:IMP:," indicating the king was the Emperor of India.

Designer and Modeller:
Portrait — T.H. Paget
(H.P. below bust)
Reverse — G.E. Kruger-Gray
(K G below right-hand
maple leaf)
Composition: .955 copper, .030 tin,
.015 zinc (1937-1942);
.980 copper, .005 tin,
.015 zinc (1942-1952)
Weight: 3.24 grams
Diameter: 19.05 mm
Edge: Plain
Die Axis: ↑↑

Date and Mint Mark	Quantity Minted	VF-20	EF-40	AU-50	MS-60	MS-63	MS-65
1937	10,040,231	.75	1.00	1.50	3.00	5.00	50.00
1938	18,365,608	.75	1.00	1.50	4.00	6.00	55.00
1939	21,600,319	.75	1.00	1.50	3.00	5.00	40.00
1940	85,740,532	.75	1.00	1.50	2.50	4.00	45.00
1941	56,336,011	1.00	1.25	3.00	10.00	20.00	250.00
1942	76,113,708	-	1.00	2.50	8.00	20.00	200.00
1943	89,111,969	-	-	2.00	4.00	10.00	125.00
1944	44,131,216	-	-	3.00	10.00	22.00	250.00
1945	77,269,591	-	-	1.50	2.50	3.50	45.00
1946	56,662,071	-	-	1.50	2.50	3.50	45.00
1947	31,093,901	-	-	1.50	3.00	4.00	40.00

MAPLE LEAF ISSUE 1947. The granting of independence to India resulted in a dilemma for the Royal Canadian Mint in the early part of 1948. New obverse coinage tools with "ET IND: IMP:" omitted would not arrive for several months, yet there was a pressing need for all denominations of coins. The mint satisfied this demand by striking coins dated 1947 and bearing an obverse with outmoded titles. To differentiate this issue from the regular strikings of 1947, a tiny maple leaf was placed after the date.

1947 Maple Leaf Issue
struck in 1948

Date and Mint Mark	Quantity Minted	EF-40	AU-50	MS-60	MS-63	MS-65
1947 ML	43,855,448	1.00	1.50	2.50	3.50	35.00

MODIFIED OBVERSE LEGEND 1948-1952. Following the arrival of the master tools with the new obverse legend lacking "ET IND: IMP:" in 1948, the 1947 Maple Leaf coinage was suspended. For the remainder of the year coins were produced with the new obverse and the true date 1948. This obverse was employed for the rest of the reign.

The physical and chemical specifications are as for the 1937-1947 issues.

Date and Mint Mark	Quantity Minted	EF-40	AU-50	MS-60	MS-63	MS-65
1948	25,767,779	1.25	2.00	3.00	6.00	75.00
1949	33,128,933	.75	1.00	2.00	3.50	45.00
1950	60,444,992	.75	1.00	1.50	2.50	45.00
1951	80,430,379	.75	1.00	1.50	2.50	45.00
1952	67,631,736	.75	1.00	1.50	2.50	45.00

ONE CENT
Elizabeth II 1953 to date

The portrait model for the new Queen Elizabeth coinages was prepared in England by a sculptress, Mrs. Mary Gillick. The relief of this model was too high, with the result that the centre portion containing two lines on the shoulder (representing a fold in the Queen's gown) did not strike up well on the coins. This first obverse variety has been commonly termed the "no shoulder strap" variety by many collectors. Later in 1953, Royal Canadian Mint authorities decided to correct the defects in the obverse design. Thomas Shingles, the Mint's Chief Engraver, lowered the relief of the model, and strengthened the shoulder and hair detail. This modified obverse (often called the "shoulder strap" variety due to the resemblance of the lines to a strap) was introduced before the end of the year and became the standard obverse. By mistake the No Shoulder Fold obverse was used to produce some of the 1954 cents for the Proof-like sets and a small quantity of 1955 cents for circulation.

Many collectors have difficulty differentiating the two varieties on slightly worn cents. The best way is to note that the "Is" on the No Shoulder Fold variety are flared at the ends and that an imaginary line drawn up through the centre of the "I" in "DEI" goes between two rim denticles. On the Shoulder Fold variety the "I's" are nearly straight sided and a line drawn up through the "I" of "DEI" runs into a rim denticle.

The reverse was a continuation of the George VI reverse.

Note: George VI small cents in VF-30 and lower, at present, are not collectable.

Designer and Modeller:
Portrait — Mrs. Mary Gillick
(M.G. on truncation)
Engraver: No Shoulder Fold Obverse —
Thomas Shingles, using the Gillick
portrait model;
Shoulder Fold Obverse —
Thomas Shingles, modifying existing
NSF coinage tools
Composition: .980 copper, .005 tin,
.015 zinc
Weight: 3.24 grams
Diameter: 19.05 mm
Edge: Plain
Die Axis: ↑↑

No Shoulder Fold Obverse note flared ends of "Is" and "I" in DEI points between two rim denticles.

Shoulder Fold Obverse note straight-sided "Is" and "I" in DEI points at a rim denticle.

Date and Mint Mark	Quantity Minted	F-12	VF-20	EF-40	AU-50	MS-60	MS-63	MS-65	PL-65
1953 NSF	67,806,016	-	-	.75	1.50	2.00	4.00	30.00	25.00
1953 SF	Incl. above	1.00	3.00	6.00	10.00	20.00	60.00	125.00	100.00
1954 NSF*		-	-	-	-	-	-	-	350.00
1954 SF	22,181,760	-	-	.75	1.50	4.00	8.00	30.00	25.00
1955 SF	56,403,193	-	-	-	.40	.75	2.00	20.00	25.00
1955 NSF	Incl. above	150.00	250.00	375.00	600.00	800.00	1,500.00	-	-
1956	78,685,535	-	-	-	.40	.75	1.50	12.00	15.00
1957	100,601,792	-	-	-	.40	.50	1.00	10.00	15.00
1958	59,385,679	-	-	-	.40	.50	1.00	10.00	15.00
1959	83,615,343	-	-	-	.25	.35	.50	5.00	12.00
1960	75,772,775	-	-	-	.25	.35	.50	5.00	2.00
1961	139,598,404	-	-	-	.25	.35	.40	5.00	2.00
1962	227,244,069	-	-	-	.20	.30	.40	5.00	2.00
1963	279,076,334	-	-	-	.20	.30	.40	5.00	2.00
1964	484,655,322	-	-	-	.20	.30	.40	4.00	2.00

TIARA PORTRAIT & MAPLE TWIG REVERSE 1965-1966. In 1964 the British government decided to introduce a more mature portrait of Queen Elizabeth for domestic and Commonwealth coinages. The new portrait model, by Arnold Machin, features the Queen wearing a tiara instead of a laurel wreath. A copy of the model was forwarded to Canada and was incorporated into the obverses for 1965.

Designer and Modeller:
Obverse — Arnold Machin
Reverse — G.E. Kruger-Gray
Composition: .980 copper, .005 tin, .015 zinc
Weight: 3.24 grams
Diameter: 19.05 mm
Edge: Plain
Die Axis: ↑↑

VARIETIES 1965. During 1965, difficulties were encountered in striking the cents, resulting in the introduction of a second variety obverse. The first variety has small beads at the rim and a flat field; the second variety has large rim beads and a field that slopes up at the rim. Another way to distinguish the two obverses is by the location of the "A" in "REGINA" relative to the rim beads: on the small beads obverse it points between two beads, whereas on the large beads obverse it points at a bead. In addition, two reverses differing in the style of 5 in the date were used in 1965. The obverses and reverses were employed in all possible combinations, creating four varieties for the year.

Small Beads Obverse
A of REGINA points between beads

Large Beads Obverse
A of REGINA points at bead

Pointed 5
Top right of 5 comes to point

Blunt 5
Top right of 5 is nearly square

Date and Mint Mark	Quantity Minted	AU-50	MS-60	MS-63	MS-65	PL-65
1965 Variety 1 (small beads, pointed 5)	304,441,082	.50	1.00	3.00	20.00	2.00
1965 Variety 2 (small beads, blunt 5)	Incl. above	-	.15	.25	4.00	-
1965 Variety 3 (large beads, blunt 5)	Incl. above	-	.25	.50	8.00	-
1965 Variety 4 (large beads, pointed 5)	Incl. above 1	15.00	25.00	50.00	200.00	-
1966	183,644,388	-	.15	.20	3.00	2.00

Note: Elizabeth II small cents except for 1953/54/55 grading EF-45 and lower, at present, are not collectible.

COMMEMORATIVE FOR CENTENNIAL OF CONFEDERATION 1967. Alex Colville's design of a rock dove was selected for the 1967 cent reverse, struck in commemoration of Canada's centennial of Confederation. The event was marked by a special design for each denomination coined for circulation, plus a special $20 gold piece for collectors only. The obverse of the cent is the same as that for the 1966 issue.

The physical and chemical specifications are as for the 1965 issue.

Date and Mint Mark	Quantity Minted		MS-60	MS-63	MS-65	PL-65
1967 Confederation Commemorative	345,140,650		.15	.30	3.00	2.00

MAPLE TWIG REVERSE RESUMED; LARGE PORTRAIT 1968-1978

The physical and chemical specifications are as for the 1965 issue.

Date and Mint Mark	Quantity Minted		MS-60	MS-63	MS-65	PL-65
1968	329,695,772		.15	.25	3.00	1.00
1969	335,240,929		.15	.25	3.00	1.00
1970	311,145,010		.15	.25	3.00	1.00
1971	298,228,936		.15	.25	3.00	1.00
1972	451,304,591		.15	.25	3.00	1.00
1973	457, 059,852		.15	.25	3.00	1.00
1974	692,058,489		.15	.25	2.00	1.00
1975	642,318,000		.15	.25	2.00	1.00
1976	701,122,890		.15	.25	2.00	1.00
1977	453,050,666		.15	.25	2.00	1.00
1978	911,170,647		.15	.25	2.00	1.00

MODIFIED TIARA PORTRAIT 1979. As part of a general standardization of the coinage, the portrait of the queen was made smaller beginning with the 1979 coinage. The purpose was to make the size of the portrait proportional to the diameter of the coin, regardless of the denomination.

Designer and Modeller:
  Obverse — Arnold Machin, Walter Ott
  Reverse — G.E. Kruger-Gray
Composition: .980 copper, .005 tin,
    .015 zinc
Weight: 3.24 grams
Diameter: 19.05 mm
Edge: Plain
Die Axis: ↑↑

Date and Mint Mark	Quantity Minted		MS-60	MS-63	MS-65	PL-65
1979	753,942,953		.15	.25	2.00	1.00

REDUCED WEIGHT 1980-1981. In 1978 the Mint struck pattern pieces, dated 1979, with a considerably reduced weight and a diameter of 16 mm. The mint was prompted by the rising price of copper which resulted in the 1-cent piece being coined at a loss. Unfortunately, the diameter of the pattern was the same as that for the tokens used by the Toronto Transit Commission and this was enough to result in the cancellation of plans for the new 16 mm cent. The mint struck cents of the old size and design during 1979. However, in 1980 it introduced a coin of the same design as before, but with a decreased diameter and thickness (hence a decreased weight).

Designer and Modeller:
Obverse — Arnold Machin
Reverse — G.E. Kruger-Gray
Composition: .980 copper, .005 tin, .015 zinc
Weight: 2.8 grams
Diameter: 19.00 mm
Thickness: 1.38 mm
Edge: Plain
Die Axis: ↑↑

Date and Mint Mark	Quantity Minted		MS-60	MS-63	MS-65	PL-65	PR-65
1980	911,800,000		.10	.25	2.00	1.00	-
1981	1,209,468,500		.15	.25	2.00	-	2.00

12-SIDED, TIARA PORTRAIT, MAPLE TWIG DESIGN, 1982-1989. In December of 1981 the Ministry of Supplies and Services announced that the Royal Canadian Mint would be modifying Canada's one-cent coin. The design was changed from a round to a twelve-sided piece. Also the rim denticles were removed to be replaced with beads.

Designer and Modeller:
Obverse — Arnold Machin
Reverse — G.E. Kruger-Gray
Composition: .980 copper, .005 tin, .015 zinc
Weight: 2.5 grams
Diameter: 19.1 mm
Edge: 12-sided, plain
Die Axis: ↑↑

Blunt Five

Pointed Five

Date and Mint Mark	Quantity Minted		MS-60	MS-63	MS-65	PR-65
1982	876,036,898		.15	.25	2.00	2.00
1983	975,510,000		.15	.25	2.00	2.00
1984	838,225,000		.15	.25	2.00	2.00
1985 BL5	771,772,500		.15	.25	2.00	2.00
1985 PT5	Incl. above		15.00	25.00	50.00	-
1986	788,285,000		.15	.25	2.00	2.00
1987	774,549,000		.15	.25	2.00	2.00
1988	482,676,752		.15	.25	2.00	2.00
1989	1,066,628,200		.15	.25	2.00	2.00

CROWNED PORTRAIT; MAPLE TWIG DESIGN; 1990 TO 1991. In line with changes in Great Britain and other commonwealth countries Canada in 1990 introduced a new portrait design for Canadian coins. Designed by Dora de Pédery-Hunt, this crowned portrait of Queen Elizabeth II is the first effigy of the queen designed by a Canadian. The diamond crown is completely circular, decorated with symbolic roses, shamrocks and thistles. It was made for George IV and worn by Queen Victoria for many of her formal portraits. Today it is worn by Queen Elizabeth for her opening of Parliament.

Designer and Modeller:
Obverse — Dora de Pédery-Hunt,
Ago Aarand
Reverse — G.E. Kruger-Gray
Composition: .980 copper, .005 tin,
.015 zinc
Weight: 2.5 grams
Diameter: 19.1 mm
Edge: 12-sided, plain
Die Axis: ↑↑

Date and Mint Mark	Quantity Minted		MS-60	MS-63	MS-65	PR-65
1990	218,035,000		.15	.25	2.00	2.00
1991	831,001,000		.15	.25	2.00	2.00

COMMEMORATIVE FOR THE 125TH ANNIVERSARY; 1867-1992. The reserve design was modified to include the bracket dates 1867-1992 for the 125th birthday of Canada.

Designer, modeller and physical characteristics are as for the 1990 and 1991 issues.

Date and Mint Mark	Quantity Minted		MS-60	MS-63	MS-65	PR-65
1992	673,512,000		.15	.25	2.00	2.00

MAPLE TWIG DESIGN RESUMED; 1993 TO 1995. In 1993 the practice of using a single date was resumed.

Designer, modeller and physical characteristics are as for the 1990 and 1991 issues.

Date and Mint Mark	Quantity Minted		MS-60	MS-63	MS-65	PR-65
1993	808,585,000		.15	.25	2.00	2.00
1994	639,516,000		.15	.25	2.00	2.00
1995	559,047,000		.15	.25	2.00	2.00

MAPLE TWIG DESIGN CONTINUED, 1996 TO DATE: In July 1996 the composition of the Canadian subsidiary coins was changed as a cost saving measure. Beside the composition change the cent was returned to the round design of the pre 1982 coinage.

Photograph not
available at
press time

Designer, Modeller and Engraver:
Obverse — Dora de Pédery-Hunt,
Ago Aarand
Reverse — G.E. Kruger-Gray
Composition: Copper plated zinc
Weight: 2.5 grams
Diameter: 19.1 mm
Edge: Plain
Die Axis: ↑↑

Date and Mint Mark	Quantity Minted	MS-60	MS-63	MS-65	PR-65
1996	N/A	.15	.25	2.00	2.00
1997	N/A	.15	.25	2.00	2.00

FIVE CENTS CIRCULATING COINAGE
Victoria 1870 - 1901

The first 5-cent pieces for the Dominion of Canada were introduced in 1870. The initial designs were identical to those used for the Province of Canada in 1858. During the reign of Queen Victoria, five obverse varieties, differing primarily in the facial features, were employed. Their detailed description and listing by year are not included in this standard catalogue. Three varieties of the reverse are known: the Wide Rim reverse (1870), the Narrow Rim, 21 Leaves reverse (1870-1881, 1890-1901) and the Narrow Rim, 22 Leaves reverse (1882-1889).

Designer, Modeller and Engraver:
Leonard C. Wyon
Composition: .925 silver, .075 copper
Weight: 1.16 grams
Diameter: 15.50 mm
Edge: Reeded
Die Axis: ↑↓

Heaton Mint issues of 1872-1883 and the Mint, Birmingham issue of 1880 have an "H" mint mark on the reverse under the wreath. London Mint strikings have no letter.

VARIETIES 1870. Before the coinage of 1870 was complete, new master tools for the 5-cent piece were introduced, with the result that two varieties were created for the year. The first has wide rims (including unusually long rim denticles) on the obverse and reverse and the second has more conventional narrow rims.

1870 Wide Rims   1870 Narrow Rims

Date and Mint Mark	Quantity Minted	G-4	VG-8	F-12	VF-20	EF-40	AU-50	MS-60	MS-63
1870 W/R	2,800,000	11.00	22.00	33.00	65.00	100.00	225.00	450.00	1,250.00
1870 N/R	Incl. above	11.00	22.00	33.00	60.00	90.00	200.00	400.00	1,000.00
1871	1,400,000	11.00	22.00	33.00	65.00	100.00	225.00	450.00	1,250.00
1872H	2,000,000	9.00	15.00	30.00	60.00	100.00	275.00	650.00	2,000.00

VARIETIES 1874H & 1875H. In 1874 and 1875 two sizes of digits were used for dating the dies. In addition, the two date sizes for 1874 also differ in the style of 4: the small date contains a plain 4 and the large date contains a crosslet 4.

Through a clerical error part of the mintage of 1874H-dated coins was assigned to the next year's production figures. Therefore the mintage figures for the two years, 800,000 and 1,000,000, respectively, have been combined.

1874H Small Date
(Plain 4)

1874H Large Date
(Crosslet 4)

1875H Small Date

1875H Large Date

Date and Mint Mark	Quantity Minted	G-4	VG-8	F-12	VF-20	EF-40	AU-50	MS-60	MS-63
1874H SD, P/4	1,800,000	18.00	35.00	65.00	120.00	175.00	325.00	750.00	2,000.00
1874H LD, C/4	Incl. above	15.00	25.00	55.00	100.00	150.00	350.00	800.00	2,250.00
1875H SD	Incl. above	90.00	150.00	250.00	450.00	800.00	1,600.00	3,000.00	7,500.00
1875H LD	Incl. above	100.00	200.00	325.00	550.00	1,000.00	2,500.00	4,500.00	10,000.00
1880H	3,000,000	6.00	9.00	18.00	40.00	80.00	200.00	500.00	1,250.00
1881H	1,500,000	7.00	10.00	20.00	40.00	80.00	200.00	550.00	1,400.00
1882H	1,000,000	7.00	12.00	25.00	45.00	80.00	200.00	550.00	1,25 0.00
1883H	600,000	16.00	30.00	60.00	110.00	250.00	550.00	1,500.00	4,500.00
1884	200,000	80.00	150.00	250.00	425.00	900.00	2,500.00	5,000.00	10,000.00

VARIETIES 1885 & 1886. During the year 1885, two markedly different styles of 5 were used in the date. One is the small 5 seen on the 1875H issue; the other is the larger 5 used in the denomination "5 CENTS." In 1886 there is either a small 6 or a large 6 used. The uppermost part of the inner portion of the small 6 comes to a point, whereas that area on the large 6 is almost square.

1885 Small 5

1885 Large 5

Note: Due to the high degree of rarity of some coins in the Victoria series, the prices shown in italics are indications only. Insufficient market data exists to fix prices with any certainty. The actual selling prices will be determined by supply and demand at the time of transaction.

1886 Small 6   1886 Large 6

Date and Mint Mark	Quantity Minted	G-4	VG-8	F-12	VF-20	EF-40	AU-50	MS-60	MS-63
1885 Small 5	1,000,000	10.00	20.00	33.00	70.00	150.00	375.00	850.00	2,750.00
1885 Large 5	Incl. above	11.00	22.00	40.00	80.00	175.00	400.00	1,000.00	3,000.00
1886 Small 6	1,700,000	7.00	10.00	20.00	40.00	75.00	200.00	550.00	1,250.00
1886 Large 6	Incl. above	9.00	12.00	25.00	50.00	100.00	250.00	650.00	1,750.00
1887	500,000	15.00	30.00	55.00	85.00	150.00	275.00	650.00	1,750.00
1888	1,000,000	6.00	9.00	15.00	30.00	55.00	125.00	300.00	800.00
1889	1,200,000	17.00	33.00	60.00	110.00	175.00	350.00	700.00	2,000.00
1890H	1,000,000	7.00	11.00	20.00	40.00	70.00	140.00	300.00	750.00
1891	1,800,000	6.00	8.00	10.00	20.00	50.00	110.00	300.00	750.00
1892	860,000	7.00	10.00	20.00	35.00	75.00	185.00	550.00	1,250.00
1893	1,700,000	6.00	8.00	10.00	22.00	50.00	100.00	325.00	800.00
1894	500,000	14.00	25.00	50.00	85.00	175.00	300.00	600.00	1,750.00
1896	1,500,000	6.00	9.00	14.00	28.00	50.00	120.00	325.00	800.00
1897	1,319,283	6.00	9.00	13.00	25.00	45.00	100.00	275.00	700.00
1898	580,717	9.00	17.00	30.00	55.00	100.00	200.00	400.00	1,250.00
1899	3,000,000	6.00	8.00	10.00	18.00	45.00	90.00	225.00	650.00

VARIETIES 1900. Two sizes of date are seen on the 1900 issue. The large date has been referred to most often as the Round 0s variety and the small date as the Oval 0s variety, but there is a greater difference in the 9s. The large date has a Wide 9 as on the 1898 issue and the small date has a Narrow 9 as on the 1899 and 1901 issues.

1900 Large Date   1900 Small Date
(Wide 0s and 9)   (Narrow 0s and 9)

Date and Mint Mark	Quantity Minted	G-4	VG-8	F-12	VF-20	EF-40	AU-50	MS-60	MS-63
1900 LD, W/0s	1,800,000	15.00	28.00	50.00	90.00	160.00	300.00	500.00	1,500.00
1900 SD, N/0s	Incl. above	6.00	9.00	11.00	20.00	45.00	90.00	225.00	650.00
1901	2,000,000	6.00	9.00	10.00	18.00	45.00	90.00	225.00	650.00

FIVE CENTS
Edward VII 1902 - 1910

In 1902, the coronation year for Edward VII, the Royal Mint was extremely busy producing new coinage tools and striking the new coins and medals. One compromise this necessitated involved the reverse of the Canadian 5-cent piece. It had been intended to transfer both the word "CANADA" from the obverse to the reverse legend and to replace the old St. Edward's crown, showing depressed arches at the top, with the Imperial State crown, showing raised arches at the top. Instead, the mint had to settle for making the legend change only. The following year the crown was changed. The 1903H issue had a reverse with 21 leaves, but a modified design with 22 leaves was instituted for the London issue. The Mint, Birmingham issue has an "H" mint mark on the reverse under the wreath. The London Mint has no letter.

Designer and Modeller:
Obverse — G.W. DeSaulles
(DES under bust)
Engraver: Reverse — G.W. DeSaulles
Composition: .925 silver, .075 copper
Weight: 1.16 grams
Diameter: 15.50 mm
Edge: Reeded
Die Axis: ↑↓

MINT MARK VARIETIES 1902. Two sizes of "H" appear on the 1902 Heaton Mint issue of this denomination. One is a small, narrow "H" not seen on any other Canadian coins and the other is a large, wide "H" similar to that on the 1903H.

1902 Large H   1902 Small H

Date and Mint Mark	Quantity Minted	VG-8	F-12	VF-20	EF-40	AU-50	MS-60	MS-63
1902	2,120,000	3.50	4.50	9.00	17.00	30.00	55.00	90.00
1902H Large H	2,200,000	3.50	5.50	10.00	20.00	35.00	70.00	135.00
1902H Small H	Incl. above	10.00	18.00	40.00	70.00	100.00	175.00	275.00

IMPERIAL CROWN; 21 LEAVES IN REVERSE WREATH 1903 (The Mint, Birmingham Issue Only). The 1903 issue for The Mint, Birmingham was essentially the same as the 1902 coinage with the St. Edward's crown replaced by the Imperial State crown. This design was employed for only the one year and at the Birmingham Mint only.

Designer and Engraver:
probably G.W. De Saulles

The physical and chemical specifications are as for the 1902 issue.

Date and Mint Mark	Quantity Minted	VG-8	F-12	VF-20	EF-40	AU-50	MS-60	MS-63
1903H	2,640,000	4.00	6.00	14.00	30.00	80.00	225.00	450.00

IMPERIAL CROWN; 22 LEAVES IN REVERSE WREATH 1903 (London Mint - 1910). In a move unprecedented in Canadian coinage the Royal Mint produced a coin (the 5-cent piece) that bore a somewhat different design than that used by its sub-contractor, The Mint, Birmingham, in 1903. The 1903 London issue features a new wreath with 22 instead of 21 leaves.

Designer and Modeller:
Obverse — G.W. De Saulles
Reverse — W.H.J. Blakemore
Composition: .925 silver, .075 copper
Weight: 1.16 grams (1903-1910);
1.17 grams (1910)
Diameter: 15.50 mm
Edge: Reeded
Die Axis: ↑↓ (1903-1907);
↑↑ (1908-1910)

Date and Mint Mark	Quantity Minted	VG-8	F-12	VF-20	EF-40	AU-50	MS-60	MS-63
1903	1,000,000	7.50	15.00	30.00	60.00	135.00	275.00	450.00
1904	2,400,000	4.50	7.00	15.00	40.00	75.00	325.00	850.00
1905	2,600,000	4.00	6.00	13.00	28.00	60.00	165.00	350.00
1906	3,100,000	3.50	5.00	9.00	18.00	50.00	135.00	350.00
1907	5,200,000	3.50	5.00	8.00	16.00	50.00	110.00	225.00
1908	1,220,524	7.50	13.00	28.00	45.00	70.00	150.00	275.00

VARIETIES 1909 & 1910. In 1909 the existing reverse was modified to create a variety in which the maple leaves have sharp points along their edges, causing them to resemble holly leaves. Both the Maple Leaves and the Holly Leaves reverses saw use in 1909 and 1910.

Maple Leaves Reverse
(1903-1910)

Holly Leaves Reverse
(1909-1910)

Date and Mint Mark	Quantity Minted	VG-8	F-12	VF-20	EF-40	AU-50	MS-60	MS-63
1909 Maple Leaves	1,983,725	4.50	7.00	18.00	45.00	100.00	325.00	850.00
1909 Holly Leaves	Incl. above	15.00	25.00	50.00	100.00	200.00	550.00	1,750.00
1910 Maple Leaves	5,580,325	18.00	30.00	60.00	135.00	275.00	650.00	2,000.00
1910 Holly Leaves	Incl. above	3.50	4.50	8.00	15.00	33.00	75.00	175.00

FIVE CENTS - SILVER
George V 1911 - 1921

"GODLESS" OBVERSE 1911. The new obverse introduced in 1911 was criticized by the public because the Latin phrase "DEI GRATIA" (or an abbreviation for it), indicating that the King ruled by the grace of God, was omitted. The coinage tools were modified during the year and a new obverse with "DEI GRA:" included in the legend appeared on the 1912 issue. The Maple Leaves design reverse was that of the previous reign.

Designer and Modeller:
   Portrait — Sir E.B. MacKennal
   (B.M. on truncation)
Composition: .925 silver, .075 copper
Weight: 1.17 grams
Diameter: 15.50 mm
Edge: Reeded
Die Axis: ↑↑

Date and Mint Mark	Quantity Minted	VG-8	F-12	VF-20	EF-40	AU-50	MS-60	MS-63
1911	3,692,350	2.50	4.00	8.00	16.00	50.00	110.00	200.00

MODIFIED OBVERSE LEGEND 1912-1921.

Composition: .925 silver, .075 copper
   (1912-1919)
   .800 silver, .200 copper
   (1920-1921)

The physical specifications are as for the 1911 issue.

Date and Mint Mark	Quantity Minted	VG-8	F-12	VF-20	EF-40	AU-50	MS-60	MS-63
1912	5,863,170	2.50	3.50	5.00	11.00	33.00	90.00	275.00
1913	5,588,048	2.00	3.00	5.00	8.00	18.00	45.00	80.00
1914	4,202,179	2.50	3.50	5.00	11.00	33.00	80.00	225.00
1915	1,172,258	10.00	18.00	28.00	60.00	160.00	350.00	700.00
1916	2,481,675	3.50	6.50	9.00	25.00	70.00	160.00	350.00
1917	5,521,373	2.00	3.00	4.00	7.50	22.00	60.00	150.00
1918	6,052,298	2.00	3.00	3.50	6.50	18.00	50.00	110.00
1919	7,835,400	2.00	3.00	3.50	6.50	18.00	50.00	110.00
1920	10,649,851	2.00	3.00	3.50	6.50	18.00	45.00	100.00

Note: Some 1920 5¢ are believed to have remained unissued and returned to the melting pot in 1922.

FIVE CENTS 1921. During 1920-1921 plans moved forward for the replacement of the small silver 5-cents piece with a larger coin of pure nickel, the same size as the U.S. nickel. The enabling legislation was passed in May 1921 and thereafter no more 5-cent pieces were coined in silver. The mint melted some 3,022,665 coins of this denomination. The presumed composition of this melt is almost all the 1921 mintage and a portion of the 1920 mintage, thus explaining the rarity of the 1921 date today. Only about 400 1921's are believed to have survived. A few are Specimen coins, issued to collectors in sets and the rest are thought to be circulation strikes sold to visitors to the Mint in the early months of 1921.

Designer and Modeller:
Portrait — Sir E.B. MacKennal
(B.M. on truncation)
Composition: .800 silver, .200 copper
Weight: 1.17 grams
Diameter: 15.50 mm
Edge: Reeded
Die Axis: ↑↑

Date and Mint Mark	Quantity Minted	G-4	VG-8	F-12	VF-20	EF-40	AU-50	MS-60	MS-63
1921	2,582,495*	1,400.	2,250.	3,000.	4,000.	5,500.	8,000.	12,500.	30,000.

*Almost all 1921 5¢ are believed to have remained unissued and returned to the melting pot in 1922.

FIVE CENTS - NICKEL
George V 1922 - 1936

The new Canadian nickel 5-cent piece was introduced in 1922 after two years of planning. The silver coin it replaced was allowed to circulate also until the 1930's, when a more active withdrawal program was instituted.

Designer and Modeller:
Portrait — Sir E.B. MacKennal
(B.M. on truncation)
Reverse — W.H.J. Blakemore
Composition: 1.00 nickel
Weight: 4.54 grams
Diameter: 21.21 mm
Edge: Plain
Die Axis: ↑↑

Date and Mint Mark	Quantity Minted	G-4	VG-8	F-12	VF-20	EF-40	AU-50	MS-60	MS-63
1922	4,794,119	-	-	1.25	3.50	15.00	40.00	75.00	150.00
1923	2,502,279	-	-	2.00	5.00	20.00	65.00	175.00	400.00
1924	3,105,839	-	-	1.25	4.00	18.00	50.00	150.00	325.00
1925	201,921	18.00	30.00	50.00	90.00	250.00	650.00	1,500.00	4,500.00

VARIETIES 1926. It was the usual practice in the George V 5-cent series to complete the date at the matrix stage, eliminating the necessity to date every reverse die and thereby assuring that there would be no difference in the positioning of the date digits on a given year's coinage. A notable exception was 1926, when the reverse punch (bearing a 6 which nearly touched the maple leaf) was retired before the conclusion of the coinage. The second variety had the 6 slightly farther from the maple leaf.

1926 Near 6	1926 Far 6
the 6 almost touches the maple leaf	the 6 is farther from the maple leaf

Date and Mint Mark	Quantity Minted	G-4	VG-8	F-12	VF-20	EF-40	AU-50	MS-60	MS-63
1926 Near 6	938,162	2.00	3.50	9.00	20.00	75.00	225.00	500.00	2,000.00
1926 Far 6	Incl. above	55.00	80.00	135.00	225.00	450.00	1,000.00	2,000.00	4,000.00
1927	5,285,627	-	-	1.25	3.50	18.00	45.00	90.00	225.00
1928	4,577,712	-	-	1.25	3.50	18.00	45.00	80.00	175.00
1929	5,611,911	-	-	1.25	3.50	18.00	45.00	90.00	250.00
1930	3,704,673	-	-	1.25	3.50	18.00	50.00	125.00	350.00
1931	5,100,000	-	-	1.25	3.50	18.00	50.00	150.00	500.00
1932	3,198,566	-	-	1.25	3.50	18.00	55.00	150.00	350.00
1933	2,597,867	-	-	2.00	5.00	20.00	90.00	350.00	900.00
1934	3,827,304	-	-	1.25	3.50	18.00	55.00	150.00	450.00
1935	3,900,000	-	-	1.25	3.50	18.00	55.00	150.00	350.00
1936	4,400,000	-	-	1.25	3.50	18.00	40.00	80.00	175.00

FIVE CENTS
George VI 1937 - 1942

In 1937 Canada introduced new coinage designs for the lower denominations, in keeping with a trend towards modernization begun in 1935 with the silver dollar. The reverse of the 5-cent piece bore a beaver on a rock-studded mound of earth rising out of the water. At the left is a log on which the beaver has been chewing. The master tools for this reverse were produced at the Paris Mint because the Royal Mint in London was pressed for time.

Designer and Modeller:
Portrait — T.H. Paget (H.P. below bust)
Reverse — G.E. Kruger-Gray
(K.G. above water at left)
Composition: 1.00 nickel
Weight: 4.54 grams
Diameter: 21.21 mm
Edge: Plain
Die Axis: ↑↑

Date and Mint Mark	Quantity Minted	VF-20	EF-40	AU-50	MS-60	MS-63	MS-65
1937 Dot	4,593,263	2.00	3.00	6.00	12.00	33.00	100.00
1938	3,898,974	2.00	9.00	30.00	80.00	200.00	750.00
1939	5,661,123	2.00	6.00	25.00	55.00	110.00	300.00
1940	13,920,197	1.00	3.00	7.00	22.00	70.00	350.00
1941	8,681,785	1.00	3.00	9.00	27.00	75.00	400.00
1942 Nickel	6,847,544	1.00	3.00	7.00	22.00	70.00	350.00

Note: All 1937 5¢ have the dot after the date.

CANADA

BEAVER DESIGN; TOMBAC COINAGE 1942. Nickel is an important component of stainless steel and other alloys needed for producing war materials, so World War II put a great strain upon Canada's nickel producers. By 1942 it was decided that nickel would have to be suspended as a coinage material for the duration of the war and experiments were initiated to find a substitute metal for the 5-cent piece. This led to the adoption of a 12-sided coin made of tombac, a kind of brass. The idea had come from the British 3-penny piece first issued in 1937. The tombac 5-cent was given its shape so that when tarnished it would still not be confused with 1-cent pieces.

Designer: Royal Canadian Mint staff, modifying existing designs
Engraver: Thomas Shingles, modifying Royal Mint coinage tools
Composition: .88 copper, .12 zinc
Weight: 4.54 grams
Diameter: c. 21.3 mm (opposite corners)
c. 20.0 mm (opposite sides)
Edge: Plain
Die Axis: ↑↑

Date and Mint Mark	Quantity Minted	VF-20	EF-40	AU-50	MS-60	MS-63	MS-65
1942 Tombac	3,396,234	1.25	2.25	3.25	4.00	18.00	85.00

TORCH & V DESIGN; TOMBAC COINAGE 1943-1944. In 1943 a new reverse design came into use for this denomination. Its purpose was to help promote the war effort. The idea for the design came from Churchill's famous "V" sign and the V denomination mark on the U.S. 5-cent pieces of 1883-1912. A novel feature was the use of an International Code message meaning, "We Win When We Work Willingly." It was placed along the rim on the reverse instead of denticles. The original master matrix was engraved entirely by hand by Royal Canadian Mint Chief Engraver Thomas Shingles. The obverse was the same as that for 1942, except rim denticles were added.

Designer, Engraver: Obverse — Thomas Shingles, modifying existing design and tools
Reverse — Thomas Shingles (T.S. at lower right of V and torch)
Composition: .88 copper, .12 zinc
Weight: 4.54 grams
Diameter: c. 21.3 mm (opposite corners)
c. 20.9 mm (opposite sides)
Edge: Plain
Die Axis: ↑↑

Date and Mint Mark	Quantity Minted	VF-20	EF-40	AU-50	MS-60	MS-63	MS-65
1943	24,760,256	.75	1.25	2.25	3.00	12.00	65.00
1944	8,000	Mid-year ANA Sale 1983 $9,500.00					

Note: Most of the 1944 5¢ tombac remained unissued and were melted.

TORCH & V DESIGN; STEEL COINAGE 1944-1945. War demands for copper and zinc forced a suspension in the use of tombac for the 5-cent piece and the institution of plated steel. The steel was plated with nickel and then returned to the plating tank for a very thin plating of chromium. The chromium was hard and helped retard wear. Unfortunately it was necessary to plate the strips prior to the blanks being punched out. This resulted in the edges of the blanks (and hence the coins) being unplated and vulnerable to rusting.

Some collectors have noted steel 5-cent pieces which have a dull gray colour instead of the normal bluish-white colour. This is due to some of the strips being plated with nickel only and not nickel and chromium. Such coins do not ordinarily command a significant premium.

Composition: Steel with .0127 mm plating of nickel and .0003 mm plating of chromium

All other statistics are as for the 1943 coinage.

Date and Mint Mark	Quantity Minted	VF-20	EF-40	AU-50	MS-60	MS-63	MS-65
1944	11,532,784	.75	1.25	2.00	3.00	7.00	35.00
1945	18,893,216	.75	1.25	2.00	3.00	7.00	40.00

BEAVER DESIGN RESUMED; "ET IND:IMP:" IN OBVERSE LEGEND 1946-1947. After the end of World War II, the Mint returned to the issue of nickel 5-cent pieces of the beaver design. However, it was decided to retain the 12-sided shape, because it had become popular. The obverse was a continuation of that of 1943-1945.

Designer, Engraver: Reverse — Thomas Shingles, modifying existing design and tools
Composition: 1.00 nickel
Weight: 4.54 grams
Diameter: c. 21.3 mm (opposite corners)
c. 20.9 mm (opposite sides)
Edge: Plain
Die Axis: ↑↑

Date and Mint Mark	Quantity Minted	VF-20	EF-40	AU-50	MS-60	MS-63	MS-65
1946	6,952,684	.75	3.00	5.00	18.00	40.00	175.00
1947	7,603,724	.75	2.25	4.50	11.00	25.00	125.00

MAPLE LEAF ISSUE 1947. The granting of independence to India provided a dilemma for the Royal Canadian Mint in the early part of 1948. The new obverse coinage tools (with "ET IND: IMP:" omitted) would not arrive for several months, yet there was a great need for all denominations of coins. Therefore, the mint struck coins dated 1947 and bearing the obverse with the outmoded titles. To differentiate this issue from the regular strikings of 1947, a tiny maple leaf was placed after the date.

CANADA

1947.

1947 Maple Leaf issue, struck in 1948
The physical and chemical specifications
are as for the 1946-1947 issues.

Date and Mint Mark	Quantity Minted	VF-20	EF-40	AU-50	MS-60	MS-63	MS-65
1947 ML	9,595,124	.75	2.00	4.00	9.00	22.00	100.00
1947 Dot		30.00	65.00	175.00	300.00	600.00	1,750.00

MODIFIED OBVERSE LEGEND; BEAVER REVERSE 1948-1950. Following the arrival of the master tools with the new obverse legend lacking "ET IND: IMP:" in 1948, the 1947 Maple Leaf coinage was suspended from production. For the remainder of the year coins were produced with the new obverse and the true date, 1948.

Designer and Engraver: Reverse —
Thomas Shingles, modifying existing
design and tools
Composition: 1.00 nickel
Weight: 4.54 grams
Diameter: c. 21.3 mm (opposite corners)
c. 20.9 mm (opposite sides)
Edge: Plain
Die Axis: ↑↑

Date and Mint Mark	Quantity Minted	VF-20	EF-40	AU-50	MS-60	MS-63	MS-65
1948	1,810,789	1.50	3.00	9.00	20.00	40.00	135.00
1949	13,037,090	.75	1.50	2.50	6.00	12.00	90.00
1950	11,970,520	.75	1.50	2.50	6.00	12.00	75.00

COMMEMORATIVE FOR ISOLATION & NAMING OF NICKEL 1951. In 1950 plans were made to strike a coin to commemorate the isolation and naming of the element nickel by the Swedish chemist A.F. Cronstedt in 1751. The three Canadian commemorative coins issued up to that time had been silver dollars, but the 5-cent piece was selected for use in 1951 because it was the only denomination struck in nickel. The design was chosen from entries submitted to the Mint in an open competition, the first of its type in Canada for a coinage that was actually issued. The winning design depicts a nickel refinery, with low buildings flanking a smoke stack in the centre. The obverse is the same as that for the 1948-1950 issues.

Some members of the public became confused and believed that the dates 1751-1951 should have read 1851-1951. This caused hoarding of these coins in the mistaken belief that they would become extremely valuable.

Designer and Modeller:
Reverse — Stephen Trenka
(ST monogram below the
building at the right)
Composition: 1.00 nickel
Weight: 4.54 grams
Diameter: c. 21.3 mm (opposite corners)
c. 20.9 mm (opposite sides)
Edge: Plain
Die Axis: ↑↑

Date and Mint Mark	Quantity Minted	VF-20	EF-40	AU-50	MS-60	MS-63	MS-65
1951 Comm.	9,028,507	.50	1.00	1.25	2.50	5.00	40.00

BEAVER DESIGN RESUMED; STEEL COINAGE 1951-1952. The Korean War placed strong demand on nickel, forcing suspension of production of the commemorative nickel 5-cent piece before the end of 1951. In its place steel coins of the beaver design were struck. It was found during trials that the beaver design was not as easy to strike in steel as in nickel, so new, lower relief coinage tools were prepared for both obverse and reverse. By mistake, a High Relief obverse die was used to strike a small proportion of the 1951 steel coinage, resulting in two varieties for the year. Aside from the difference in relief the High and Low Relief obverses differ in the position of the last A of "GRATIA" relative to the rim denticles. On the High Relief variety the "A" points to a rim denticle; on the Low Relief variety it points between denticles. The entire 1952 issue was coined with the Low Relief obverse.

Modeller: Thomas Shingles, modifying existing models
Composition: Steel with .0127 mm plating of nickel and .0003 mm plating of chromium
Weight: 4.54 grams
Diameter: c. 21.3 mm (opposite corners)
c. 20.9 mm (opposite sides)
Edge: Plain
Die Axis: ↑↑

A in GRATIA points to a rim denticle

1951 High Relief Obverse

A in GRATIA points between rim denticles

1951 Low Relief Obverse

Date and Mint Mark	Quantity Minted	VG-8	F-12	VF-20	EF-40	AU-50	MS-60	MS-63	MS-65
1951 High Relief	4,313,310	-	650.00	900.00	1,750.00	3,000.00	4,000.00	-	-
1951 Low Relief	Incl. above	-	-	.75	1.50	2.25	3.50	8.00	40.00
1952	10,891,148	-	-	.75	1.50	2.25	3.50	8.00	40.00

FIVE CENTS:
Elizabeth II 1953 to date

STEEL FIVE CENTS (12 sided) 1953-1954. Two obverse varieties, termed the No Shoulder Fold and Shoulder Fold obverses, saw use during 1953 (see 1-cent Elizabeth II, 1953 to date, for full explanation). On the 5-cent piece these varieties are best distinguished on worn coins by observing the styles of the letters in the obverse legends: they are more flared (particularly the I's) on the No Shoulder Fold variety. The reverses combined with the two obverses also show slight differences.

Designer and Modeller:
    Portrait — Mrs. Mary Gillick,
    (M.G. on truncation)
Engraver: No Shoulder Fold Obverse —
    Thomas Shingles, using the Gillick
    portrait model
    Shoulder Fold Obverse —
    Thomas Shingles, modifying
    existing NSF coinage tools
Composition: Steel with .0127 mm
    plating of nickel and .0003 mm plating
    of chromium
Weight: 4.54 grams
Diameter: c. 21.3 mm (opposite corners)
            c. 20.9 mm (opposite sides)
Edge: Plain
Die Axis: ↑↑

No Shoulder Fold Obverse
note flared ends of Is

Shoulder Fold Obverse
note straight-sided Is

Date and Mint Mark	Quantity Minted	EF-40	AU-50	MS-60	MS-63	MS-65	PL-65
1953 NSF	16,635,552	.75	2.50	4.00	9.00	30.00	125.00
1953 SF	Incl. above	.75	3.00	5.00	11.00	35.00	60.00
1954	6,998,662	1.00	3.50	7.00	13.00	40.00	25.00

NICKEL 12-SIDED COINAGE 1955-1962. The mint returned to nickel for the 5-cent piece in 1955. The reverse for the George VI coinage of 1946-1950 was continued.

Composition: 1.00 nickel

The other specifications are as for the 1953-1954 issues.

Date and Mint Mark	Quantity Minted	AU-50	MS-60	MS-63	MS-65	PL-65
1955	5,355,028	1.75	3.50	6.00	25.00	15.00
1956	9,399,854	1.25	2.25	5.00	20.00	12.00
1957	7,387,703	.75	2.00	5.00	15.00	10.00
1958	7,607,521	.75	2.00	5.00	15.00	10.00
1959	11,552,523	.40	.75	2.00	10.00	8.00
1960	37,157,433	.40	.50	1.50	6.00	6.00
1961	47,889,051	.40	.50	1.50	5.00	4.00
1962	46,307,305	.40	.50	1.50	5.00	4.00

LAUREATED BUST; ROUND COINAGE 1963-1964. For strictly economic reasons the production of round 5-cent pieces was resumed in 1963 for the first time since 1942. It was cheaper to make round coins because the collars for the coining presses lasted longer.

Engraver: Thomas Shingles, using existing coining tools
Composition: 1.00 nickel
Weight: 4.54 grams
Diameter: 21.21 mm
Edge: Plain
Die Axis: ↑↑

Date and Mint Mark	Quantity Minted	MS-60	MS-63	MS-65	PL-65
1963	43,970,320	.25	1.00	5.00	4.00
1964	78,075,068	.25	1.00	5.00	4.00

TIARA PORTRAIT; BEAVER REVERSE 1965-1966. A new obverse with the Queen showing more mature facial features and wearing a tiara was introduced on all denominations in 1965.

Designer and Modeller:
Portrait — Arnold Machin

The physical and chemical specifications are as for the 1963-1964 issues.

Date and Mint Mark	Quantity Minted	MS-60	MS-63	MS-65	PL-65
1965	84,876,019	.25	1.00	5.00	4.00
1966	27,678,469	.25	1.00	5.00	4.00

CANADA

COMMEMORATIVE FOR CENTENNIAL OF CONFEDERATION 1967. A reverse design showing a hopping rabbit was selected for the 1967 5-cent piece. It was by Alex Colville, who also designed the reverses of the other Confederation commemoratives issued for circulation. The obverse was a continuation of the 1965-1966 design.

Designer: Reverse — Alex Colville
Modeller: Reverse — Myron Cook

The physical and chemical specifications are as for the 1963-1966 issues.

Date and Mint Mark	Quantity Minted	MS-60	MS-63	MS-65	PL-65
1967	36,876,574	.25	1.00	5.00	6.00

TIARA PORTRAIT: BEAVER REVERSE RESUMED 1968-1978

Designer and Modeller:
Obverse — Arnold Machin
Reverse — G.E. Kruger-Gray
Composition: 1.00 nickel
Weight: 4.54 grams
Diameter: 21.21 mm
Edge: Plain
Die Axis: ↑↑

Date and Mint Mark	Quantity Minted	MS-60	MS-63	MS-65	PL-65
1968	99,253,330	.25	1.00	2.00	1.00
1969	27,830,229	.25	1.00	2.00	1.00
1970	5,726,010	.50	2.00	4.00	1.00
1971	27,312,609	.25	1.00	2.00	1.00
1972	62,417,387	.25	1.00	2.00	1.00
1973	53,507,435	.25	1.00	2.00	1.00
1974	94,704,645	.25	1.00	2.00	1.00
1975	138,882,000	.25	1.00	2.00	1.00
1976	55,140,213	.25	1.00	2.00	1.00
1977	89,120,791	.25	1.00	2.00	1.00
1978	137,079,273	.25	1.00	2.00	1.00

MODIFIED TIARA PORTRAIT; BEAVER REVERSE 1979-1989. Beginning on the 1979 coinage and as part of a general standardization of the coinage, the portrait of the Queen was made smaller. The purpose was to make the size of the portrait proportional to the diameter of the coin, regardless of the denomination.

Designer and Modeller:
Obverse — Arnold Machin, Walter Ott
Reverse — G.E. Kruger-Gray
Composition: 1.00 nickel (1979-1981)
.75 copper, .25 nickel
(1982-1989)
Weight: 4.54 grams
Diameter: 21.21 mm
Edge: Plain
Die Axis: ↑↑

Date and Mint Mark	Quantity Minted		MS-60	MS-63	MS-65	PL-65
1979	186,295,825		.25	.50	2.00	1.00
1980	134,878,000		.25	.50	2.00	1.00

Note: Beginning in 1981 the Royal Canadian Mint ceased production of proof-like coins. They are replaced in the listings by proof coins from the prestige set.

Date and Mint Mark	Quantity Minted		MS-60	MS-63	MS-65	PR-65
1981	99,107,900		.25	.50	2.00	2.00
1982	105,539,898		.25	.50	2.00	2.00
1983	72,596,000		.25	.50	2.00	2.00
1984	84,088,000		.25	.50	2.00	2.00
1985	126,618,000		.25	.50	2.00	2.00
1986	156,104,000		.25	.50	2.00	2.00
1987	106,299,000		.25	.50	2.00	4.00
1988	75,025,000		.25	.50	2.00	4.00
1989	141,435,538		.25	.50	2.00	4.00

CROWNED PORTRAIT; BEAVER REVERSE; 1990 TO 1991. A new obverse portrait of the Queen wearing a diamond diadem and jewellery was introduced on all denominations in 1990.

Designer and Modeller:
Obverse —Dora de Pédery-Hunt
Ago Aarand
Reverse —G.E. Kruger-Gray
Composition: Cupro-nickel
.75 copper, .25 nickel
Weight: 4.6 grams
Diameter: 21.2 mm
Edge: Plain
Die Axis: ↑↑

Date and Mint Mark	Quantity Minted		MS-60	MS-63	MS-65	PR-65
1990	42,537,000		.25	.50	2.00	4.00
1991	10,931,000		.25	.50	2.00	4.00

CANADA

COMMEMORATIVE FOR THE 125TH ANNIVERSARY; 1867-1992. The reverse design was modified to include the bracket dates 1867-1992 for the 125th birthday of Canada

Designer, modeller and physical specification are as for the 1990 and 1991 issues.

Date and Mint Mark	Quantity Minted		MS-60	MS-63	MS-65	PR-65
1992	53,732,000		.25	.50	2.00	4.00

BEAVER REVERSE RESUMED; 1993 TO 1997. In 1993 the practice of using a single date was resumed. The transition from rim denticles to beads, which began in 1982 on the one cent piece, was carried out on the five cent piece in 1993.

Designer, modeller and physical specification are as for the 1990 and 1991 issues.

Date and Mint Mark	Quantity Minted		MS-60	MS-63	MS-65	PR-65
1993	86,877,000		.25	.50	2.00	4.00
1994	99,352,000		.25	.50	2.00	4.00
1995	78,528,000		.25	.50	2.00	4.00
1996	N/A		.25	.50	2.00	4.00
1997	N/A		.25	.50	2.00	4.00

TEN CENT CIRCULATING COINAGE
Victoria 1870 - 1901

The initial designs for the Victoria 10-cent pieces issued by the Dominion government were identical to the 1858 Province of Canada issue. During the reign, six obverse varieties were used. They differed primarily in the features of the Queen's face. A detailed description and listing by year is not included in this standard catalogue. Two major varieties of the reverse exist; only in 1891 were both used for the same year's coinage (see below).

Designer, Modeller and Engraver:
  Leonard C. Wyon
Composition: .925 silver, .075 copper
Weight: 2.33 grams
Diameter: 18.03 mm
Edge: Reeded
Die Axis: ↑↓

Heaton Mint issues of 1871-1883 and the Mint, Birmingham issue of 1890 have an "H" mint mark on the reverse under the wreath. London Mint strikings have no letter.

VARIETIES 1870. Two styles of 0 appear in the date of the 1870 issue. The Narrow 0 with sides of equal thickness is more common than the Wide 0, on which the right-hand side is thicker.

1870 Narrow 0
Sides of equal thickness

1870 Wide 0
Right side is thicker

Date and Mint Mark	Quantity Minted	G-4	VG-8	F-12	VF-20	EF-40	AU-50	MS-60	MS-63
1870 Narrow 0	1,600,000	16.00	30.00	55.00	100.00	175.00	275.00	500.00	1,500.00
1870 Wide 0	Incl. above	18.00	35.00	65.00	120.00	225.00	325.00	600.00	1,750.00
1871	800,000	16.00	30.00	60.00	120.00	225.00	400.00	800.00	2,500.00
1871H	1,870,000	20.00	35.00	65.00	150.00	275.00	450.00	700.00	2,250.00
1872H	1,000,000	65.00	120.00	190.00	375.00	750.00	1,400.00	2,500.00	6,000.00

CANADA

MINTAGE FIGURES 1874H & 1875H. Through a clerical error part of the mintage of 1874H-dated coins was assigned to the next year's production figures. Therefore, the mintage figures for the two years, 600,000 and 1,000,000, respectively, have been combined.

Date and Mint Mark	Quantity Minted	G-4	VG-8	F-12	VF-20	EF-40	AU-50	MS-60	MS-63
1874H	1,600,000	10.00	17.00	30.00	65.00	150.00	250.00	500.00	1,500.00
1875H	Incl. above	175.00	325.00	550.00	1,100.00	2,250.00	4,500.00	8,000.00	17,500.00
1880H	1,500,000	9.00	15.00	28.00	60.00	115.00	225.00	450.00	1,500.00
1881H	950,000	10.00	20.00	35.00	75.00	165.00	275.00	550.00	1,600.00
1882H	1,000,000	10.00	20.00	40.00	75.00	165.00	300.00	650.00	1,750.00
1883H	300,000	25.00	50.00	100.00	250.00	375.00	700.00	1,200.00	2,750.00
1884	150,000	135.00	250.00	550.00	1,100.00	2,750.00	5,000.00	10,000.00	25,000.00
1885	400,000	20.00	40.00	70.00	200.00	500.00	1,500.00	3,000.00	8,000.00

VARIETIES 1886. For the 1886 coinage three distinctly different styles of 6 were used: a small 6, a large 6 with a point on its tail, and a large 6 with a large knob on its tail.

Photo
not
available

1886 Small 6	1886 Large, Pointed 6	1886 Large, Knobbed 6

Date and Mint Mark	Quantity Minted	G-4	VG-8	F-12	VF-20	EF-40	AU-50	MS-60	MS-63
1886 Small 6	800,000	16.00	25.00	50.00	125.00	250.00	500.00	1,250.00	3,000.00
1886 Lg., Pt. 6	Incl. above	16.00	30.00	60.00	125.00	250.00	500.00	1,100.00	2,750.00
1886 Lg., Knb. 6	Incl. above	16.00	30.00	60.00	125.00	250.00	500.00	1,100.00	2,750.00
1887	350,000	22.00	45.00	90.00	225.00	500.00	1,000.00	2,000.00	6,000.00
1888	500,000	9.00	13.00	30.00	65.00	125.00	225.00	500.00	1,500.00
1889	600,000	375.00	650.00	1,400.00	2,750.00	5,000.00	8,000.00	15,000.00	-
1890H	450,000	12.00	22.00	45.00	90.00	200.00	325.00	650.00	1,750.00

VARIETIES 1891 - 1893. The two major reverse varieties seen on this denomination differ in the number of leaves in the wreath. The first (1870-1881 & 1891) has 21 leaves and the second (1882-1901) has 22 leaves. The 21-leaf reverse in 1891 occurs with small digits in the date, whereas the 22-leaf reverse in 1891 has a large date.

One 1891 large date die was carried over into 1892 and the 1 was overdated with a 2. Aside from the overpunching, the 1892 over 1 differs from the non-overdate 1892's in the style of the 9. The overdate has the large 9 of the 22 leaves, 1891 variety, and the non-overdates have the small 9 of the 21 leaves, 1891 variety.

Dating varieties continued into 1893. In that year one or two dies were dated with a large 9 and round-top 3, while the rest were dated with a medium 9 and a flat-top 3.

1891 21 Leaves, Small Date

1891 22 Leaves, Large Date

1892 2 over 1, Large 9

1892 Normal Date, Small 9

1893 Flat-top 3, Medium 9

1893 Round-top 3, Large 9
The 3 on this variety is often weakly struck.

Date and Mint Mark	Quantity Minted	G-4	VG-8	F-12	VF-20	EF-40	AU-50	MS-60	MS-63
1891 21 Lvs.	800,000	12.00	22.00	45.00	100.00	225.00	375.00	650.00	1,600.00
1891 22 Lvs.	Incl. above	12.00	22.00	45.00	100.00	225.00	375.00	650.00	1,600.00
1892 2 over 1	520,000	22.00	45.00	70.00	135.00	300.00	600.00	1,250.00	2,750.00
1892	Incl. above	10.00	20.00	35.00	75.00	165.00	325.00	650.00	1,750.00
1893 F-Top 3	500,000	15.00	27.00	65.00	135.00	275.00	500.00	1,000.00	3,000.00
1893 R-Top 3	Incl. above	400.00	650.00	1,650.00	3,000.00	5,000.00	7,500.00	12,500.00	25,000.00
1894	500,000	16.00	30.00	55.00	110.00	225.00	325.00	650.00	1,750.00
1896	650,000	8.00	15.00	28.00	55.00	110.00	225.00	450.00	1,000.00
1898	720,000	8.00	15.00	30.00	60.00	120.00	225.00	500.00	1,250.00

VARIETIES 1899. During the production of the 1899 10-cent pieces, two styles of 9 were used for dating the dies: a small, narrow 9 and a large, wide 9. The upper centre of the wide 9 is almost round, compared with the tall, square centre of the narrow 9.

1899 Small 9s   1899 Large 9s

Date and Mint Mark	Quantity Minted	G-4	VG-8	F-12	VF-20	EF-40	AU-50	MS-60	MS-63
1899 Small 9's	1,200,000	8.00	11.00	22.00	55.00	110.00	200.00	375.00	1,000.00
1899 Large 9's Incl. above		11.00	22.00	35.00	50.00	175.00	325.00	700.00	2,000.00
1900	1,100,000	7.00	10.00	22.00	50.00	100.00	165.00	300.00	750.00
1901	1,200,000	7.00	10.00	22.00	50.00	100.00	165.00	300.00	850.00

TEN CENTS
Edward VII 1902 - 1910

The reverse first employed for the 10-cent pieces of this reign was adapted from the 22-leaf Victorian reverse. The Imperial State crown replaced the St. Edward's crown at the top and the word "CANADA" was transferred from the obverse legend.

Designer and Modeller:
Obverse — G.W. DeSaulles
(DES. under the bust);
Broad Leaves Reverse
(1909-10) — W.H.J. Blakemore
Engraver: Victorian Leaves Reverse
(1902-09) — G.W. DeSaulles
Composition: .925 silver, .075 copper
Weight: 2.32 grams (1902-10);
2.33 grams (1910)
Diameter: 18.03 mm
Edge: Reeded
Die Axis: ↑↓ (1902-07);
↑↑ (1908-10)

The Mint, Birmingham issues (1902-1903) have an "H" mint mark on the reverse under the wreath. London Mint issues have no letter.

Date and Mint Mark	Quantity Minted	G-4	VG-8	F-12	VF-20	EF-40	AU-50	MS-60	MS-63
1902	720,000	4.00	8.00	18.00	45.00	100.00	175.00	500.00	1,000.00
1902H	1,100,000	3.00	6.00	11.00	25.00	55.00	85.00	175.00	425.00
1903	500,000	9.00	17.00	35.00	100.00	250.00	600.00	1,500.00	4,000.00
1903H	1,320,000	4.00	8.00	15.00	40.00	80.00	175.00	400.00	850.00
1904	1,000,000	7.00	11.00	20.00	55.00	120.00	200.00	400.00	850.00
1905	1,000,000	6.00	10.00	20.00	65.00	150.00	225.00	700.00	1,750.00
1906	1,700,000	4.00	7.00	13.00	40.00	75.00	150.00	350.00	750.00
1907	2,620,000	4.00	7.00	13.00	35.00	65.00	150.00	350.00	650.00
1908	776,666	7.00	11.00	22.00	55.00	120.00	175.00	350.00	600.00

VARIETIES 1909. In 1909 an entirely new model was prepared for this denomination. The variety thus created has been called the Broad Leaves variety because of its broad leaves with strong, detailed venation.

1909 Victorian Leaves

1909 Broad Leaves

Date and Mint Mark	Quantity Minted	G-4	VG-8	F-12	VF-20	EF-40	AU-50	MS-60	MS-63
1909 Victorian	1,697,200	3.50	8.00	20.00	50.00	100.00	225.00	500.00	1,500.00
1909 Broad	Incl. above	6.00	11.00	25.00	60.00	125.00	275.00	600.00	1,500.00
1910	4,468,331	2.50	6.00	11.00	25.00	55.00	85.00	200.00	475.00

TEN CENTS
George V 1911 - 1936

"GODLESS" OBVERSE 1911. The obverse combined with the 1911 reverse aroused criticism because it lacked reference to the king's ruling "by the grace of God." The coinage tools were modified during 1911 and a new legend containing the Latin abbreviation "DEI GRA." appeared on the 1912 and subsequent issues. The first reverse was a continuation of the Broad Leaves design introduced in 1909. It was replaced during 1913 (see below).

Designer and Modeller:
Portrait — Sir E.B. MacKennal
(B.M. on truncation);
Small Leaves Reverse
W.H.J. Blakemore
Composition: .925 silver, .075 copper
Weight: 2.32 grams
Diameter: 18.03 mm
Edge: Reeded
Die Axis: ↑↑

Date and Mint Mark	Quantity Minted	G-4	VG-8	F-12	VF-20	EF-40	AU-50	MS-60	MS-63
1911	2,737,584	2.50	6.50	15.00	25.00	65.00	90.00	175.00	400.00

MODIFIED OBVERSE LEGEND 1912-1936

Composition: .925 Silver, .075 copper
(1912-19);
.800 silver, .200 copper
(1920-1936)

The physical specifications are as for the 1911 issue.

Date and Mint Mark	Quantity Minted	VG-8	F-12	VF-20	EF-40	AU-50	MS-60	MS-63
1912	3,235,557	2.50	4.00	9.00	33.00	110.00	325.00	850.00

VARIETIES 1913. The reverse that replaced the Broad Leaves design during 1913 has smaller leaves with less venations. It is from a completely new model.

1913 Broad Leaves   1913 Small Leaves

Date and Mint Mark	Quantity Minted	VG-8	F-12	VF-20	EF-40	AU-50	MS-60	MS-63
1913 Small	3,613,937	2.00	3.50	8.00	30.00	80.00	225.00	650.00
1913 Broad	Incl. above	125.00	250.00	500.00	1,250.00	3,500.00	7,500.00	20,000.00
1914	2,549,811	2.00	3.50	8.00	30.00	80.00	225.00	700.00
1915	688,057	6.00	16.00	33.00	125.00	275.00	550.00	1,100.00
1916	4,218,114	1.00	2.00	6.00	16.00	55.00	125.00	375.00
1917	5,011,988	.75	1.50	4.00	13.00	45.00	80.00	175.00
1918	5,133,602	.75	1.50	4.00	13.00	40.00	70.00	150.00
1919	7,877,722	.75	1.50	4.00	13.00	40.00	70.00	150.00
1920	6,305,345	.75	1.50	4.00	13.00	45.00	80.00	200.00
1921	2,469,562	1.50	2.50	5.00	20.00	55.00	135.00	375.00
1928	2,458,602	1.00	2.00	5.00	16.00	45.00	90.00	275.00
1929	3,253,888	1.00	2.00	5.00	16.00	45.00	80.00	200.00
1930	1,831,043	1.00	2.50	6.00	20.00	55.00	80.00	200.00
1931	2,067,421	1.00	2.00	5.00	16.00	45.00	80.00	175.00
1932	1,154,317	2.00	3.00	8.00	30.00	70.00	125.00	275.00
1933	672,368	2.50	4.50	12.00	40.00	90.00	275.00	650.00
1934	409,067	4.00	8.00	33.00	90.00	200.00	450.00	800.00
1935	384,056	4.00	8.00	25.00	75.00	175.00	400.00	700.00
1936	2,460,871	.75	1.50	4.00	13.00	40.00	65.00	125.00

TEN CENTS
George VI 1936 - 1952

COINAGE USING GEORGE V DIES 1936. Early in 1937, while the Royal Canadian Mint was awaiting the arrival of the master tools for the new coinage for George VI, an emergency coinage of 10-cent pieces dated 1936 and from George V dies is said to have taken place. To mark the special nature of the coinage the dies bore a small raised dot on the reverse under the wreath.

Although the mintage of the 1936 dot variety is claimed to be nearly 200,000, only four examples seem to survive today. All are specimen strikes, adding to the suspicion that circulation strikes were either never produced or were all melted. No genuine circulation strike has been confirmed.

NOTE: Lower grade silver coins, which do not have price listings are priced based on silver bullion on the day of purchase or sale. These lower grade coins do not have a numismatic premium at this time.

The physical and chemical specifications are as for the 1911-1936 issues.	1936 With Raised Dot Below Date, struck in 1937

Date and Mint Mark	Quantity Minted	SPECIMEN
1936 Dot	191,237	Only four known to exist

CANADA

COINAGE OF GEORGE VI 1937-1952. The new reverse design introduced in 1937 was destined to become one of the most loved and most controversial of Canada's coinage designs. It features a "fishing schooner under sail," as the official proclamation states. Proud Nova Scotians, believing the ship represents the famous fishing and racing schooner "Bluenose" have continually pressed for official acknowledgment. Available information indicates that the designer, Emanuel Hahn, used that ship as his primary model, but that strictly speaking the design must be considered a composite. The original master tools for the reverse were prepared at the Paris Mint. To improve the wearing qualities of the date, larger size digits were introduced in 1938.

"ET IND: IMP:" IN OBVERSE LEGEND 1937-1947. The intial obverse bore a legend containing the Latin abbreviation "ET IND: IMP:" to indicate that the King was the Emperor of India.

Designer and Modeller:
Portrait — T.H. Paget
(H.P. below bust);
Reverse — Emanuel Hahn
(H above waves at left)
Composition: .800 silver, .200 copper
Weight: 2.33 grams
Diameter: 18.03 mm
Edge: Reeded
Die Axis: ↑↑

Date and Mint Mark	Quantity Minted	F-12	VF-20	EF-40	AU-50	MS-60	MS-63	MS-65
1937	2,500,095	1.25	2.50	4.00	8.00	20.00	30.00	125.00
1938	4,197,323	2.25	3.50	10.00	30.00	65.00	110.00	450.00
1939	5,501,748	1.75	2.50	10.00	25.00	60.00	100.00	400.00
1940	16,526,470	.75	1.50	4.00	9.00	22.00	40.00	150.00
1941	8,716,386	1.75	3.50	9.00	25.00	60.00	110.00	450.00
1942	10,214,011	.75	1.50	6.00	16.00	40.00	65.00	250.00
1943	21,143,229	.75	1.50	5.00	9.00	18.00	40.00	150.00
1944	9,383,582	1.25	2.50	7.00	13.00	35.00	65.00	175.00
1945	10,979,570	.75	1.50	5.00	9.00	18.00	30.00	125.00
1946	6,300,066	1.25	2.50	7.00	13.00	35.00	65.00	200.00
1947	4,431,926	1.75	3.50	10.00	20.00	45.00	75.00	225.00

MAPLE LEAF ISSUE 1947. The granting of independance to India posed a problem for the Royal Canadian Mint in the early part of 1948. The new obverse coinage tools (with the Latin phrase "ET IND: IMP:" omitted to indicate that the king was no longer the Emperor of India) would not arrive for several months, yet there was a need for all denominations of coins. The mint satisfied the demand by striking coins dated 1947 bearing the obverse with the outmoded titles. To differentiate this issue from the regular strikings of 1947, a tiny maple leaf was placed after the date.

1947 Maple Leaf Issue,
struck in 1948

Date and Mint Mark	Quantity Minted	F-12	VF-20	EF-40	AU-50	MS-60	MS-63	MS-65
1947 Maple Leaf	9,638,793	.75	1.75	4.50	7.00	15.00	25.00	100.00

MODIFIED OBVERSE LEGEND 1948-1952. Following the arrival of the master tools with the obverse legend ommitting "ET IND: IMP:" production of the 1947 Maple Leaf coinage was suspended. For the remainder of the year coins were produced with the new obverse and the true date, 1948. This obverse was employed for the rest of the reign.

Designer and Modeller:
Obverse — T.H. Paget
Reverse — Emanuel Hahn
Composition: .800 silver, .200 copper
Weight: 2.33 grams
Diameter: 18.03 mm
Edge: Reeded
Die Axis: ↑↑

Date and Mint Mark	Quantity Minted	F-12	VF-20	EF-40	AU-50	MS-60	MS-63	MS-65
1948	422,741	4.50	10.00	22.00	35.00	60.00	90.00	350.00
1949	11,336,172	.75	2.00	3.50	5.50	10.00	18.00	100.00
1950	17,823,075	.75	1.25	2.25	3.50	9.00	15.00	75.00
1951	15,079,265	.75	1.25	2.25	3.50	7.00	13.00	55.00
1952	10,474,455	.75	1.25	2.25	3.50	7.00	12.00	45.00

NOTE: Lower grade silver coins, which do not have price listings, are based on silver bullion on the day of purchase or sale. These lower grade coins do not have a numismatic premium at this time.

TEN CENTS
Elizabeth II 1953 to Date

LAUREATED PORTRAIT 1953-1964. Two obverse varieties, termed the No Shoulder Fold and the Shoulder Fold obverses, saw use during 1953 (see 1-cent Elizabeth II 1953 to date for full explanation). On heavily circulated 10-cent pieces these varieties are most easily distinguished by observing the lettering styles in the legend. The No Shoulder Fold obverse has thicker letters with more flared ends (note the ls). The use of the George VI reverse was continued.

Designer and Modeller:
Portrait — Mrs. Mary Gillick
(M.G. on truncation)
Engraver: No Shoulder Fold Obverse —
Thomas Shingles, using the Gillick
portrait model;
Shoulder Fold Obverse — Thomas
Shingles, modifying existing NSF
coinage tools
Composition: .800 silver, .200 copper
Weight: 2.33 grams
Diameter: 18.03 mm
Edge: Reeded
Die Axis: ↑↑

No Shoulder Fold Obverse 1953,
note the flared ends of the letters.

Shoulder Fold Obverse 1953-1954,
the ends of letters are not as flared.

Date and Mint Mark	Quantity Minted	EF-40	AU-50	MS-60	MS-63	MS-65	PL-65
1953 NSF	17,706,395	1.25	2.00	4.00	7.00	55.00	125.00
1953 SF	Incl. above	1.75	3.00	5.00	9.00	70.00	75.00
1954	4,493,150	2.00	3.50	8.00	13.00	45.00	35.00
1955	12,237,294	.75	1.50	4.50	7.00	25.00	20.00
1956	16,732,844	.75	1.50	4.00	5.50	20.00	15.00
1957	16,110,229	.75	1.00	1.50	3.00	12.00	12.00
1958	10,621,236	.75	1.00	1.50	3.00	12.00	10.00
1959	19,691,433	-	1.00	1.25	2.00	10.00	10.00
1960	45,466,835	-	1.00	1.25	2.00	7.00	7.00
1961	26,850,859	-	1.00	1.25	2.00	6.00	5.00
1962	41,864,335	-	1.00	1.25	2.00	6.00	5.00
1963	41,916,208	-	-	1.25	1.50	6.00	5.00
1964	49,518,549	-	-	1.25	1.50	6.00	5.00

TIARA PORTRAIT, FISHING SCHOONER REVERSE 1965-1966. A new obverse with the Queen showing more mature facial features and wearing a tiara was introduced on all denominations in 1965.

Designer and Modeller:
　Obverse — Arnold Machin
　Reverse — Emanuel Hahn
Composition: .800 silver, .200 copper
Weight: 2.33 grams
Diameter: 18.03 mm
Edge: Reeded
Die Axis: ↑↑

Date and Mint Mark	Quantity Minted	MS-60	MS-63	MS-65	PL-65
1965	56,965,392	1.00	2.00	6.00	5.00
1966	34,330,199	1.00	2.00	6.00	5.00

COMMEMORATIVE FOR CENTENNIAL OF CONFEDERATION 1967. A reverse design showing a mackerel was chosen as part of the group of commemorative designs for the centennial of Confederation. During the year, the rising price of silver forced a reduction in the silver content to .500 from .800. The two varieties are not distinguishable by eye. The obverse is the same as on the 1965-1966 issues.

Designer and Modeller:
　Obverse — Arnold Machin
　Reverse — Alex Colville, Myron Cook
Composition: .800 silver, .200 copper
　　　　　　　　.500 silver, .500 copper
Weight: 2.33 grams
Diameter: 18.03 mm
Edge: Reeded
Die Axis: ↑↑

Date and Mint Mark	Quantity Minted	MS-60	MS-63	MS-65	PL-65
1967 .800 silver	32,309,135	1.00	1.50	6.00	6.00
1967 .500 silver	30,689,080	1.00	1.50	6.00	6.00

TIARA PORTRAIT: SCHOONER REVERSE RESUMED 1968. During 1968 the use of silver in circulation coins was discontinued. Nickel was used in its place. The nickel coins are darker and are attracted to a magnet. In addition about half of the 1968 nickel 10-cent pieces were coined at the Philadelphia Mint in the United States because of the pressure of other work at the Royal Canadian Mint. The Philadelphia and Ottawa issues differ only in the number and shape of the grooves in the edge of the coins; the grooves have square bottoms on the Philadelphia coins and V-shaped bottoms on the Ottawa strikings.

Designer and Modeller:
　Obverse — Arnold Machin
　Reverse — Emanuel Hahn
Composition: .500 silver, .500 copper
　　　　　　　　1.00 nickel
Weight: Silver - 2.33 gms, Nickel - 2.07 gms
Diameter: 18.03 mm
Edge: Reeded
Die Axis: ↑↑

Philadelphia Mint	Royal Canadian Mint
Edge grooves have flat bottoms	Edge grooves have V-shaped bottoms

Date and Mint Mark	Quantity Minted	MS-60	MS-63	MS-65	PL-65
1968 .500 silver	70,460,000	1.25	1.75	6.00	5.00
1968 Nickel, Philadelphia Mint	85,170,000	.40	.50	1.00	1.00
1968 Nickel, Ottawa Mint	87,412,930	.40	.50	1.00	1.00

MODIFIED SCHOONER REVERSE 1969. The 1969 Large Schooner-Large Date design is a rare variety. A small quantity was struck early in the year before it was discovered that the original designs had deteriorated so much that it was no longer useable. A completely new model with a noticeably smaller schooner and small date replaced the original designs in early 1969. The obverse is as on the 1965-1968 issues.

Designer and Modeller:
Obverse — Arnold Machin
Reverse — Emanuel Hahn,
Myron Cook
Composition: 1.00 nickel
Weight: 2.07 grams
Diameter: 18.03 mm
Edge: Reeded
Die Axis: ↑↑

1969 Large Date	1969 Small Date

NOTE: As of this edition only four examples of this extremely rare variety are known.

Date and Mint Mark	Quantity Minted	VF-20	EF-40	AU-50	MS-60	MS-63	MS-65	PL-65
1969 Large Date	Incl. Below	10,000.	15,000.	17,500.	-	-	-	-
1969 Small Date	55,833,929	-	-	-	.40	.50	1.00	1.00

SMALL SCHOONER REVERSE, LARGE PORTRAIT; 1970 - 1978.

Date and Mint Mark	Quantity Minted		MS-60	MS-63	MS-65	PL-65
1970	5,249,296		.50	1.00	4.00	2.00
1971	41,016,968		.40	.50	2.00	1.00
1972	60,169,387		.40	.50	2.00	1.00
1973	167,715,435		.40	.50	2.00	1.00
1974	201,566,565		.40	.50	2.00	1.00
1975	207,680,000		.40	.50	2.00	1.00
1976	95,018,533		.40	.50	2.00	1.00
1977	128,452,206		.40	.50	2.00	1.00
1978	170,366,431		.40	.50	2.00	1.00

MODIFIED TIARA PORTRAIT, SCHOONER REVERSE; 1979-1989. With the 1979 issue a general standardization of the coinage was started. The portrait of the Queen was reduced to make it proportional to the diameter of the coin, regardless of the denomination.

Designer and Modeller:
Obverse — Arnold Machin, Walter Ott
Reverse — Emanuel Hahn,
Composition: 1.00 nickel
Weight: 2.07 grams
Diameter: 18.03 mm
Edge: Reeded
Die Axis: ↑↑

Date and Mint Mark	Quantity Minted		MS-60	MS-63	MS-65	PL-65
1979	236,910,479		.40	.50	2.00	1.00
1980	169,910,479		.40	.50	2.00	1.00

Note: Beginning in 1981 the Royal Canadian Mint ceased production of proof-like coins. They are replaced in the listings by proof coins from the prestige set.

Date and Mint Mark	Quantity Minted		MS-60	MS-63	MS-65	PR-65
1981	123,912,900		.40	.50	2.00	3.00
1982	93,960,898		.40	.50	2.00	3.00
1983	111,501,710		.40	.50	2.00	3.00
1984	119,080,000		.40	.50	2.00	3.00
1985	142,800,000		.40	.50	2.00	3.00
1986	168,620,000		.40	.50	2.00	3.00
1987	147,309,000		.40	.50	2.00	3.00
1988	162,998,558		.40	.50	2.00	3.00
1989	198,693,414		.40	.50	2.00	3.00

CROWNED PORTRAIT; SCHOONER REVERSE; 1990 to 1991. A new obverse portrait of the Queen wearing a diamond diadem and jewellery was introduced on all denominations in 1990.

Designer and Modeller:
Obverse — Dora de Pédery-Hunt
   — Ago Aarand
Reverse — Emanuel Hahn,
Composition: Nickel
Weight: 2.07 grams
Diameter: 18.03 mm
Edge: Reeded
Die Axis: ↑↑

Date and Mint Mark	Quantity Minted		MS-60	MS-63	MS-65	PR-65
1990	65,023,000		.40	.50	2.00	6.00
1991	50,397,000		.40	.50	2.00	12.00

COMMEMORATIVE FOR THE 125TH ANNIVERSARY; 1867-1992. The reversed design was modified to include the bracket dates 1867-1992 for the 125th birthday of Canada.

Designer, modeller and physical specifications are the same as 1990 and 1991 issues.

Date and Mint Mark	Quantity Minted		MS-60	MS-63	MS-65	PR-65
1992	174,476,000		.40	.50	2.00	6.00

SCHOONER REVERSE RESUMED; 1993 TO 1997. In 1993 the practice of using a single date was resumed. The transition to beads from rim denticles which began in 1982 on the one cent piece, was completed on the ten cent piece in 1993.

Designer, modeller and physical specifications are the same as 1990 and 1991 issues.

Date and Mint Mark	Quantity Minted		MS-60	MS-63	MS-65	PR-65
1993	135,569,000		.40	.50	2.00	6.00
1994	145,800,000		.40	.50	2.00	6.00
1995	115,394,000		.40	.50	2.00	6.00
1996	N/A		.40	.50	2.00	6.00
1997	N/A		.40	.50	2.00	6.00

TWENTY-FIVE CENT CIRCULATING COINAGE
Victoria 1870 - 1901

The Province of Canada did not issue this denomination so new coinage tools were required for the Dominion of Canada issue. During Victoria's reign, five obverse and two reverse device varieties were employed. Their detailed description and listing by year are not included in this standard catalogue. The basic design for the reverse is the same as all other silver denominations: crossed boughs of sweet maple, tied at the bottom by a ribbon and surmounted by St. Edward's crown.

Designer, Modeller and Engraver:
Leonard C. Wyon
Composition: .925 silver, .075 copper
Weight: 5.81 grams
Diameter: 23.62 mm
Edge: Reeded
Die Axis: ↑↓

Heaton Mint issues of 1871-1883 and the Mint, Birmingham issue of 1890 have an "H" mint mark on the reverse under the wreath. London Mint strikings have no letter.

Date and Mint Mark	Quantity Minted	G-4	VG-8	F-12	VF-20	EF-40	AU-50	MS-60	MS-63
1870	900,000	11.00	20.00	40.00	110.00	225.00	450.00	900.00	2,500.00
1871	400,000	12.00	25.00	50.00	150.00	325.00	650.00	1,400.00	3,500.00
1871H	748,000	14.00	28.00	55.00	175.00	375.00	700.00	1,400.00	2,750.00
1872H	2,240,000	7.00	13.00	25.00	65.00	150.00	325.00	750.00	2,250.00

MINTAGE FIGURES 1874H & 1875H. Through a clerical error part of the mintage of 1874H-dated coins was assigned to the next year's production figures. Therefore the mintage figures for the two years, 1,600,000 and 1,000,000 respectively, have been combined.

Date and Mint Mark	Quantity Minted	G-4	VG-8	F-12	VF-20	EF-40	AU-50	MS-60	MS-63
1874H	2,600,000	7.00	13.00	20.00	65.00	150.00	300.00	650.00	1,750.00
1875H	Incl. above	200.00	350.00	750.00	2,250.00	4,500.00	7,500.00	15,000.00	-

CANADA

VARIETIES 1880H. Two styles of 0 were utilized for dating the dies for the 1880 issue of the denomination. Both the Narrow 0 and the Wide 0 occur alone, but in addition there is a scarce variety with the Narrow 0 punched over the Wide 0. Since the Narrow over Wide 0 variety looks like the plain, Wide 0 when it is worn, it is not listed separately and is considered part of the Wide 0 group.

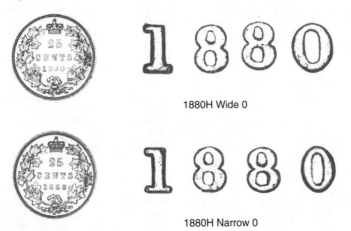

1880H Wide 0

1880H Narrow 0

Date and Mint Mark	Quantity Minted	G-4	VG-8	F-12	VF-20	EF-40	AU-50	MS-60	MS-63
1880H Wide 0	400,000	95.00	165.00	300.00	600.00	1,500.00	2,500.00	3,500.00	6,000.00
1880H Nar. 0	Incl. above	33.00	55.00	110.00	325.00	650.00	900.00	1,500.00	4,000.00
1881H	820,000	10.00	22.00	55.00	125.00	325.00	650.00	1,750.00	3,500.00
1882H	600,000	12.00	28.00	60.00	150.00	350.00	700.00	1,750.00	3,500.00
1883H	960,000	9.00	20.00	40.00	100.00	250.00	500.00	900.00	2,500.00
1885	192,000	75.00	135.00	275.00	600.00	1,500.00	2,750.00	5,000.00	10,000.00

VARIETIES 1886. A very interesting and long unrecognized overdate occurs on the 1886 25-cents. The overdate 1886/3 seems unlikely in view of the fact that the 1885 date came in between and the 1883 coins were all produced at The Mint, Birmingham with the H mint mark; however, in an article it is proved conclusively that the overdate here illustrated is indeed 6/3.

6 over 3

Date and Mint Mark	Quantity Minted	G-4	VG-8	F-12	VF-20	EF-40	AU-50	MS-60	MS-63
1886 6 over 3	540,000	11.00	22.00	55.00	135.00	400.00	800.00	2,000.00	4,500.00
1886	Incl. above	9.00	20.00	45.00	125.00	350.00	700.00	1,750.00	4,000.00
1887	100,000	75.00	135.00	275.00	550.00	1,500.00	2,500.00	5,000.00	10,000.00
1888	400,000	9.00	20.00	40.00	110.00	275.00	500.00	1,000.00	3,250.00
1889	66,324	90.00	165.00	300.00	600.00	1,750.00	3,000.00	6,000.00	12,500.00
1890H	200,000	13.00	28.00	55.00	150.00	375.00	700.00	1,500.00	3,000.00
1891	120,000	50.00	80.00	150.00	350.00	750.00	1,250.00	2,000.00	4,500.00
1892	510,000	9.00	17.00	35.00	100.00	275.00	500.00	1,000.00	3,500.00
1893	100,000	65.00	125.00	225.00	450.00	1,000.00	1,600.00	2,500.00	4,750.00
1894	220,000	13.00	30.00	60.00	150.00	350.00	600.00	1,100.00	2,750.00
1899	415,580	6.00	11.00	22.00	60.00	165.00	375.00	950.00	2,250.00
1900	1,320,000	5.00	10.00	20.00	60.00	140.00	275.00	650.00	1,750.00
1901	640,000	5.00	10.00	20.00	60.00	140.00	300.00	750.00	1,750.00

TWENTY-FIVE CENTS
Edward VII 1902-1910

SMALL CROWN REVERSE 1902-1905. The initial reverse for the Edward VII coins of this denomination has an almost unaltered wreath from the Victorian issues coupled with a small Imperial State crown and a new legend containing "CANADA" (it was formerly on the obverse).

Designer and Modeller:
  Obverse — G.W. DeSaulles
  (DES. under the bust)
Engraver: Small Crown reverse —
  G.W. DeSaulles
Composition: .925 silver, .075 copper
Weight: 5.81 grams
Diameter: 23.62 mm
Edge: Reeded
Die Axis: ↑↓

The Mint, Birmingham issue of 1902 has an "H" mint mark on the reverse under the wreath. London Mint issues have no letter.

Date and Mint Mark	Quantity Minted	VG-8	F-12	VF-20	EF-40	AU-50	MS-60	MS-63
1902	464,000	11.00	25.00	65.00	175.00	375.00	1,000.00	3,000.00
1902H	800,000	8.00	15.00	55.00	110.00	200.00	375.00	800.00
1903	846,150	11.00	25.00	65.00	175.00	375.00	850.00	2,500.00
1904	400,000	20.00	50.00	150.00	400.00	900.00	2,000.00	7,500.00
1905	800,000	12.00	27.00	100.00	300.00	900.00	2,250.00	10,000.00

LARGE CROWN REVERSE 1906 - 1910. The reverse for the 1906 coinage was modified to improve die life and impart a better overall appearance to the coins. The wreath was extensively retouched and a larger crown was placed at the top.

Engraver: Reverse — W.H.J. Blackmore
Weight: 5.81 grams (1906-10)
          5.83 grams (1910)
Die Axis: ↑↓ (1906-1907);
         ↑↑ (1908-1910)

The other specifications are as for the 1902-1905 issues.

Date and Mint Mark	Quantity Minted	VG-8	F-12	VF-20	EF-40	AU-50	MS-60	MS-63
1906	1,237,843	9.00	18.00	55.00	150.00	325.00	700.00	2,250.00
1907	2,088,000	8.00	16.00	50.00	150.00	300.00	650.00	1,750.00
1908	495,016	12.00	25.00	70.00	275.00	350.00	500.00	1,250.00
1909	1,335,929	10.00	20.00	60.00	225.00	450.00	900.00	2,750.00
1910	3,577,569	8.00	15.00	55.00	110.00	200.00	400.00	1,100.00

TWENTY - FIVE CENTS
George V 1911 - 1936

"GODLESS" OBVERSE 1911. The obverse issued on the 1911 coins provoked public outcry because it lacked reference to the King's ruling "by the grace of God." The coinage tools were modified during the year and a new legend including the Latin abbreviation "DEI GRA:" appeared on the 1912 and subsequent issues. The reverse was a continuation of the Large Crown variety of Edward VII.

Designer and Modeller:
    Portrait — Sir E.B. MacKennal
    (B.M. on truncation)
Composition: .925 silver, .075 copper
Weight: 5.83 grams
Diameter: 23.62 mm
Edge: Reeded
Die Axis: ↑↑

Date and Mint Mark	Quantity Minted	VG-8	F-12	VF-20	EF-40	AU-50	MS-60	MS-63
1911	1,721,341	9.00	22.00	50.00	125.00	200.00	400.00	800.00

MODIFIED OBVERSE LEGEND 1912 - 1936

Composition: .925 silver, .075 copper
(1912-1919);
.800 silver, .200 copper
(1920-1936)

The physical specifications are as for the
1911 issue.

Date and Mint Mark	Quantity Minted	VG-8	F-12	VF-20	EF-40	AU-50	MS-60	MS-63
1912	2,544,199	3.25	5.50	20.00	60.00	150.00	550.00	2,250.00
1913	2,213,595	3.25	5.50	20.00	60.00	120.00	425.00	1,750.00
1914	1,215,397	3.50	6.50	25.00	65.00	225.00	850.00	3,250.00
1915	242,382	15.00	35.00	160.00	500.00	1,750.00	3,500.00	8,500.00
1916	1,462,566	2.75	5.50	20.00	50.00	80.00	350.00	900.00
1917	3,365,644	2.25	4.50	15.00	30.00	55.00	200.00	375.00
1918	4,175,649	2.25	4.50	15.00	30.00	50.00	135.00	325.00
1919	5,852,262*	2.25	4.50	15.00	30.00	50.00	135.00	350.00
1920	1,975,278	2.75	5.00	17.00	40.00	70.00	275.00	750.00
1921	597,337	11.00	27.00	100.00	225.00	700.00	1,750.00	4,500.00
1927	468,096	27.00	45.00	125.00	325.00	650.00	1,250.00	2,750.00
1928	2,114,178	2.75	4.00	20.00	50.00	70.00	225.00	575.00
1929	2,690,562	2.25	3.75	20.00	45.00	65.00	225.00	575.00
1930	968,748	3.25	5.50	18.00	40.00	75.00	350.00	850.00
1931	537,815	3.25	4.50	25.00	55.00	100.00	375.00	900.00
1932	537,994	3.75	6.50	30.00	60.00	100.00	350.00	800.00
1933	421,282	4.50	7.00	25.00	55.00	100.00	275.00	575.00
1934	384,350	5.50	10.00	35.00	75.00	150.00	325.00	750.00
1935	537,772	5.50	9.00	30.00	65.00	125.00	275.00	550.00
1936	972,094	2.25	3.50	15.00	35.00	55.00	125.00	325.00

*51,494 25¢ pieces, .925 fine and presumably all dated 1919, were melted in 1920.

TWENTY-FIVE CENTS
George VI 1937 - 1952

COINAGE USING GEORGE V DIES 1936. Early in 1937, while the Royal Canadian Mint was
awaiting the arrival of the master tools for the new coinage for George VI, an emergency issue
of 25-cent pieces occurred to satisfy urgent demands for this denomination. To mark the
special nature of the coinage the dies bore a small raised dot on the reverse under the wreath.
That such an emergency issue even took place was generally not known until 1940, when
collectors began noticing that some of the 25-cent pieces dated 1936 had a dot under the
wreath. It was learned that supposedly 1- and 10-cent pieces were issued also, but no
circulated examples of the two latter denominations have been proved genuine.

The physical and chemical specifications are as for the 1911-1936 issues.

1936 With raised dot below date struck in 1937.

Date and Mint Mark	Quantity Minted	VG-8	F-12	VF-20	EF-40	AU-50	MS-60	MS-63
1936 Dot	153,322	40.00	90.00	225.00	425.00	675.00	1,250.00	2,750.00

COINAGE OF GEORGE VI 1937 - 1952. The design chosen for the reverse of the new George VI coinage in 1937 was Emanuel Hahn's caribou head. This design was part of the government's program of modernizing the coinage. The original master tools were prepared at the Paris Mint due to a heavy work load at the Royal Mint in London at that time.

"ET IND: IMP:" IN OBVERSE LEGEND 1937 - 1947. The initial obverse bore a legend containing an abbreviation for the Latin phrase, "ET INDIAE IMPERATOR'" meaning "and Emperor of India," referring to the fact that the British monarch had held that position since Queen Victoria was made Empress of India in 1876.

Designer and Modeller:
Portrait — T.H. Paget
(H.P. below bust);
Reverse — Emanuel Hahn
(H in front of caribou's neck at bottom)
Composition: .800 silver, .200 copper
Weight: 5.83 grams
Diameter: 23.62 mm
Edge: Reeded
Die Axis: ↑↑

Date and Mint Mark	Quantity Minted	F-12	VF-20	EF-40	AU-50	MS-60	MS-63	MS-65
1937	2,690,176	1.75	5.00	7.00	9.00	18.00	50.00	225.00
1938	3,149,245	1.75	6.00	9.00	40.00	90.00	175.00	650.00
1939	3,532,495	1.75	4.00	8.00	33.00	80.00	150.00	550.00
1940	9,583,650	1.25	3.00	5.00	9.00	18.00	45.00	225.00
1941	6,654,672	1.25	3.00	5.00	9.00	22.00	50.00	225.00
1942	6,935,871	1.25	3.00	5.00	9.00	22.00	50.00	225.00
1943	13,559,575	1.25	3.00	5.00	9.00	22.00	50.00	225.00
1944	7,216,237	1.25	3.00	6.00	16.00	35.00	90.00	250.00
1945	5,296,495	1.25	3.00	5.00	7.00	18.00	45.00	225.00
1946	2,210,810	1.50	4.00	7.00	22.00	55.00	100.00	300.00
1947	1,524,554	1.50	4.00	9.00	33.00	65.00	135.00	350.00

MAPLE LEAF ISSUE 1947. In early 1948 the Royal Canadian Mint was faced with a problem resulting from India's recent independence. The new obverse coinage tools, with the Latin abbreviation "ET IND: IMP." ommited to indicate that the King's titles had changed, would not arrive for several months, yet there was a great need for all denominations of coins. The mint satisfied the demand by striking coins dated 1947 and bearing outmoded titles on the obverse. To distinguish this issue from the regular strikings of 1947, a tiny maple leaf was placed after the date.

1947 Maple Leaf Issue
struck in 1948

Date and Mint Mark	Quantity Minted	F-12	VF-20	EF-40	AU-50	MS-60	MS-63	MS-65
1947 Maple Leaf	4,393,938	1.25	3.00	5.00	7.00	22.00	40.00	150.00
1947 Dot		60.00	90.00	160.00	250.00	400.00	750.00	1,500.00

MODIFIED OBVERSE LEGEND 1948 - 1952. Following the arrival of the master tools with the new obverse legend lacking "ET IND: IMP:" in 1948, production of the 1947 Maple Leaf coinage was suspended. For the remainder of the year coins were produced with the new obverse and the true date, 1948.

Designer and Modeller:
Portrait — T.H. Paget
(H.P. below bust);
Reverse — Emanuel Hahn
(H in front of caribou's neck at bottom)
Composition: .800 silver, .200 copper
Weight: 5.83 grams
Diameter: 23.62 mm
Edge: Reeded
Die Axis: ↑↑

Date and Mint Mark	Quantity Minted	F-12	VF-20	EF-40	AU-50	MS-60	MS-63	MS-65
1948	2,564,424	2.25	4.00	7.00	22.00	75.00	160.00	350.00
1949	7,988,830	1.25	2.00	3.00	6.00	13.00	35.00	175.00
1950	9,673,335	1.25	2.00	3.00	5.00	11.00	25.00	150.00

VARIETIES 1951 - 1952. In an attempt to improve the appearance of the obverse of this denomination a fresh reduction was made to produce an obverse with a slightly larger, lower relief portrait. Both varieties were used in 1951 and 1952. Aside from the difference in relief and the size of the portrait, the two varieties can be distinguished by the lettering. The High Relief variety has a plain lettering style in the legend, and the first "A" in "GRATIA" points to a rim denticle. On the Low Relief variety the letters are more flared and the first "A" in "GRATIA" points between rim denticles.

High Relief Obverse

Low Relief Obverse

Date and Mint Mark	Quantity Minted	VF-20	EF-40	AU-50	MS-60	MS-63	MS-65
1951 Low Relief	8,290,719	2.00	3.00	5.00	9.00	20.00	125.00
1951 High Relief	Incl. above	2.00	3.00	5.00	9.00	20.00	125.00
1952 Low Relief	8,859,642	2.00	3.00	5.00	9.00	20.00	125.00
1952 High Relief	Incl. above	2.00	3.00	5.00	9.00	20.00	125.00

TWENTY-FIVE CENTS
Elizabeth II 1953 to Date

LAUREATED PORTRAIT 1953-1964. Two obverse varieties, called the No Shoulder Fold and Shoulder Fold obverses, saw use during 1953 (see 1-cent Elizabeth II, 1953 to date for full explanation). On the 25-cents these obverses are combined with reverses that are readily distinguishable. The No Shoulder Fold obverse comes with a Large Date reverse (carried over from George VI) and the Shoulder Fold was used with a Small Date reverse.

1953 No Shoulder Fold Obverse, Large Date Reverse

Designer and Modeller:
 Portrait — Mrs. Mary Gillick
 (M.G. on truncation);
 Small Date Reverse — Thomas
 Shingles, modifying existing models
Engraver: No Shoulder Fold Obverse —
 Thomas Shingles, using the Gillick
 portrait model;
 Shoulder Fold Obverse — Thomas
 Shingles, modifying existing NSF
 coinage tools
Composition: .800 silver, .200 copper
Weight: 5.83 grams
Diameter: 23.62 mm (1953 Lg. Date);
 23.88 mm (1953 Sm. Date - '64)
Edge: Reeded
Die Axis: ↑↑

1953 Shoulder Fold Obverse,
Small Date Reverse

Date and Mint Mark	Quantity Minted	VF-20	EF-40	AU-50	MS-60	MS-63	MS-65	PL-65
1953 LD, NSF	10,456,769	2.00	2.50	4.50	7.00	15.00	40.00	175.00
1953 SD, SF	Incl. above	2.00	2.50	5.50	10.00	25.00	75.00	100.00
1954	2,318,891	3.00	8.00	14.00	30.00	60.00	125.00	75.00
1955	9,552,505	-	-	3.00	6.00	15.00	40.00	35.00
1956	11,269,353	-	-	3.00	5.00	10.00	30.00	25.00
1957	12,770,190	-	-	2.50	4.00	8.00	25.00	20.00
1958	9,336,910	-	-	2.50	4.00	7.00	20.00	15.00
1959	13,503,461	-	-	2.50	4.00	6.00	15.00	12.00
1960	22,835,327	-	-	2.00	2.50	4.00	15.00	5.00
1961	18,164,368	-	-	2.00	2.50	4.00	15.00	5.00
1962	29,559,266			2.00	2.50	4.00	15.00	5.00
1963	21,180,652			2.00	2.50	4.00	15.00	5.00
1964	36,479,343			2.00	2.50	4.00	15.00	5.00

TIARA PORTRAIT; CARIBOU REVERSE 1965 - 1966. A new obverse with the Queen showing more mature facial features and wearing a tiara was introduced on all denominations in 1965.

Designer and Modeller:
 Portrait - Arnold Machin

The physical and chemical specifications are as for the 1954 - 1964 issues.

Date and Mint Mark	Quantity Minted	MS-60	MS-63	MS-65	PL-65
1965	44,708,869	2.00	4.00	15.00	5.00
1966	25,626,315	2.00	4.00	15.00	5.00

CANADA

COMMEMORATIVE FOR CENTENNIAL OF CONFEDERATION 1967. A reverse design featuring a walking wildcat (bobcat) was selected as part of the commemorative set of coins for this year. During the year, the rising price of silver entailed reducing the silver content from .800 to .500. The two varieties are not distinguishable by eye.

Designer: Reverse — Alex Colville
Modeller: Reverse — Myron Cook
Composition: .800 silver, .200 copper or
.500 silver, .500 copper

The other physical specifications are as for the 1954-1964 issues.

Date and Mint Mark	Quantity Minted	MS-60	MS-63	MS-65	PL-65
1967 Commemorative .800 silver	49,136,303	2.00	4.00	15.00	5.00
1967 Commemorative .500 silver	Incl. above	2.00	4.00	15.00	5.00

CARIBOU REVERSE RESUMED 1968 - 1972. During the 1968 coining it was necessary to discontinue the use of silver and substitute nickel for it. Nickel coins are darker in colour and are attracted to a magnet.

Designer and Modeller:
Portrait — Arnold Machin
Composition: 1968 — .500 silver,
.500 copper
1968-1972 — 1.00 nickel
Weight: Silver — 5.83 grams
Nickel — 5.07 grams
Diameter: 23.88 mm
Edge: Reeded
Die Axis: ↑↑

Date and Mint Mark	Quantity Minted	MS-60	MS-63	MS-65	PL-65
1968 .500 Silver	71,464,000	2.00	4.00	15.00	-
1968 Nickel	88,686,931	.75	1.00	1.50	1.00
1969	133,037,929	.75	1.00	1.50	1.00
1970	10,302,010	1.00	2.00	6.00	3.00
1971	48,170,428	.75	1.00	1.50	1.00
1972	43,743,387	.75	1.00	1.50	1.00

COMMEMORATING THE CENTENNIAL OF THE FOUNDING OF THE R.C.M.P. 1973. The special reverse on the 1973 25-cent piece commemorates the centennial of the founding of the North West Mounted Police, which later became the Royal Canadian Mounted Police. A new obverse with a smaller, more detailed portrait and fewer rim denticles placed farther from the rim was prepared for use with the commemorative reverse. However, a small quantity of coins was struck with the 1972 obverse, creating two varieties for the year. The quantity of the Large Bust variety struck for circulation is believed not to exceed 10,000.

Designer: Reverse — Paul Cedarberg (PC behind horse)
Modeller: Small Bust Obverse — Patrick Brindley, modifying the existing Machin Portrait
Reverse — Walter Ott
Composition: 1.00 nickel
Weight: 5.07 grams
Diameter: 23.88 mm
Edge: Reeded
Die Axis: ↑↑

Small Bust   Large Bust

Date and Mint Mark	Quantity Minted	F-12	VF-20	EF-40	AU-50	MS-60	MS-63	MS-65	PL-65
1973 Sm. Bust	134,958,589	-	-	-	-	.75	1.00	2.00	1.00
1973 Lge. Bust	Incl. above	80.00	90.00	100.00	110.00	140.00	165.00	200.00	175.00

CARIBOU REVERSE RESUMED; TIARA PORTRAIT; 1974 - 1978. With the return to the caribou reverse for the 25-cent piece in 1974, the use of the Large Portrait obverse was resumed.

The physical and chemical specifications are as for the 1968-1972 issues.

Date and Mint Mark	Quantity Minted	MS-60	MS-63	MS-65	PL-65
1974	192,360,598	.75	1.00	2.00	1.00
1975	141,148,000	.75	1.00	2.00	1.00
1976	86,898,261	.75	1.00	2.00	1.00
1977	99,634,555	.75	1.00	2.00	1.00

1978 Far Canada 148 Small Denticles	1978 Near Canada 120 Large Denticles

Date and Mint Mark	Quantity Minted	MS-60	MS-63	MS-65	PL-65
1978 Small Denticles	176,475,408	2.00	4.00	5.00	-
1978 Large Denticles	Incl. above	.75	1.00	2.00	1.00

CARIBOU REVERSE; MODIFIED DESIGN; 1979 - 1989. Beginning with the 1979 issue and as part of a general standardization of the coinage, the portrait of the Queen was reduced. The intention was to make the size of the portrait proportional to the diameter of the coin, regardless of the denomination. This obverse is not the same as that employed in connection with the 1973 R.C.M.P. commemorative.

Designer and Modeller:
Obverse — Arnold Machin,
Walter Ott
Reverse — Emanuel Hahn
Composition: 1.00 Nickel
Weight: 5.07 grams
Diameter: 23.88 mm
Edge: Reeded
Die Axis: ↑↑

Date and Mint Mark	Quantity Minted	MS-60	MS-63	MS-65	PL-65
1979	131,042,905	.75	1.00	2.00	1.00
1980	76,178,000	.75	1.00	2.00	1.00

Note: Beginning in 1981 the Royal Canadian Mint ceased production of proof-like coins. They are replaced in the listings by proof coins from the prestige set.

Date and Mint Mark	Quantity Minted	MS-60	MS-63	MS-65	PR-65
1981	131,583,900	.75	1.00	2.00	1.50
1982	171,926,000	.75	1.00	2.00	1.50
1983	13,162,000	2.00	2.50	5.00	1.50
1984	119,212,000	.75	1.00	2.00	1.50
1985	158,734,000	.75	1.00	2.00	1.50
1986	132,220,000	.75	1.00	2.00	2.00
1987	53,408,000	1.00	1.25	2.50	4.00
1988	80,368,473	.75	1.00	2.00	6.00
1989	119,624,307	.75	1.00	2.00	6.00

CROWNED PORTRAIT; CARIBOU REVERSE; 1990 TO 1991. A new obverse portrait of the Queen wearing a diamond diadem and jewellery was introduced on all denominations in 1990.

Designer and Modeller:
Obverse — Dora de Pédery-Hunt
Ago Aarand
Reverse — Emanuel Hahn
Composition: 1.00 Nickel
Weight: 5.07 grams
Diameter: 23.88 mm
Edge: Reeded
Die Axis: ↑↑

Date and Mint Mark	Quantity Minted		MS-60	MS-63	MS-65	PR-65
1990	31,258,000		.75	1.00	2.00	7.00
1991	459,000		6.00	8.00	15.00	25.00

COMMEMORATIVE FOR 125TH ANNIVERSARY; 1867-1992. The reverse design was modified to include the bracket dates 1867-1992 for the 125th birthday of Canada.

Designer, modeller and physical specifications are as for the 1990 and 1991 issues.

Date and Mint Mark	Quantity Minted		PL-65	PR-65
1992	442,986		4.00	8.00

Note: No 1867 - 1992 dated quarters were issued for circulation. The double dated caribou can only be found in the uncirculated set, specimen set, or the seven coin proof set, all issued by the numismatic department of the R.C.M.

Note: A potential 1991 twenty-five cent variety exists. At present they are classified as wide and narrow rim varieties. The narrow rim being the scarcer. However, there are questions as to how these varieties came about, and if they are true varieties. One school has the varieties originating from the different treatment of the planchets, while the other is based on the use of two different reverse hubs.

CANADA

125TH ANNIVERSARY OF CONFEDERATION; 1867-1992. During each month of 1992 the Royal Canadian Mint issued a twenty-five cent coin bearing a unique design to represent one of the twelve provinces and territories. Each coin was launched at a special event organized in the capital city of the province or territory commemorated by the design. The designs for the thirteen coins issued to celebrate the 125th birthday (a one dollar coin was issued for Canada Day 1992) were chosen by a national contest.

The obverse and physical specifications are common to all twelve coins

Designer and Modeller:
Obverse — Dora de Pédery-Hunt
Ago Aarand
Reverse — See below
Composition: 1.00 Nickel
Weight: 5.07 grams
Diameter: 23.88 mm
Edge: Reeded
Die Axis: ↑↑ ↑↓

New Brunswick
January 9, 1992
Ronald Lambert
Sheldon Beveridge

Northwest Territories
February 6, 1992
Beth McEachen
A. Aarand/C.Saffioti

Newfoundland
March 5, 1992
Christopher Newhook
Sheldon Beveridge

Manitoba
April 7, 1992
Muriel Hope
Ago Aarand

Yukon
May 7, 1992
Libby Dulac
William Woodruff

Alberta
June 4, 1992
Mel Heath
William Woodruff

Prince Edward Island
July 7, 1992
Nigel Roe
Sheldon Beveridge

Ontario
August 6, 1992
Greg Salmela
Susan Taylor

Nova Scotia
September 9, 1992
Bruce Wood
Terry Smith

Quebec
October 1,1992
Romualdas Bukauskas
Stan Witten

Saskatchewan
November 5, 1992
Brian Cobb
Terry Smith

British Columbia
November 9, 1992
Carla Egan
Sheldon Beveridge

Date and Mint Mark	Description	Quantity Minted	MS-60	MS-63	MS-65
1992	New Brunswick, Medal	12,174,000	1.00	1.50	2.00
1992	New Brunswick, Coinage	Inc. Above	5.00	10.00	20.00
1992	Northwest Territories	12,580,000	1.00	1.50	2.00
1992	Newfoundland	11,405,000	1.00	1.50	2.00
1992	Manitoba	11,349,000	1.00	1.50	2.00
1992	Yukon	10,388,000	1.00	1.50	2.00
1992	Alberta	12,133,000	1.00	1.50	2.00
1992	Prince Edward Island	13,001,000	1.00	1.50	2.00
1992	Ontario	14,263,000	1.00	1.50	2.00
1992	Nova Scotia	13,600,000	1.00	1.50	2.00
1992	Quebec	13,607,000	1.00	1.50	2.00
1992	Saskatchewan	14,165,000	1.00	1.50	2.00
1992	British Columbia	14,001,000	1.00	1.50	2.00

Note: For the proof-like nickel map set and proof silver set please see page no. 214.

CARIBOU REVERSE RESUMED; 1993 TO 1997. In 1993 the practice of using a single date was resumed. The transition to beads from rim denticles, which began in 1982 on the one cent piece, was completed in 1993 by the use of beads on the twenty-five cent coin.

Designer, modeller and physical specifications are as for the 1990 and 1991 issues.

Date and Mint Mark	Quantity Minted	MS-60	MS-63	MS65	PR-65
1993	73,758,000	.75	1.00	1.25	7.00
1994	77,670,000	.75	1.00	1.25	7.00
1995	72,302,000	.75	1.00	1.25	7.00
1996	N/A	.75	1.00	1.25	7.00
1997	N/A	.75	1.00	1.25	7.00

FIFTY CENT CIRCULATING COINAGE
Victoria 1870 - 1901

Since the Province of Canada did not issue this denomination, new coinage tools had to be produced when the Dominion placed its first order for coins. For the obverse L.C. Wyon used the same portrait model as he did for the 25-cents: a crowned effigy of Victoria based on a model by William Theed. The reverse featured the St. Edward's crown atop crossed boughs of sweet maple, tied at the bottom by a ribbon. By the end of the reign four major obverses and two reverses had been utilized. With the exception of the first two obverses (see below), a detailed description and listing of these varieties by year does not appear in this standard catalogue.

Designer, Modeller and Engraver:
Leonard C. Wyon
Composition: .925 silver, .075 copper
Weight: 11.62 grams
Diameter: 29.72 mm
Edge: Reeded
Die Axis: ↑↓

Heaton Mint issues of 1871-1881 and the Mint, Birmingham issue of 1890 have an "H" on the reverse under the wreath. London Mint strikings have no letter

VARIETIES 1870. The initial obverse for this denomination lacked the initial of the designer on the truncation of the queen's neck. The second obverse, also employed for the 1870 coinage, has the "L.C.W.," as well as a shamrock just behind the front cross in the Queen's tiara.

No Shamrock Behind Front Cross   1870 Without L.C.W.

Shamrock behind front cross

1870 L.C.W. on Truncation

Date and Mint Mark	Quantity Minted	G-4	VG-8	F-12	VF-20	EF-40	AU-50	MS-60	MS-63
1870 No L.C.W.	450,000	450.00	875.00	1,500.00	3,000.00	6,000.00	10,000.00	-	-
1870 L.C.W.	Incl. above	50.00	80.00	175.00	350.00	700.00	2,000.00	7,000.00	17,500.00
1871	200,000	60.00	110.00	250.00	500.00	1,000.00	3,000.00	10,000.00	22,500.00
1871H	45,000	85.00	175.00	350.00	750.00	1,600.00	3,500.00	12,500.00	35,000.00

VARIETIES 1872H. Numerous repunching varieties exist on the 1872H coinage, but the only one interesting enough to include in this catalogue involves a blundered obverse die. While repunching defective letters in the obverse legend the engraver inadvertantly used an "A" punch to repair a defective "V" in "VICTORIA," converting the queen's name into "∀ICTORIA."

1872 Inverted A in VICTORIA

Date and Mint Mark	Quantity Minted	G-4	VG-8	F-12	VF-20	EF-40	AU-50	MS-60	MS-63
1872H Normal	80,000	50.00	80.00	175.00	350.00	700.00	2,000.00	7,500.00	17,500.00
1872H A/V	Incl. above	100.00	200.00	400.00	850.00	1,750.00	3,500.00	10,000.00	27,500.00
1881H	150,000	50.00	95.00	175.00	350.00	900.00	2,000.00	9,000.00	30,000.00
1888	60,000	120.00	225.00	425.00	900.00	1,750.00	3,500.00	10,000.00	25,000.00
1890H	20,000	650.00	1,100.00	2,200.00	4,000.00	7,000.00	10,000.00	20,000.00	50,000.00
1892	151,000	55.00	110.00	225.00	500.00	1,250.00	3,000.00	11,000.00	35,000.00
1894	29,036	250.00	450.00	800.00	1,750.00	3,500.00	6,500.00	15,000.00	40,000.00
1898	100,000	55.00	110.00	250.00	500.00	1,000.00	2,500.00	10,000.00	35,000.00
1899	50,000	95.00	200.00	400.00	900.00	2,250.00	4,500.00	12,500.00	40,000.00
1900	118,000	45.00	75.00	150.00	325.00	750.00	2,000.00	8,500.00	35,000.00
1901	80,000	45.00	75.00	150.00	325.00	750.00	2,000.00	8,000.00	25,000.00

FIFTY CENTS
Edward VII 1902 - 1910

The reverse of the Edward VII 50-cents followed the same design as the lower silver denominations: the word "CANADA" was made part of the legend, moved from it's former position at the bottom of the obverse, and the Imperial State crown replaced St. Edward's crown. The first reverse used the Victorian maple wreath almost untouched.

CANADA

Designer and Modeller:
Obverse — G.W. DeSaulles
(DES. under the bust)
Engraver: Victorian Leaves Reverse —
G.W. DeSaulles;
Edwardian Leaves Reverse —
W.H.J. Blakemore
Composition: .925 silver, .075 copper
Weight: 11.62 grams (1902-1910)
11.66 grams (1910)
Diameter: 29.72 mm
Edge: Reeded
Die Axis: ↑↓ (1902-1907)
↑↑ (1908-1910)

The Mint, Birmingham issue of 1903 has an "H" mint mark on the reverse under the wreath. London Mint issues (1902-1907) and Ottawa Mint issues (1908-1910) have no letter.

Date and Mint Mark	Quantity Minted	G-4	VG-8	F-12	VF-20	EF-40	AU-50	MS-60	MS-63
1902	120,000	8.00	17.00	50.00	150.00	400.00	800.00	2,250.00	5,500.00
1903H	140,000	17.00	33.00	80.00	175.00	400.00	800.00	2,250.00	5,500.00
1904	60,000	65.00	135.00	300.00	550.00	1,250.00	2,500.00	5,000.00	12,500.00
1905	40,000	85.00	165.00	400.00	800.00	2,000.00	4,000.00	8,000.00	17,500.00
1906	350,000	11.00	22.00	50.00	150.00	400.00	800.00	2,250.00	5,500.00
1907	300,000	8.00	17.00	45.00	150.00	400.00	800.00	2,500.00	6,000.00
1908	128,119	15.00	40.00	75.00	225.00	450.00	850.00	1,750.00	3,500.00
1909	203,118	11.00	28.00	75.00	250.00	700.00	1,500.00	4,000.00	12,500.00

VARIETIES 1910. Because the Victorian Leaves variety 50-cent pieces being coined at the Ottawa Mint had almost no rim, it was requested that the parent Royal Mint in London make new reverse tools. In addition to a wider rim the new variety (Edwardian Leaves reverse) had several altered leaves and a different cross atop the crown. The most noticeable difference is the two outside leaves at the right side of the date. On the Victorian Leaves reverse these leaves have long points which nearly touch the denticles, but on the Edwardian Leaves reverse these leaves have shorter, more curved points farther from the denticles.

1910 Victorian Leaves Reverse

1910 Edwardian Leaves Reverse

Date and Mint Mark	Quantity Minted	G-4	VG-8	F-12	VF-20	EF-40	AU-50	MS-60	MS-63
1910 Victorian	649,521	8.00	17.00	45.00	150.00	400.00	800.00	2,250.00	6,000.00
1910 Edwardian	Incl. above	8.00	17.00	45.00	150.00	400.00	800.00	2,250.00	6,000.00

FIFTY CENTS
George V 1911 - 1936

"GODLESS" OBVERSE 1911. Public outcry greeted the new George V coins issued in 1911 because the obverse legend lacked reference to the King's ruling "by the grace of God." The coinage tools were modified during the year and a new legend containing the Latin abbreviation "DEI GRA:" appeared on the 1912 and subsequent issues. The reverse was a continuation of the Edwardian Leaves variety of the previous reign.

Designer and Modeller:
   Sir E.B. MacKennal
   (B.M. on truncation)
Composition: .925 silver, .075 copper
Weight: 11.66 grams
Diameter: 29.72 mm
Edge: Reeded
Die Axis: ↑↑

Date and Mint Mark	Quantity Minted	VG-8	F-12	VF-20	EF-40	AU-50	MS-60	MS-63
1911	209,972	13.00	75.00	350.00	750.00	1,100.00	2,250.00	6,000.00

MODIFIED OBVERSE LEGEND 1912 - 1936.

Composition: .925 silver, .075 copper
   (1912-1919);
   .800 silver, .200 copper
   (1920-1936)

The physical specifications are as for the 1911 issue.

Date and Mint Mark	Quantity Minted	VG-8	F-12	VF-20	EF-40	AU-50	MS-60	MS-63
1912	285,867	7.00	25.00	125.00	350.00	700.00	1,750.00	4,500.00
1913	265,889	7.00	27.00	150.00	375.00	850.00	3,000.00	8,500.00
1914	160,128	18.00	70.00	225.00	650.00	1,750.00	4,500.00	13,500.00
1916	459,070	4.50	20.00	80.00	200.00	450.00	1,500.00	3,750.00
1917	752,213	4.50	16.00	55.00	150.00	325.00	850.00	2,250.00
1918	854,989	4.50	12.00	35.00	110.00	250.00	750.00	1,750.00
1919	1,113,429*	4.50	12.00	35.00	110.00	250.00	750.00	2,250.00
1920	584,429**	4.50	13.00	50.00	200.00	400.00	850.00	2,250.00

*144,200 fifty-cent pieces of .925 silver were melted in 1920; it is believed they were all dated 1919.
** In 1929 480,392 pieces of this denomination, consisting of 1920 and 1921 dates, were melted.

FIFTY CENTS 1921. This popular and very scarce coin was originally minted in considerable quantity. During the early and mid-1920s the demand for 50-cent pieces was very light; only 28,000 pieces were issued between 1921 and 1929. These are assumed to have been almost entirely 1920s. When a greater demand for this denomination arose later in 1929, the Master of the Ottawa Mint decided to melt the stock of 1920 and 1921 coins (amounting to some 480,392 pieces) and recoin the silver into 1929 coins. He took this decision because he feared that the public would suspect they were receiving counterfeits if a large quantity of coins with "old" dates were issued. It is believed that the 75 or so 1921s that have survived came from specimen sets sold to collectors or from circulation strikes sold to Mint visitors.

Composition:
.925 silver, .075 copper
(1912-1919);
.800 silver, .200 copper
(1920-1936)

Date and Mint Mark	Quantity Minted	G-4	VG-8	F-12	VF-20	EF-40	AU-50	MS-60	MS-63
1921	206,398	9,000.	13,500.	18,000.	25,000.	35,000.	45,000.	—	—
1929	228,328	-	5.00	16.00	55.00	160.00	325.00	1,000.00	2,250.00
1931	57,581	-	11.00	35.00	110.00	350.00	800.00	1,750.00	3,750.00
1932	19,213	-	50.00	135.00	325.00	800.00	1,750.00	4,500.00	13,500.00
1934	39,539	-	16.00	40.00	110.00	325.00	700.00	1,200.00	2,500.00
1936	38,550	-	13.00	33.00	90.00	275.00	500.00	900.00	1,750.00

Note: In 1929 480,392 pieces of this denomination, consisting of 1920 and 1921 dates, were melted.

FIFTY CENTS
George VI 1937 - 1952

"ET IND; IMP;" OBVERSE 1937-1947. A stylized Canadian coat-of-arms designed by George Edward Kruger-Gray was selected for the George VI 50-cent piece, first issued in 1937. The initial obverse bore a legend containing an abbreviation for the Latin phrase, "ET INDIAE IMPERATOR," meaning "and Emperor of India," denoting the King was emperor of that vast country.

Designer and Modeller:
Portrait — T.H. Paget
(H.P. below bust)
Reverse — G.E. Kruger-Gray
(K.G. flanking lower part of
crown on shield)
Composition: .800 silver,
.200 copper
Weight: 11.66 grams
Diameter: 29.72 mm
Edge: Reeded
Die Axis: ↑↑

Date and Mint Mark	Quantity Minted	F-12	VF-20	EF-40	AU-50	MS-60	MS-63	MS-65
1937	192,016	5.00	9.00	13.00	22.00	45.00	100.00	600.00
1938	192,018	9.00	20.00	45.00	75.00	175.00	475.00	2,250.00
1939	287,976	6.00	11.00	27.00	55.00	125.00	325.00	1,250.00
1940	1,996,566	2.50	4.00	7.00	12.00	30.00	100.00	600.00
1941	1,714,874	2.50	4.00	7.00	12.00	30.00	100.00	600.00
1942	1,974,165	2.50	4.00	7.00	12.00	30.00	100.00	600.00
1943	3,109,583	2.50	4.00	7.00	12.00	30.00	100.00	600.00
1944	2,460,205	2.50	4.00	7.00	12.00	30.00	100.00	600.00
1945	1,959,528	2.50	4.00	7.00	12.00	30.00	100.00	600.00
1946	950,235	3.00	6.00	10.00	22.00	75.00	175.00	750.00

VARIETIES 1947. There are two styles of 7 for the 1947 issue. The first is a tall figure with a tail curving to the left at the bottom (Straight 7), similar to that on the 1937 issue. The second (Curved 7) has a bottom that curves to the right.

1947 Straight 7	1947 Curved 7

Date and Mint Mark	Quantity Minted	F-12	VF-20	EF-40	AU-50	MS-60	MS-63	MS-65
1947 Straight 7	424,885	4.00	7.00	18.00	50.00	110.00	275.00	1,000.00
1947 Curved 7	Incl. above	4.00	7.00	18.00	50.00	110.00	275.00	1,000.00

MAPLE LEAF ISSUE 1947. With the granting of independence to India, the Royal Canadian Mint was faced with a dilemma in early 1948. The new obverse coinage tools with the Latin abbreviation "ET IND: IMP" ommitted would not arrive for several months, yet there was a great need for all denominations of coins. The Mint satisfied the demand by striking coins dated 1947 and bearing an obverse with outmoded titles. To differentiate this issue from the regular strikings of 1947, a tiny maple leaf was placed after the date. Both styles of 7 (see above) were employed for the Maple Leaf coinage, creating four varieties of the 1947 date in all.

1947 Maple Leaf, Straight 7	1947 Maple Leaf, Curved 7

Date and Mint Mark	Quantity Minted	VG-8	F-12	VF-20	EF-40	AU-50	MS-60	MS-63	MS-65
1947 ML,S7	38,433	15.00	22.00	40.00	75.00	110.00	250.00	425.00	800.00
1947 ML,C7	Incl. above	1,400.00	1,800.00	2,400.00	3,000.00	3,500.00	5,000.00	7,500.00	-

MODIFIED OBVERSE LEGEND 1948 - 1952. In 1948, following the arrival of the master tools with the new obverse legend, production of the 1947 Maple Leaf coinage was suspended. For the remainder of the year coins were produced with the new obverse and true date, 1948.

The physical and chemical specifications are as for the 1937-1947 issues.

Date and Mint Mark	Quantity Minted	VG-8	F-12	VF-20	EF-40	AU-50	MS-60	MS-63	MS-65
1948	37,784	45.00	65.00	90.00	110.00	175.00	250.00	350.00	750.00
1949	858,991	-	4.00	7.00	13.00	22.00	50.00	175.00	550.00
1950	2,384,179	-	-	3.00	5.00	7.00	15.00	35.00	200.00
1951	2,421,730	-	-	2.50	4.00	6.00	10.00	30.00	150.00
1952	2,596,465	-	-	2.50	4.00	6.00	10.00	25.00	150.00

NOTE: Lower grade silver coins, which do not have price listings, are priced based on silver bullion on the day of purchase or sale. These lower grade coins do not have a numismatic premium at this time.

FIFTY CENTS
Elizabeth II 1953 to date

LAUREATED PORTRAIT; LARGE COAT-OF-ARMS REVERSE 1953-1943. During 1953 two obverse varieties were employed. Known as No Shoulder Fold and Shoulder Fold varieties (see 1-cent Elizabeth II, 1953 to date for full description), they were combined with two major reverse varieties. The No Shoulder Fold obverse was used with both Small and Large Date reverses, though only a modest quantity were struck. The Small Date reverse was carried over from George VI issues. The Shoulder Fold obverse appeared only with the Large Date reverse.

Designer and Modeller: Portrait — Mrs. Mary Gillick, (M.G. on truncation);
   Large Date Reverse — Thomas Shingles, copying existing model
Engraver: No Shoulder Fold Obverse — Thomas Shingles, using the Gillick portrait model;
   Shoulder Fold Obverse — Thomas Shingles, modifying existing NSF coinage tools
Composition: .800 silver, .200 copper
Weight: 11.66 grams
Diameter: 29.72 mm
Edge: Reeded
Die Axis: ↑↑

No Shoulder Fold Obverse 1953
letters have pronounced flaring

Shoulder Fold Obverse 1953-1964
letters have subdued flaring

Small Date Reverse 1953

Large Date Reverse 1953-1964

Date and Mint Mark	Quantity Minted	F-12	VF-20	EF-40	AU-50	MS-60	MS-63	MS-65	PL-65
1953 SD,NSF	1,630,429	2.00	2.50	3.00	6.00	7.00	20.00	100.00	300.00
1953 LD,NSF	Incl. above	4.00	7.00	18.00	50.00	110.00	175.00	400.00	-
1953 LD,SF	Incl. above	2.50	5.00	7.00	10.00	25.00	45.00	150.00	200.00
1954	506,305	3.00	6.00	10.00	15.00	35.00	45.00	150.00	100.00

MODIFIED REVERSE 1955 - 1958. Continuing difficulties with the coat-of-arms reverse design resulted in the introduction of a major modification in 1955. The problem was the obverse portrait tended to draw away too much metal at the moment the coin was struck, leaving insufficient metal to completely fill the design on the reverse die. Thus, the coins sometimes showed a weakness in the design at and around the crown and top of the shield. This problem was largely solved by a new reverse with a smaller version of the coat-of-arms.

Designer and Modeller:
Thomas Shingles, copying existing models

The physical and chemical specifications are as for the 1953-1954 issues.

Date and Mint Mark	Quantity Minted	VF-20	EF-40	AU-50	MS-60	MS-63	MS-65	PL-65
1955	763,511	4.00	7.00	9.00	20.00	33.00	125.00	75.00
1956	1,379,499	2.50	3.00	4.00	6.00	15.00	75.00	40.00
1957	2,171,689	2.00	2.50	3.50	5.00	9.00	50.00	20.00
1958	9,957,266	2.00	2.50	3.00	4.00	8.00	40.00	20.00

NEW COAT-OF-ARMS REVERSE; LAUREATED OBVERSE 1959 - 1964. In 1959 the new Canadian coat-of-arms which had been approved for government issue in 1957 was adapted for the 50-cent piece. One of the major changes compared to the previous design was the addition of a ribbon at the bottom bearing "A MARI USQUE AD MARE," meaning "from sea to sea" and making reference to the territorial extent of the country. The 1959 issue had horizontal lines in the bottom panel, indicating the colour incorrectly as blue. To indicate the correct colour, white, these lines were removed from the 1960 and subsequent issues. The obverse continued unchanged.

Designer and Modeller:
Reverse — Thomas Shingles
(TS flanking shield at bottom)
Composition: .800 silver, .200 copper
Weight: 11.66 grams
Diameter: 29.72 mm
Edge: Reeded
Die Axis: ↑↑

Date and Mint Mark	Quantity Minted	MS-60	MS-63	MS-65	PL-65
1959	3,095,535	4.00	6.00	35.00	15.00
1960	3,488,897	3.00	5.00	30.00	7.00
1961	3,584,417	3.00	5.00	30.00	7.00
1962	5,208,030	3.00	5.00	30.00	7.00
1963	8,348,871	3.00	5.00	30.00	7.00
1964	9,177,676	3.00	5.00	30.00	7.00

TIARA PORTRAIT; NEW COAT-OF-ARMS REVERSE 1965 - 1966. A new obverse with the Queen showing more mature facial features and wearing a tiara was introduced in 1965.

Designer and Modeller:
Portrait — Arnold Machin

The physical and chemical specifications are as for the 1959-1964 issues.

Date and Mint Mark	Quantity Minted		MS-60	MS-63	MS-65	PL-65
1965	12,629,974		3.00	5.00	30.00	7.00
1966	7,683,228		3.00	5.00	30.00	7.00

COMMEMORATIVE FOR CENTENNIAL OF CONFEDERATION 1967. A design for the reverse showing a howling wolf was chosen as part of the set of commemorative coins for this year. The obverse continued unchanged.

Designer: Reverse — Alex Colville
Modeller: Reverse — Myron Cook

The physical and chemical specifications are as for the 1959-1966 issues.

Date and Mint Mark	Quantity Minted	MS-60	MS-63	MS-65	PL-65
1967 Confederation Commemorative	4,211,395	4.00	6.00	30.00	8.00

NEW COAT-OF-ARMS REVERSE RESUMED; REDUCED SIZE NICKEL COINAGE 1968-1976. When the coat-of-arms reverse design was resumed in 1968, the strikes were in nickel. In order to make the coins easier to strike in the harder metal the diameter was considerably reduced.

Designer and Modeller:
Obverse — Arnold Machin
Reverse — Thomas Shingles
Composition: 1.00 nickel
Weight: 8.10 grams
Diameter: 27.13 mm
Edge: Reeded
Die Axis: ↑↑

Date and Mint Mark	Quantity Minted	MS-60	MS-63	MS-65	PL-65
1968	3,966,932	1.00	2.00	5.00	2.00
1969	7,113,929	1.00	2.00	5.00	2.00
1970	2,429,516	1.00	2.00	5.00	2.00
1971	2,166,444	1.00	2.00	5.00	2.00
1972	2,515,632	1.00	2.00	5.00	2.00
1973	2,546,096	1.00	2.00	5.00	2.00
1974	3,436,650	1.00	2.00	5.00	2.00
1975	3,710,000	1.00	2.00	5.00	2.00
1976	2,940,719	1.00	2.00	5.00	2.00

COAT-OF-ARMS REVERSE; MODIFIED DESIGN OF 1977. The 1977 coinage featured pronounced changes on both sides. The obverse bears a smaller bust with increased hair detail, smaller lettering, and larger beads placed farther from the rim. The reverse shows a smaller coat-of-arms and for the first time beads instead of denticles at the rim.

Modeller: Obverse — Patrick Brindley, modifying the Machin portrait

The physical and chemical specifications are as for the 1968-1976 issues.

Date and Mint Mark	Quantity Minted	MS-60	MS-63	MS-65	PL-65
1977	709,939	1.50	3.00	8.00	2.00

COAT-OF-ARMS REVERSE; MODIFIED DESIGN 1978 - 1989. In 1978 the Mint's attempts to settle upon standard designs continued. The beaded motif for the reverse was dropped and a design essentially the same as that for 1968-1976 was restored. Two minor varieties of the 1978 reverse are known. The 1978 obverse was a combination of the 1968-1976 and 1977 designs. The unmodified Machin portrait was restored, but the smaller lettering of 1977 was retained.

Designer and Modeller:
Obverse — Arnold Machin
Reverse — Thomas Shingles
Composition: 1.00 nickel
Weight: 8.10 grams
Diameter: 27.13 mm
Edge: Reeded
Die Axis: ↑↑

Square Jewels   Round Jewels

Date and Mint Mark	Quantity Minted	MS-60	MS-63	MS-65	PL-65
1978 Square Jewels	3,341,892	1.00	1.50	5.00	2.00
1978 Round Jewels	Incl. above	5.00	6.00	12.00	-
1979	3,425,000	1.00	1.25	5.00	2.00
1980	1,943,155	1.00	1.25	5.00	2.00

1982 with 123
Small Beads

1982 with 118
Large Beads

Note: Beginning in 1981 the Royal Canadian Mint ceased production of proof-like coins. They are replaced in the listings by proof coins from the prestige set.

Date and Mint Mark	Quantity Minted	MS-60	MS-63	MS-65	PR-65
1981	2,588,900	1.00	1.25	3.00	4.00
1982 Small Beads	2,884,572	1.00	1.25	3.00	4.00
1982 Large Beads	Incl. above	1.00	1.25	3.00	-
1983	1,177,000	1.00	1.25	3.00	4.00
1984	1,502,989	1.00	1.25	3.00	4.00
1985	2,188,374	1.00	1.25	3.00	4.00
1986	781,400	1.00	1.25	3.00	4.00
1987	373,000	1.00	1.25	3.00	4.00
1988	220,000	1.00	1.25	3.00	4.00
1989	266,419	1.00	1.25	3.00	4.00

CROWNED PORTRAIT; COAT-OF-ARMS REVERSE; 1990 TO 1991. A new obverse portrait of the Queen wearing a diamond diadem and jewellery was introduced on all denominations in 1990.

Designer and Modeller:
Obverse — Dora DePedery-Hunt
Ago Aarand
Reverse — Thomas Shingles
Composition: 1.00 Nickel
Weight: 8.10 grams
Diameter: 27.13 mm
Edge: Reeded
Die Axis: ↑↑

Date and Mint Mark	Quantity Minted	MS-60	MS-63	MS-65	PR-65
1990	207,000	1.00	1.25	3.00	4.00
1991	490,000	1.00	1.25	3.00	15.00

CANADA

COMMEMORATIVE FOR 125TH ANNIVERSARY; 1867-1992. The reverse design was modified to include the bracket dates 1867-1992 for the 125th birthday of Canada.

Designer, modeller and physical specifications are as for the 1990 and 1991 issues.

Date and Mint Mark	Quantity Minted		MS-60	MS-63	MS-65	PR-65
1992	248,000		1.00	1.25	3.00	4.00

COAT OF ARMS REVERSED RESUMED; 1993 TO 1997. In 1993 the practice of using a single date was resumed. Also, the transition to beads from rim denticles, which began in 1982 on the one cent coin, was completed in 1993 on the fifty cent piece.

Designer, modeller and physical specifications are as for the 1990 and 1991 issue.

Date and Mint Mark	Quantity Minted		MS-60	MS-63	MS-65	PR-65
1993	393,000		1.00	1.25	3.00	4.00
1994	987,000		1.00	1.25	3.00	4.00
1995	626,000		1.00	1.25	3.00	4.00
1996	N/A		1.00	1.25	3.00	4.00
1997	N/A		1.00	1.25	3.00	4.00

Note: For the 1995 and 1996 silver proof issue of the 50 cent wildlife series please see page no. 215

ONE DOLLAR CIRCULATING COINS

ONE DOLLAR - SILVER
George V 1935 - 1936

SILVER JUBILEE COMMEMORATIVE 1935. Canada's first silver dollar for circulation, also the first commemorative coin, marked the 25th anniversary of the accession of King George V. The Bank of Canada $25 bill also commemorated the special event. The reverse of the silver dollar was a modern design by sculptor Emanuel Hahn, showing an Indian and a voyageur, a travelling agent for a fur company, paddling a canoe by an islet on which there are two wind-swept trees. In the canoe are bundles of goods; the bundle at the right has HB, representing the Hudson's Bay Company. The vertical lines in the background represent the northern lights. This modern design began a trend which produced the beautiful reverses for 1937.

The obverse was the commemorative side of the coin with the Latin legend indicating the King was in the 25th year of his reign. The portrait was by Percy Metcalfe and was never used for any other Canadian coinage, but had been used previously for the obverses of some New Zealand and Australian coinages.

Generally, the coins were issued in cardboard tubes of 20.

Designer and Modeller: Portrait — Percy Metcalfe;
      Reverse — Emanuel Hahn (EH in water left end of canoe)
Composition: .800 silver, .200 copper
Weight: 23.33 grams
Diameter: 36.00 mm
Edge: Reeded
Die Axis: ↑↑

Date and Mint Mark	Quantity Minted	VF-20	EF-40	AU-50	MS-60	MS-63	MS-64	MS-65
1935	428,707	25.00	40.00	50.00	60.00	100.00	150.00	300.00

STANDARD OBVERSE 1936. In 1936 the issue of silver dollars continued, with the new reverse remaining unchanged. The obverse was the regular MacKennal design used for 1- to 50-cent pieces of 1912-1936. The tools for this obverse had already been prepared in 1911 for use on the 1911 dollar (see DC-6 in the chapter on Patterns).

Designer & Modeller: Portrait - Sir E.B. MacKennal (B.M. on trucation)

The physical and chemical specifications are as for the 1935 issue.

Date and Mint Mark	Quantity Minted	VF-20	EF-40	AU-50	MS-60	MS-63	MS-64	MS-65
1936	339,600	20.00	25.00	30.00	50.00	125.00	250.00	700.00

ONE DOLLAR - SILVER
George VI 1937 - 1952

VOYAGEUR REVERSE 1937-1938. New reverse designs were under consideration for the 1937 issues; however, it was decided to retain the voyageur design, since it was already modern.

Designer and Modeller: Portrait — T.H. Paget (H.P. below bust)
Composition: .800 silver, .200 copper
Weight: 23.33 grams
Diameter: 36.00 mm
Edge: Reeded
Die Axis: ↑↑

Date and Mint Mark	Quantity Minted	VF-20	EF-40	AU-50	MS-60	MS-63	MS-64	MS-65
1937	207,406	16.00	20.00	25.00	40.00	100.00	300.00	1,500.00
1938	90,304	55.00	70.00	85.00	100.00	250.00	600.00	1,600.00

COMMEMORATIVE FOR ROYAL VISIT 1939. Canada's second commemorative coin was created when the reverse of the 1939 silver dollar was used to mark the visit of George VI and Queen Elizabeth to Canada. The design consists of the centre block of the Parliament buildings in Ottawa and the Latin phrase, "FIDE SVORVM REGNAT," meaning "He reigns by the faith of his people."

The usual means of issuing coins was through the Bank of Canada, but for this special coinage it was decided to make them available through the Post Office as well. Consequently, 369,500 of the original mintage of nearly 1.4 million were issued direct to the Post Office. This mintage proved to be larger than public demand and between 1939 and 1945 nearly 160,000 pieces were returned to the Mint and melted.

Designer and Modeller: Reverse — Emanuel Hahn (E H flanked the building in the original model, but was removed by order of Canadian government officials)

The physical and chemical specifications are as for the 1937-1938 issues.

Date and Mint Mark	Quantity Minted	VF-20	EF-40	AU-50	MS-60	MS-63	MS-64	MS-65
1939	1,363,816*	8.00	10.00	14.00	18.00	40.00	100.00	250.00

* 158,084 pieces were returned to the Mint and melted between 1939 and 1945.

VOYAGEUR REVERSE RESUMED; "ET IND; IMP;" OBVERSE 1945-1947. Beginning with the 1945 silver dollar a more brilliant appearance was achieved. This was due to the use of chromium-plated coinage dies. For previous issues unplated dies with a rougher surface had been used.

The chemical and physical specifications are as for the 1937-1939 issues.

Date and Mint Mark	Quantity Minted	VF-20	EF-40	AU-50	MS-60	MS-63	MS-64	MS-65
1945	38,391	150.00	175.00	200.00	400.00	850.00	1,250.00	3,000.00
1946	93,055	30.00	50.00	70.00	100.00	300.00	1,300.00	2,500.00

CANADA

VARIETIES 1947. Two styles of 7 were used to date the 1947 dies; a tall figure with the lower tail pointing back to the right (Pointed 7); and a shorter 7 with the lower tail pointing almost straight down (Blunt 7).

1947 Pointed 7   1947 Blunt 7

Date and Mint Mark	Quantity Minted	VF-20	EF-40	AU-50	MS-60	MS-63	MS-64	MS-65
1947 Pointed 7	65,595	120.00	135.00	200.00	350.00	1,750.00	3,500.00	6,500.00
1947 Blunt 7	Incl.	90.00	135.00	160.00	175.00	450.00	900.00	2,250.00

MAPLE LEAF ISSUE 1947. In early 1948 the Royal Canadian Mint was faced with a problem. New obverse coinage tools with the Latin abbreviation "ET IND: IMP:" ommited to indicate that the King's titles had been changed to concur with India's recently granted independance would not arrive for several months. Yet, there was a great need for all denominations of coins. The Mint satisfied the demand by striking coins dated 1947 and bearing an obverse with outmoded titles. To differentiate this issue from the regular strikings of 1947, a tiny maple leaf was placed after the date. Only the Blunt 7 was employed for dating this issue.

1947 Maple Leaf Issue,
struck in 1948

Date and Mint Mark	Quantity Minted	VF-20	EF-40	AU-50	MS-60	MS-63	MS-64	MS-65
1947 Maple Leaf	21,135	170.00	200.00	250.00	325.00	1,000.00	1,750.00	4,000.00

MODIFIED OBVERSE LEGEND; VOYAGEUR REVERSE 1948. Following the arrival in 1948 of the master tools with the new obverse legend, production of the 1947 Maple Leaf coinage was suspended. For the remainder of the year coins were produced with the new obverse and the true date, 1948.

Designer and Modeller: Portrait — T.H. Paget (H.P. below bust)
Composition: .800 silver, .200 copper
Weight: 23.33 grams
Diameter: 36.00 mm
Edge: Reeded
Die Axis: ↑↑

Date and Mint Mark	Quantity Minted	VF-20	EF-40	AU-50	MS-60	MS-63	MS-64	MS-65
1948	18,780	700.00	850.00	900.00	1,000.00	1,850.00	3,500.00	6,500.00

COMMEMORATIVE FOR ENTRY OF NEWFOUNDLAND INTO CONFEDERATION 1949.
On December 31, 1949 Newfoundland became the tenth province of the Dominion of Canada. This historic event was recognized on the Canadian coinage with a special reverse for the 1949 silver dollar. The design shows the ship *Matthew* in which it is thought John Cabot discovered Newfoundland in 1497. Below it is the Latin phrase, "FLOREAT TERRA NOVA," meaning "May the new found land flourish." The design was inspired by Newfoundland's commemorative postage stamp of 1947, based on a model of the ship by Ernest Maunder. The obverse continued unchanged from that of 1948.

The 1949 dollars were struck more carefully than those of previous years and were issued in plastic or cardboard tubes of 20 to protect them. Many of these coins remain in proof-like condition today. Thomas Shingles was the engraver, doing his work entirely by hand, without the aid of a "reducing" machine.

It was decided to strike these coins, dated 1949, as long as there was a demand for them. In 1950 some 40,718 pieces were coined. The 1949 and 1950 strikings have been combined to give the total production for the type.

Designer: Reverse — Thomas Shingles, based upon Ernest Maunder's
Model of the "Matthew" (T.S. above horizon at right)
Engraver: Reverse — Thomas Shingles

The physical and chemical specifications are as for the 1948 issues.

Date and Mint Mark	Quantity Minted	VF-20	EF-40	AU-50	MS-60	MS-63	MS-64	MS-65	PL-65
1949	672,218	20.00	30.00	35.00	40.00	45.00	50.00	75.00	100.00

VOYAGEUR REVERSE RESUMED 1950-1952; ARNPRIOR DOLLARS. During the year 1950 a technical problem arose that was to plague the Mint throughout the 1950's. At each end of the canoe are four (not three as is so often claimed) shallow water lines. In the process of polishing or repolishing the dies, parts of these lines tended to disappear, creating differences within a given year's coinage. Collectors have decided arbitrarily that a certain pattern of partial water lines at the right-hand end of the canoe should be collected separately and command a premium over dollars with perfect water lines or other partial lines configurations.

The so-called Arnprior configuration (see One Dollar, Queen Elizabeth II 1955 for more details) consists of 2 1/2 (often incorrectly called 1 1/2) water lines at the right. Any trace of the bottom water line disqualifies a coin from being an Arnprior. One should also beware of coins that have had part of the water lines fraudulently removed.

Normal (4) Water Lines at Right   Arnprior (2 1/2) Water Lines at Right

Date and Mint Mark	Quantity Minted	VF-20	EF-40	AU-50	MS-60	MS-63	MS-64	MS-65	PL-65
1950	261,002	12.00	16.00	20.00	30.00	40.00	70.00	150.00	400.00
1950 Arn	Incl.	14.00	18.00	22.00	40.00	135.00	325.00	600.00	-
1951	416,395	7.00	9.00	11.00	15.00	45.00	90.00	250.00	400.00
1951 Arn	Incl.	40.00	50.00	70.00	150.00	350.00	600.00	1,250.00	-

VARIETIES 1952. In 1952 a modified reverse, with no water lines at all, was put into use. In addition to removing the water lines, this reverse differs from the Water Lines variety in having a remodeled (larger) islet tip at the right end of the canoe. This variety is fundamentally different from the Arnpriors in that it is was deliberately, not accidentally created. The Water Lines variety was also used in 1952.

1952 Water Lines Variety   1952 No Water Lines Variety

Date and Mint Mark	Quantity Minted	VF-20	EF-40	AU-50	MS-60	MS-63	MS-64	MS-65	PL-65
1952	406,148	7.00	9.00	11.00	15.00	35.00	110.00	250.00	-
1952 No Lines	Incl.	7.00	9.00	11.00	15.00	35.00	150.00	400.00	400.00

ONE DOLLAR - SILVER
Elizabeth II 1953 - 1967

LAUREATED PORTRAIT; VOYAGEUR REVERSE 1953-1957. As was true of all the lower denominations, the 1953 silver dollars came with two obverses, called the No Shoulder Fold and Shoulder Fold varieties (see one cent, Queen Elizabeth II, 1953 to date for full explanation). On this denomination these obverses are combined with different reverses. The No Shoulder Fold variety appears with the Wire Edge reverse, the Water Lines reverse of 1950-1952, and the Shoulder Fold obverse with the Wide Border reverse.

No Shoulder Fold Obverse 1953
letters have pronounced flaring

Shoulder Fold Obverse 1953-1964
letters have subdued flaring

Designer and Modeller: Portrait — Mrs. Mary Gillick (M.G. on truncation)
Engraver: No Shoulder Fold Obverse — Thomas Shingles, using the Gillick portrait; Shoulder Fold Obverse — Thomas Shingles, modifying existing NSF coinage tools
Composition: .800 silver, .200 copper
Weight: 23.33 grams
Diameter: 36.00 mm
Edge: Reeded
Die Axis: ↑↑

Date and Mint Mark	Quantity Minted	VF-20	EF-40	AU-50	MS-60	MS-63	MS-64	MS-65	PL-65
1953 NSF	1,073,218	5.00	7.00	8.00	12.00	25.00	90.00	250.00	600.00
1953 SF	Incl.	5.00	7.00	8.00	12.00	25.00	90.00	250.00	450.00
1954	241,306	12.00	16.00	18.00	20.00	40.00	110.00	350.00	200.00

ARNPRIOR DOLLAR 1955. In December,1955 the Mint made up an order of 2,000 silver dollars for a firm in Arnprior, Ontario. These coins had 2 1/2 water lines at the right of the canoe, similar to the configuration which occured on some of the 1950 - 1951 dollars. It was the 1955 dollars that first attracted the attention of collectors, but the term Arnprior has been applied to any dollar with a similar configuration of defective water lines. See the 1950-1951 silver dollars issues for additional comments.

1955 Normal (4) Water Lines at Right   1955 Arnprior (2 1/2) Water Lines at Right

Date and Mint Mark	Quantity Minted	VF-20	EF-40	AU-50	MS-60	MS-63	MS-64	MS-65	PL-65
1955	260,155	12.00	16.00	18.00	20.00	40.00	110.00	350.00	150.00
1955 Arn	Incl.	90.00	100.00	125.00	135.00	225.00	450.00	900.00	250.00
1956	198,880	13.00	18.00	20.00	25.00	75.00	160.00	400.00	100.00

ONE WATER LINE DOLLAR 1957. Part of the 1957 issue was struck from dies that retained only one of the long water lines at the right end of the canoe. This difference arose in the same way as the Arnprior dollars (see 1950-1951 issues for commentary) and is of questionable importance.

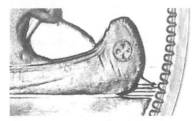 

1957 Normal (4) Water Lines at Right   1957 One Water Line at Right

Date and Mint Mark	Quantity Minted	EF-40	AU-50	MS-60	MS-63	MS-64	MS-65	PL-65
1957 Normal Water Lines	480,899	6.00	7.00	9.00	25.00	60.00	200.00	40.00
1957 One Water Line	Incl.	9.00	11.00	15.00	50.00	125.00	250.00	-

BRITISH COLUMBIA COMMEMORATIVE 1958. The reverse of the 1958 dollar commemorates the centenary of the Caribou gold rush and the establishment of British Columbia as a crown colony. The design shows a totem pole section with mountains in the background. The top element in the totem is a raven, used by some Indians to symbolize death. As a result, it was rumoured that those Indians disliked the dollars, causing them to be called "death dollars." The obverse was the same as that on the 1954-1957 issues.

Designer and Modeller: Reverse — Stephan Trenka (ST on right-hand of lower base of totem pole)
Composition: .800 silver, .200 copper
Weight: 23.33 grams
Diameter: 36.00 mm
Edge: Reeded
Die Axis: ↑↑

Date and Mint Mark	Quantity Minted	EF-40	AU-50	MS-60	MS-63	MS-64	MS-65	PL-65
1958	3,039,630	7.00	8.00	9.00	18.00	60.00	200.00	40.00

VOYAGEUR REVERSE RESUMED 1959-1963. During this period minor changes were made in the reverse details, the description of which is not listed in this standard catalogue. The obverse was continued from the previous year.

Date and Mint Mark	Quantity Minted	EF-40	AU-50	MS-60	MS-63	MS-64	MS-65	PL-65
1959	1,398,342	5.00	7.00	8.00	12.00	50.00	200.00	20.00
1960	1,337,758	5.00	7.00	8.00	12.00	50.00	200.00	15.00
1961	1,141,303	5.00	7.00	8.00	12.00	50.00	200.00	12.00
1962	1,636,248	5.00	7.00	8.00	12.00	50.00	200.00	10.00
1963	3,126,446	5.00	7.00	8.00	12.00	40.00	200.00	10.00

CONFEDERATION MEETINGS COMMEMORATIVE 1964. The reverse of the 1964 silver dollar carried a special design marking the centennial of the 1864 meetings in Charlottetown, P.E.I. and Quebec City, Quebec which prepared the way for Confederation in 1867. The design depicts, conjoined within a circle, the French fleur-de-lis, the Irish shamrock, the Scottish thistle and the English rose. The obverse coupled with the commemorative reverse was a reworking of the Shoulder Fold variety.

Designer: Reverse — Dinko Vodanovic (D.V. near the Q of Quebec)
Modeller: Reverse — Thomas Shingles (T.S. near the C of Quebec)
Obverse — Myron Cook, modifying existing model

The physical and chemical specifications are as for the 1958-1963 issues.

Date and Mint Mark	Quantity Minted	EF-40	AU-50	MS-60	MS-63	MS-64	MS-65	PL-65
1964	4,434,391	5.00	7.00	8.00	12.00	40.00	200.00	10.00

TIARA PORTRAIT; VOYAGEUR REVERSE 1965-1966. A new obverse with the Queen showing more mature facial features and wearing a tiara was introduced on all denominations in 1965. The first obverse for the dollar had to be replaced because it gave such poor die life. The difficulty was a flat field (Small Beads variety). A single trial die (Medium Beads variety) established that an obverse with the field sloping up at the edge was preferable, so new master tools were prepared (Large Beads variety) and those dies became the standard variety. In addition two reverses, bearing slightly different 5s were employed, creating five varieties in all for 1965. Through an error a small quantity of 1966 dollars were struck with the outmoded Small Beads obverse.

Designer: Portrait — Arnold Machin

The physical and chemical specifications are as for the 1958-1964 issues.

Small Beads Obverse 1965-1966
rear jewel in tiara is well attached

Medium Beads Obverse 1965
rear jewel in tiara is nearly detached

Large Beads Obverse
rear jewel in tiara is well attached

1965 Pointed 5 (at bottom)	1965 Blunt 5 (at bottom)

Date and Mint Mark	Quantity Minted	EF-40	AU-50	MS-60	MS-63	MS-64	MS-65	PL-65
1965 SB Pt5 (V-1)	7,863,885	5.00	7.00	8.00	12.00	40.00	200.00	10.00
1965 SB Bl5 (V-2)	Incl. above	5.00	7.00	8.00	12.00	40.00	200.00	10.00
1965 MB Pt5 (V-5)	Incl. above	9.00	13.00	18.00	60.00	150.00	350.00	-
1965 LB Bl5 (V-3)	Incl. above	5.00	7.00	8.00	12.00	40.00	200.00	175.00
1965 LB Pt5 (V-4)	Incl. above	5.00	7.00	9.00	12.00	50.00	200.00	125.00
1966 LB	9,239,315	5.00	7.00	8.00	12.00	40.00	200.00	10.00
1966 SB	Incl. above	1,500.00	1,750.00	2,000.00	2,400.00	2,800.00	3,000.00	-

COMMEMORATIVE FOR CENTENNIAL OF CONFEDERATION 1967. A design for the reverse showing a Canada goose in flight was chosen as part of the set of commemorative coins for this year. The obverse was the Large Beads variety of 1965-1966.

Designer: Reverse — Alex Colville
Modeller: Reverse — Myron Cook
Composition: .800 silver, .200 copper
Weight: 23.33 grams
Diameter: 36.00 mm
Edge: Reeded
Die Axis: ↑↑

Date and Mint Mark	Quantity Minted	EF-40	AU-50	MS-60	MS-63	MS-64	MS-65	PL-65
1967	5,816,176	5.00	7.00	8.00	12.00	50.00	200.00	12.00

Note: 141,741 pieces were melted in 1967.

ONE DOLLAR - NICKEL
Elizabeth II 1968 to 1987

VOYAGEUR REVERSE RESUMED; REDUCED SIZE COINAGE 1968-1969. When the voyageur reverse design was resumed in 1968, the strikes were in nickel. In order to make coining easier for the harder metal the diameter was reduced considerably.

Engraver: Myron Cook, using existing models
Composition: 1.00 Nickel
Weight: 15.62 grams
Diameter: 32.13 mm
Edge: Reeded
Die Axis: ↑↑

Island	Small Island	No Island	Extra Water Line

Date and Mint Mark	Quantity Minted	MS-60	MS-63	MS-65	PL-65
1968 Island	4,755,080	1.50	3.00	5.00	2.00
1968 Small Island	Incl.	6.00	10.00	15.00	10.00
1968 No Island	Incl.	3.00	6.00	8.00	-
1968 Extra Line	Incl.	25.00	40.00	60.00	-
1969	4,215,055	1.50	3.00	5.00	2.00

MANITOBA CENTENNIAL COMMEMORATIVE 1970. The year 1970 saw Canada's first commemorative nickel dollar, with a special reverse featuring a prairie crocus in recognition of the centenary of Manitoba's entry into Confederation. The obverse continued unchanged from the 1968-1969 issues.

Designer: Reverse —
Raymond Taylor
(RT to right of crocus plant)
Modeller: Reverse - Walter Ott

The physical and chemical specifications are as for the 1968-1969 issues.

Date and Mint Mark	Quantity Minted	MS-60	MS-63	MS-65	PL-65
1970	3,493,189	1.50	3.00	6.00	3.00

BRITISH COLUMBIA CENTENNIAL COMMEMORATIVE 1971. The nickel dollar for 1971 commemorates the entry in 1871 of British Columbia into Confederation. Its design is based on the arms of the province, with a shield at the bottom and dagwood blossoms at the top. The obverse was the same as on previous nickel issues.

Designer and Modeller:
Obverse — Arnold Machin
Reverse — Thomas Shingles
(TS at bottom of shield)
Composition: 1.00 Nickel
Weight: 15.62 grams
Diameter: 32.13 mm
Edge: Reeded
Die Axis: ↑↑

Date and Mint Mark	Quantity Minted	MS-60	MS-63	MS-65	PL-65
1971	3,659,045	1.50	3.00	6.00	3.00

VOYAGEUR REVERSE RESUMED 1972. In 1972 the standard voyageur reverse was resumed; it and the obverse were the same as on the 1968-1969 issues.

The physical and chemical specifications are as for the 1968-1969 issues.

Date and Mint Mark	Quantity Minted	MS-60	MS-63	MS-65	PL-65
1972	2,193,000	1.50	3.00	6.00	3.00

P.E.I. CENTENNIAL COMMEMORATIVE 1973. The special reverse on the nickel dollar of 1973 marks the 100th anniversary of the entry of Prince Edward Island into Confederation. The design depicts the provincial legislature building. A new obverse with a smaller, more detailed portrait, and fewer rim denticles placed farther from the rim is brought into use with this reverse.

Designer and Modeller:
Obverse — Arnold Machin
Patrick Brindley
Reverse — Terry Manning
(TM at left of building)
Reverse — Walter Ott
(WO at right of building)
Composition: 1.00 Nickel
Weight: 15.62 grams
Diameter: 32.13 mm
Edge: Reeded
Die Axis: ↑↑

Date and Mint Mark	Quantity Minted	MS-60	MS-63	MS-65	PL-65
1973	2,683,000	1.50	3.00	6.00	3.00

CANADA

WINNIPEG COMMEMORATIVE 1974. The 1974 issue of nickel dollars commemorates the centenary of the city of Winnipeg, Manitoba. The design consists of a large 100; in the first 0 is a view of Main Street in 1874 and in the second 0 is a view of the same location 100 years later. For the first time the special collectors issue of silver dollars for that year had the same design.

1974 Single Yoke   1974 Double Yoke

Designer and Modeller:
Obverse — Arnold Machin
Patrick Brindley
Reverse — Paul Pederson
(PP above the date)
Patrick Brindley
(B below Winnipeg)
Composition: 1.00 Nickel
Weight: 15.62 grams
Diameter: 32.13 mm
Edge: Reeded
Die Axis: ↑↑

Date and Mint Mark	Quantity Minted	MS-60	MS-63	MS-65	PL-65
1974 Single Yoke	2,286,027	1.50	4.00	6.00	3.00
1974 Double Yoke	Incl. above	20.00	35.00	70.00	-

VOYAGEUR REVERSE RESUMED 1975-1976. The designs employed for the voyageur dollars of 1975-1976 were essentially continuations of previous designs, except for some minor variations on the obverse. The physical and chemical specifications are as for the 1974 issues.

Date and Mint Mark	Quantity Minted	MS-60	MS-63	MS-65	PL-65
1975	3,256,000	1.50	3.00	6.00	3.00
1976	1,717,010	1.50	3.00	6.00	3.00

MODIFIED REVERSE 1977. A major alteration was made in the reverse of the 1977 dollar. A new model was prepared in which the size of the device was reduced and the legend was in small lettering, much farther from the rim. The rim denticles were replaced with beads.

Designer and Modeller:
Obverse — Arnold Machin
Patrick Brindley
Reverse — E. Hahn
Terry Smith
Composition: 1.00 Nickel
Weight: 15.62 grams
Diameter: 32.13 mm
Edge: Reeded
Die Axis: ↑↑

Date and Mint Mark	Quantity Minted	MS-60	MS-63	MS-65	PL-65
1977	1,393,745	1.50	3.00	6.00	3.00

MODIFIED DESIGNS 1978-1981. Continued major changes occurred in the nickel dollar coinage in 1978. In a reversal of design policy, the Mint returned to designs more like those used prior to 1977. On the obverse the unmodified Machin portrait was restored, but the beads were farther from the rim than on the 1968-1972 issues. The reverse had a design similar to that of 1975-1976, complete with rim denticles instead of beads, but the northern lights were rendered as raised lines, as they were for the 1977 issue.

Designer and Modeller:
Obverse — Arnold Machin
Reverse — E. Hahn
Composition: 1.00 Nickel
Weight: 15.62 grams
Diameter: 32.13 mm
Edge: Reeded
Die Axis: ↑↑

Date and Mint Mark	Quantity Minted	MS-60	MS-63	MS-65	PL-65
1978	2,948,488	1.50	3.00	6.00	3.00
1979	2,544,000	1.50	3.00	6.00	3.00
1980	2,922,000	1.50	3.00	6.00	5.00
1981	2,778,900	1.50	3.00	6.00	4.00

CONSTITUTION COMMEMORATIVE DOLLAR 1982. On June 10,1982, a one dollar pure nickel circulating coin was struck to commemorate the new Canadian Constitution. The obverse of the coin depicts the effigy of Queen Elizabeth II and the year 1982. The reverse features a faithful reproduction of the celebrated painting of the Fathers of Confederation. It commemorates the Constitution with the inscription "1867 CONFEDERATION" above the painting and "CONSTITUTION 1982" beneath it. This is the first time a commemorative and a voyageur dollar were issued in the same year for circulation. For the collector's edition of this dollar please see page no. 229.

Designer and Modeller:
Obverse — Arnold Machin
RCM Staff
Reverse — Ago Aarand
RCM Staff
Composition: 1.00 Nickel
Weight: 15.62 grams
Diameter: 32.13 mm
Edge: Reeded
Die Axis: ↑↑, ↑↓

Date and Mint Mark	Quantity Minted	MS-60	MS-63	MS-65	PL-65
1982 Constitution, Medal	11,812,000	1.50	3.00	6.00	4.00
1982 Constitution, Coinage	Incl. Above	5.00	10.00	12.00	-

CANADA

VOYAGEUR REVERSE; MODIFIED DESIGN; 1982-1983. The modified designs of 1978 were continued between 1982 and 1983.

Date and Mint Mark	Quantity Minted		MS-60	MS-63	MS-65	PR-65
1982	1,544,398		1.50	3.00	6.00	3.00
1983	2,267,525		1.50	3.00	6.00	7.50

JACQUES CARTIER; COMMEMORATIVE DOLLAR 1984. The four hundred and fiftieth year of Jacques Cartier's landing at Gaspe, Quebec was honoured on July 24, 1984 by the issuing of a commemorative nickel dollar. Again, as in 1982 a commemorative and a voyageur design were issued for circulation in the same year. For the collector's edition of this dollar please see page no. 230.

Designer and Modeller:
Obverse — Arnold Machin
RCM Staff
Reverse — Hector Greville,
Victor Cote
Composition: 1.00 Nickel
Weight: 15.62 grams
Diameter: 32.13 mm
Edge: Reeded
Die Axis: ↑↑

Date and Mint Mark	Quantity Minted		MS-60	MS-63	MS-65	PR-65
1984 Jacques Cartier	6,141,503		2.00	4.00	6.00	7.00

VOYAGEUR REVERSE; MODIFIED DESIGN; 1984 TO 1987. The modified designs of 1978 were continued between 1984 and 1987. The 1987 issue of the nickel dollar appeared only in uncirculated sets sold by the numismatic department of the Mint.

Date and Mint Mark	Quantity Minted		MS-60	MS-63	MS-65	PR-65
1984	1,223,486		1.50	3.00	6.00	6.00
1985	3,104,592		1.50	3.00	6.00	6.00
1986	3,089,225		1.50	3.00	6.00	6.00
1987	Only in sets		1.50	3.00	6.00	6.00

ONE DOLLAR - NICKEL/BRONZE
Elizabeth II 1987 to date

TIARA PORTRAIT; LOON REVERSE; 1987 - 1989. The increased costs associated with the production of the one dollar bank note lead the Bank of Canada to request from the Mint a high denomination coin that would circulate, eventually replacing the paper note. The previous silver and nickel dollar issues did not. The new loon reverse is of reduced size, eleven-sided and new composition allowing the coin to be easily distinguishable from other circulating denominations. And of course, lighter in weight to facilitate the use of pocket change. In 1987 two different size dollar coins were in circulation. See page no. 222 for the collector's issue.

Designer and Modeller:
Obverse — Arnold Machin
Reverse — Robert R. Carmichael
Modeller: Reverse — Terrence Smith
Composition: Nickel electroplated with bronze
Weight: 7.00 grams
Diameter: 26.72 mm, 11 sided
Thickness: 1.95 mm
Edge: Plain
Die Axis: ↑↑

Date and Mint Mark	Quantity Minted	MS-60	MS-63	MS-65	PR-65
1987	205,405,000	1.50	3.00	6.00	6.00
1988	138,893,539	1.50	3.00	6.00	6.00
1989	184,773,902	1.50	3.00	6.00	10.00

CROWNED PORTRAIT; LOON REVERSE; 1990 TO 1991. A new obverse portrait of the Queen wearing a diamond diadem and jewellery was introduced on all denominations in 1990.

Designer and Modeller:
Obverse — Dora de Pédery-Hunt
Ago Aarand
Reverse — Robert R. Carmichael
Terrence Smith
Composition: Nickel electroplated with bronze
Weight: 7.00 grams
Diameter: 26.50 mm, 11 sided
Edge: Plain
Die Axis: ↑↑

Date and Mint Mark	Quantity Minted	MS-60	MS-63	MS-65	PR-65
1990	68,402,000	1.50	2.00	3.00	10.00
1991	23,156,000	1.50	2.00	3.00	10.00

COMMEMORATIVE FOR 125TH ANNIVERSARY; 1867-1992. The reverse design was modified to include the bracket dates 1867-1992 for the 125th birthday of Canada.

Designer, modeller and physical specifications are as for the 1990 issues.

Date and Mint Mark	Quantity Minted		MS-60	MS-63	MS-65	PR-65
1992	4,242,085		1.50	2.00	3.00	10.00

125TH ANNIVERSARY OF CONFEDERATION; 1867-1992. Issued as part of the "Canada 125" coin program celebrating Canada's 125th birthday. The design features the centre block of the Parliament Buildings and three children seated on the ground. One child holds a Canadian flag while another points to the Peace Tower clock which reads 1:25. For the collector's issue see page no. 235.

Designer and Modeller:
Obverse — Dora de Pédery-Hunt
Ago Aarand
Reverse — Rita Swanson
Ago Aarand
Composition: Nickel electroplated with bronze
Weight: 7.00 grams
Diameter: 26.50 mm, 11 sided
Edge: Plain
Die Axis: ↑↑

Date and Mint Mark	Quantity Minted		MS-60	MS-63	MS-65
1992	23,010,915		1.50	2.00	3.00

LOON REVERSE RESUMED; 1993 TO 1994. In 1993 the practice of using the current date was resumed.

Designer, modeller and physical specifications are as for the 1990 issues.

Date and Mint Mark	Quantity Minted		MS-60	MS-63	MS-65	PR-65
1993	33,662,000		1.50	2.00	3.00	10.00
1994	40,406,000		1.50	2.00	3.00	10.00

REMEMBRANCE REVERSE; 1994. The National War Memorial in Ottawa, unveiled by King George VI in May of 1939, commemorates the Canadians in WWI. The National War Memorial was rededicated in 1982 for WWII and the Korean War. For the collector's issue see page 237.

Designer and Modeller:
Obverse — Dora de Pédery-Hunt
Ago Aarand
Reverse — Royal Canadian Mint Staff
Composition: Nickel - bronze
Weight: 7.00 grams
Diameter: 26.50 mm, 11-sided
Thickness: 1.95 mm
Edge: Plain
Die Axis: ↑↑

Date and Mint Mark	Quantity Minted		MS-60	MS-63	MS-65
1994	15,000,000		1.50	2.00	3.00

PEACEKEEPING REVERSE; 1995. Commemorating Canada's commitment to world peace and the 50th anniversary of the founding of the United Nations. The reverse depicts the Peacekeeping Monument in Ottawa, unveiled in 1992. For the collector's issue see page 238.

Designer and Modeller:
Obverse — Dora de Pédery-Hunt,
Ago Aarand
Reverse — J. K. Harman,
R. G. Henriquez, C. H. Oberlander
Composition: Nickel - bronze
Weight: 7.00 grams
Diameter: 26.50 mm, 11-sided
Thickness: 1.95 mm
Edge: Plain
Die Axis: ↑↑

Date and Mint Mark	Quantity Minted		MS-60	MS-63	MS-65
1995	N\A		1.50	2.00	3.00

LOON REVERSE CONTINUED; 1995 TO 1997

Designer and Modeller:
Obverse — Dora de Pédery-Hunt,
Ago Aarand
Reverse — Robert R. Carmichael
Terrence Smith
Composition: Nickel - bronze
Weight: 7.00 grams
Diameter: 26.50 mm, 11-sided
Edge: Plain
Die Axis: ↑↑

Date and Mint Mark	Quantity Minted	MS-60	MS-63	MS-65	PR-65
1995	41,813,000	1.50	2.00	3.00	15.00
1996	N/A	1.50	2.00	3.00	15.00
1997	N/A	1.50	2.00	3.00	15.00

TWO DOLLAR CIRCULATING COINAGE

TWO DOLLAR BI-METALIC
Elizabeth II 1996 to date

CROWNED PORTRAIT; POLAR BEAR REVERSE; 1996 TO DATE. On February 19, 1996, Canada's new two dollar coin was officially launched. The lifespan of a coin is over twenty years, while that of a bank note is only a year. The economies are obvious. The new coin is bi-metallic with a nickel outer ring and an aluminum bronze core. The reverse features a polar bear along the edge of a floe, and the obverse features the effigy of Her Majesty Queen Elizabeth II. See the Collector section on page 240 for collector issues of the two dollar coin.

Designer and Modeller:
  Obverse: Dora de Pédery-Hunt
             Ago Aarand
  Reverse: Brent Townsend
             Ago Aarand
Composition:
  Outer Ring: Nickel
  Inner Core: Aluminum Bronze
Weight: 7.3 grams
Diameter:
  Outer Ring: 28 mm
  Inner Core: 16.8 mm
Thickness: 1.80 mm
Edge: Interrupted serration
Die Axis: ↑↑

Date and Mint Mark	Quantity Mnted	MS-60	MS-63	MS-65
1996	17,600,000	3.00	4.00	5.00

OTTAWA MINT SOVEREIGNS

The British £1 pieces (sovereigns) coined at the Ottawa Mint between 1908 and 1919 occupy a controversial position in Canadian numismatics. Some argue that these pieces are Canadian and must be collected as part of the Canadian series, while others claim that they are British and are separate from the decimal series of the Dominion of Canada.

From the time of the opening of the Ottawa Mint it was the intention of the Dominion government to Mint decimal gold coins; however, the fact that the Ottawa Mint was a branch of the Royal Mint in London meant it was obligated to mint sovereigns on request. And while sovereigns were legal tender in Canada, so were gold coins of the United States. Neither type of gold circulated to any significant degree in Canada in the 20th century. Most companies who requested the Ottawa Mint to strike sovereigns did so because they wanted the coins for export purposes. Finally, the fact that some sovereigns were coined at the Ottawa Mint does not automatically make them Canadian, any more than other coinages (e.g. Newfoundland or Jamaica) produced there.

ONE POUND (SOVEREIGNS)

Edward VII 1908 - 1910

As with all other branch mint sovereigns of the period, the Edward VII Canadian sovereigns are identical to the corresponding London mint issues except for the branch mint mark. The 1908 strikes were Specimen coins only and the tiny mintage was merely to establish the series.

Designer and Modeller:
Portrait — G.W. DeSalles
(DES below bust)
Reverse — Benedetto Pistrucci
(B.P. below ground line at right)
Composition: .917 gold, .083 copper
Weight: 7.99 grams
Diameter: 22.05 mm
Edge: Reeded
Die Axis: ↑↑

The "C" mint mark (for Canada) is on the ground line above the centre of the date.

Date and Mint Mark	Quantity Minted	VF-20	EF-40	AU-50	MS-60	MS-63	MS-64
1908C	636	2,750.00	3,250.00	3,750.00	4,000.00	5,000.00	6,500.00
1909C	16,273	300.00	375.00	500.00	800.00	3,000.00	6,000.00
1910C	28,012	250.00	300.00	400.00	800.00	4,000.00	8,000.00

ONE POUND (SOVEREIGNS)
George V 1911 - 1919

The mintages for the Ottawa mint sovereigns of George V continued the modest trend set in the previous reign. The total of all sovereigns from Ottawa barely equalled the yearly mintage at London or one of the Australian branch mints.

The 1916C issue is rare, with about fifty or so pieces known. The rarity of this issue is probably because most of the mintage was melted, although this is by no means an established fact. Until the last few years the 1916 London issue was also rare, but thousands of them were released from a British bank.

The reverse of the George V sovereigns is the same as that for Edward VII.

Designer and Modeller:
Portrait — E.B. Mackennal
(B.M. on truncation)
Composition: .917 gold, .083 copper
Weight: 7.99 grams
Diameter: 22.05 mm
Edge: Reeded
Die Axis: ↑↑

Date and Mint Mark	Quantity Minted	VF-20	EF-40	AU-50	MS-60	MS-63	MS-64
1911C	256,946	135.00	140.00	150.00	165.00	350.00	1,000.00
1913C	3,715	700.00	950.00	1,300.00	1,800.00	4,500.00	8,000.00
1914C	14,891	350.00	450.00	600.00	850.00	1,750.00	3,000.00
1916C	6,111	15,000.	17,500.	21,500.	25,000.	40,000.00	75,000.00
1917C	58,845	140.00	145.00	160.00	190.00	1,000.00	2,750.00
1918C	106,516	140.00	145.00	160.00	190.00	1,500.00	3,500.00
1919C	135,889	140.00	145.00	160.00	190.00	1,250.00	2,750.00

FIVE DOLLARS — GOLD
George V 1912 - 1914

From the first year of operation of the Ottawa Mint it was planned that gold should be coined in dollar denominations as well as British sovereigns. However, the preparations proceeded slowly and it was not until 1911 that final designs were decided upon (see DC-7 and DC-8 in the chapter on patterns) for the $5 and $10 coins. Originally it had been planned to strike denominations of $2.50, $5, $10 and $20, but sometime in 1911 these plans were modified to include only the two middle denominations.

Coins for circulation were first issued in 1912. Their production was halted in 1914, when Canada adopted new wartime legislation to restrict the flow of gold. At that time notes issued by the Dominion government ceased to be redeemable in gold. This redeemability was not restored until 1926.

The design for the reverse features the old Canadian coat-of-arms superimposed upon two boughs of maple.

Designer: Portrait — Sir E.B. Mackennal (B.M. on truncation) Reverse — W.H.J. Blakemore
Composition: .900 gold, .100 copper
Weight: 8.36 grams
Diameter: 21.59 mm
Edge: Reeded
Die Axis: ↑↑

Date and Mint Mark	Quantity Minted	VF-20	EF-40	AU-50	MS-60	MS-63	MS-64
1912	165,680	200.00	250.00	300.00	425.00	1,250.00	2,750.00
1913	98,832	200.00	250.00	300.00	425.00	1,400.00	4,000.00
1914	31,122	450.00	525.00	750.00	1,250.00	4,000.00	7,500.00

TEN DOLLARS — GOLD:
George V 1912 - 1914

The designs of this denomination are the same as those of the $5 except for the change in value.

Designer: Portrait — Sir E.B. Mackennal (B.M. on truncation) Reverse - W.H.J. Blakemore
Composition: .900 gold, .100 copper
Weight: 16.72 grams
Diameter: 26.92 mm
Edge: Reeded
Die Axis: ↑↑

Date and Mint Mark	Quantity Minted	VF-20	EF-40	AU-50	MS-60	MS-63	MS-64
1912	74,759	450.00	550.00	700.00	1,200.00	4,000.00	9,000.00
1913	149,232	450.00	550.00	725.00	1,250.00	5,500.00	12,500.00
1914	140,068	525.00	625.00	825.00	1,400.00	5,000.00	10,000.00

MAPLE LEAF BULLION COINS

In 1979 the Canadian Government introduced a gold bullion coin to compete with similar pieces issued by other countries (such as the Krugerrand of South Africa). From 1979 to 1981 only the 50 dollar coin (Maple Leaf) in the one troy ounce size was produced. The Maple Leaf during this period was issued with a gold fineness of .999. During November 1982 the range of the Maple Leaf bullion offering was expanded to three sizes. Now included in the offering was the five dollar or 1/10 maple and the ten dollar or 1/4 maple. With the event of the two fractional Maple Leafs all sizes were upgraded in gold content to .9999 fine. July of 1986 saw the offering range expanded once again to include the 20 dollar or 1/2 maple. All four coins are produced from 24 karat gold and are legal tender coinage of Canada. In 1988 the Royal Canadian Mint, again expanding on their bullion program introduced five new coins; four platinum (1/10, 1/4, 1/2 and one maple) and one silver (one maple). In 1993 the Royal Canadian Mint added to the series of bullion coin by issuing a 1/20 of an ounce ($1.00) size in gold and platinum. Again in 1994 the $2.00 denomination was added to the bullion coin series (1/15 of an ounce) in both platinum and gold.

GOLD AND PLATINUM MAPLE LEAFS

Designer and Modeller:
Obverse: Arnold Machin,
    Walter Ott
Reverse: Royal Canadian
    Mint, Walter Ott
Edge: Reeded
Die Axis: ↑↑

Twenty Dollars   1/2 Maple

Common Physical and Chemical Specifications

GOLD

Specification	$1.00 1/20	$2.00 1/15	$5.00 1/10	$10.00 1/4	$20.00 1/2	$50.00 Maple
Fineness (1979-1982)						.999
Fineness (1982 to date)	.9999	.9999	.9999	.9999	.9999	.9999
Weight (gms)	1.555	2.070	3.131	7.797	15.575	31.150
Diameter (mm)	14.1	15.0	16.00	20.00	25.00	30.00
Thickness (mm)	0.92	0.98	1.22	1.70	2.23	2.80
Nominal Value	1.00	2.00	5.00	10.00	20.00	50.00

PLATINUM

Specification	$1.00 1/20	$2.00 1/15	$5.00 1/10	$10.00 1/4	$20.00 1/2	$50.00 Maple
Fineness	.9995	.9995	.9995	.9995	.9995	.9995
Weight (gms)	1.555	2.070	3.131	7.797	15.575	31.150
Diameter (mm	14.10	15.0	16.00	20.00	25.00	30.00
Thickness (mm)	0.92	0.94	1.01	1.50	2.02	2.52
Nominal Value	1.00	$2.00	5.00	10.00	20.00	50.00

In 1990 the reverse hub of the one ounce gold Maple Leaf was re-engraved, enhancing veins in the maple leaf design. Other changes included a more slender stem on the maple leaf and wider spacing of the letters in the legend "Fine Gold 1 oz Or Pur."

Quantities of Gold and Platinum Leafs Minted

The production of maple leafs is on an order basis, unlike the production of coinage for circulation where the Mint will anticipate the number of coins required to fulfill the needs of the economy.

Composition	Date	$1.00 1/20	$2.00 1/15	$5.00 1/10	$10.00 1/4	$20.00 1/2	$50.00 Maple
Gold	1979			Not issued in			1,000,000
	1980			1/20, 1/10, 1/4 and 1/2 maple			1,215,000
	1981			sizes			863,000
	1982			184,000	246,000		883,000
	1983			224,000	130,000		695,000
	1984			226,000	355,200		1,098,000
	1985			476,000	607,200		1,747,500
	1986			483,000	879,200	386,400	1,093,500
	1987			459,000	376,800	332,800	978,000
	1988			412,000	380,000	521,600	800,500
	1989			539,000	328,800	259,200	856,000
	1990			476,000	253,600	174,400	815,000
	1991			322,000	166,400	96,200	290,000
	1992			384,000	179,600	116,000	368,900
	1993	37,080		248,630	158,452	99,492	321,413
	1994	78,860	3,540	313,150	148,792	104,766	180,357
	1995	85,900	4,275	294,890	127,596	103,162	208,729
	1996	N/A	N/A	N/A	N/A	N/A	N/A
	1997	N/A	N/A	N/A	N/A	N/A	N/A
Platinum	1988			46,000	87,200	23,600	26,000
	1989			18,000	3,200	4,800	10,000
	1990			9,000	1,600	2,600	31,900
	1991			13,000	7,200	5,600	31,900
	1992			16,000	11,600	12,800	40,500
	1993	2,120		14,020	8,048	6,022	17,666
	1994	4,260	135	19,190	9,456	6,710	36,245
	1995	460	1335	8940	6524	6308	25,829
	1996	N/A	N/A	N/A	N/A	N/A	N/A
	1997	N/A	N/A	N/A	N/A	N/A	N/A

Pricing:

Buying and selling prices are based on the interday spot price of bullion plus a small percentage premium for striking and handling. The smaller the unit the larger the percentage premium.

SILVER MAPLE LEAFS

The first silver one ounce maple leafs were issued in 1988. The design is a continuation of the gold maple leafs.

Designer and Modeller:
    Obverse — Arnold Machin, Walter Ott
    Reverse — Royal Canadian Mint, Walter Ott

Composition: Silver (.9999)   **Thickness:** 3.21 mm
Weight: 31.15 grams, 1 oz   **Nominal Value:** $5.00
Diameter: 38.00 mm

Date	Mintage	Price
1988	1,062,000	9.00
1989	3,332,200	9.00
1990	1,708,800	9.00
1991	644,300	15.00
1992	343,800	10.00
1993	889,946	9.00
1994	1,133,900	9.00
1995	326,244	9.00
1996	N/A	9.00
1997	N/A	9.00

Note: Please remember that the above maple leafs are linked to the price of silver and can be priced higher, or lower, than prices shown depending on market conditions.

SPECIMEN COINS OF CANADA

The sets of Specimen coins produced between 1858 and 1952 are among the most spectacular items in Canadian numismatics and are keenly sought after. These coins were usually beautifully struck and represent Canadian coinage at its finest.

The finish imparted to specimen coins has varied over the years. During the Victorian period, it consisted of frosted, raised elements with bright, mirror fields. In the reigns of Edward VII and George V an overall satin (sometimes called matte) finish was in vogue. The 1937 coins of George VI came with both finishes. Between 1938 and the mid-1940s the specimen coins tended to have an overall polished appearance.

Specimen sets were often issued in official cases. These cases are sometimes encountered without coins and so are numbered, described and priced as separate entities in the listings that follow. These listings are a beginning and are not in anyway definitive. We will, over the next few editions, strive to complete this list. If you have any additions or corrections, please write, and tell us, so that all specimen coins will be recorded.

These prices are only an indication, specimen coins are very rare with only a few examples known, conditions higher than SP-65 will naturally command higher prices.

PROVINCE OF NEWFOUNDLAND

SPECIMEN COINAGE OF 1864 AND 1865

Struck by the Royal Mint with mirror finishes.

CHARLTON NUMBER	INTENDED CONTENTS	EXTERIOR COLOUR & DIMENSIONS	INTERIOR COLOURS	PRICE FOR EMPTY CASE
4	Newfoundland 1864(1¢);1865(others) 1¢,5¢,10¢,20¢,$2 1¢,5¢,10¢,20¢,$2	Details unknown. May be the same as case #1	Unknown	$1,000.00

DATE	DENOMIN.	DESCRIPTION	SP-60	SP-63	SP-65
1864	1¢	Plain (NF-18)	1,500.00	3,500.00	6,000.00
1864	10¢	Plain		British Museum	
1865	5¢	Plain	1,750.00	4,000.00	10,000.00
1865	10¢	Plain	2,250.00	5,000.00	12,000.00
1865	20¢	Plain	2,250.00	7,500.00	20,000.00
1865	20¢	Reeded	2,750.00	10,000.00	25,000.00
1865	$2.00	Plain	5,000.00	15,000.00	40,000.00
1865	Set	Single, 5 coins*	12,500.00	35,000.00	90,000.00
1865	Set	Double, 10 coins*	25,000.00	70,000.00	180,000.00

Note: The 1865 Set contains the 1864 Pattern cent. A double set sold in the W.W.C. Wilson Sale of 1925 for $28.00.

SPECIMEN COINAGE OF 1870

Struck at the Royal Mint with mirror finishes, the 1870 set was possibly issued in a case identical to No.5. The issue comes with plain or reeded edges.

DATE	DENOM.	DESCRIPTION	SP-60	SP-63	SP-65
1870	5¢	Plain	1,250.00	4,500.00	10,000.00
1870	5¢	Reeded	1,250.00	4,500.00	10,000.00
1870	10¢	Plain	4,000.00	10,000.00	25,000.00
1870	10¢	Reeded	4,000.00	10,000.00	25,000.00
1870	20¢	Plain	2,250.00	7,500.00	20,000.00
1870	20¢	Reeded	2,250.00	7,500.00	20,000.00
1870	50¢	Plain	4,500.00	12,500.00	35,000.00
1870	50¢	Reeded	4,500.00	12,500.00	35,000.00
1870	$2.00	Plain	Rare - Price Not Established		
1870	Set	4 Coins, Reeded	12,000.00	35,000.00	90,000.00
1870	Set	5 Coin, Plain	Rare - Price Not Established		

SPECIMEN COINAGE OF 1872

Struck at the Heaton Mint in Birmingham, England. The coinage of 1872 carrying the "H" mint mark was issued with a mirror finish.

DATE	DENOM.	DESCRIPTION	SP-60	SP-63	SP-65
1872H	1¢	Plain	175.00	400.00	1,500.00
1872H	5¢	Plain	Rare - Price Not Established		
1872H	5¢	Reeded	1,250.00	4,000.00	8,500.00
1872H	10¢	Plain	Rare - Price Not Established		
1872H	10¢	Reeded	1,250.00	5,000.00	12,500.00
1872H	20¢	Plain	Rare - Price Not Established		
1872H	20¢	Reeded	1,750.00	6,000.00	17,500.00
1872H	50¢	Plain	Rare - Price Not Established		
1872H	50¢	Reeded	4,000.00	12,500.00	35,000.00
1872	$2.00	Reeded	9,000.00	25,000.00	60,000.00
1872H	Set	5 Coins, Reeded	9,000.00	27,500.00	75,000.00
1872H	Set	6 Coins, ($2.00 gold)	18,000.00	50,000.00	135,000.00

SPECIMEN COINAGE OF 1873 AND 1874

Struck at the Royal Mint with mirror finishes. No case of issue.

DATE	DENOM.	DESCRIPTION	SP-60	SP-63	SP-65
1873	1¢	Plain			
1873	5¢	Reeded			
1873	10¢	Reeded			
1873	20¢	Reeded	Rare - Price Not Established		
1873	50¢	Reeded			
1873	Set	5 Coins			
1874	50¢	Reeded			50,000.00

Note: * Price not established. In a great many cases with the early specimen coins there is insufficient pricing data available to assign a value with any degree of confidence. As with any rare collectable or antique pricing is best left to the buyer and seller.

SPECIMEN COINAGE OF 1880

Struck at the Royal Mint in London with mirror finishes. No case of issue.

DATE	DENOM.	DESCRIPTION	SP-60	SP-63	SP-65
1880	1¢	Plain, Oval 0	1,750.00	3,600.00	7,500.00
1880	1¢	Plain, Round 0	1,750.00	3,600.00	7,500.00
1880	5¢	Plain	Rare - Price Not Established		
1880	5¢	Reeded	1,250.00	3,500.00	8,500.00
1880	10¢	Plain	Rare - Price Not Established		
1880	20¢	Plain	Rare - Price Not Established		
1880	20¢	Reeded	2,250.00	7,500.00	15,000.00
1880	50¢	Plain	Rare - Price Not Established		
1880	50¢	Reeded	3,250.00	10,000.00	40,000.00
1880	$2.00	Plain	Rare - Price Not Established		
1880	Set	Plain, 6 coins	Rare - Price Not Established		

SPECIMEN COINAGE OF 1881

Struck at the Royal Mint with mirror finishes.

DATE	DENOM.	DESCRIPTION	SP-60	SP-63	SP-65
1881	5¢	Reeded	1,750.00	4,000.00	10,000.00
1881	20¢	Reeded	2,250.00	7,500.00	15,000.00
1881	50¢	Reeded	3,250.00	10,000.00	40,000.00
1881	$2.00	Reeded	Rare - Price Not Established		
1881	Set	4 coins	Rare - Price Not Established		

SPECIMEN COINAGE OF 1882

Struck at the Heaton Mint with mirror finishes. No case of issue.

DATE	DENOM.	DESCRIPTION	SP-60	SP-63	SP-65
1882H	5¢	Reeded	800.00	3,000.00	7,500.00
1882H	10¢	Reeded	1,000.00	3,500.00	8,500.00
1882H	20¢	Reeded	1,750.00	5,000.00	15,000.00
1882H	50¢	Reeded	3,250.00	8,000.00	30,000.00
1882H	$2.00	Reeded	4,500.00	17,500.00	40,000.00
1882H	Set	5 coins	11,000.00	37,000.00	100,000.00

SPECIMEN COINAGE OF 1885 AND 1888

Struck at the Royal Mint with mirror finishes. No known case of issue.

DATE	DENOM.	DESCRIPTION	SP-60	SP-63	SP-65
1885	1¢	Plain			
1885	5¢	Reeded			
1885	10¢	Reeded			
1885	20¢	Reeded			
1885	50¢	Reeded			
1885	$2.00	Reeded	All Rare - Price Not Established		
1885	Set	6 coins			
1888	5¢	Reeded			
1888	10¢	Reeded			
1888	20¢	Reeded			
1888	50¢	Reeded			
1888	$2.00	Reeded			

SPECIMEN COINAGE OF 1890 AND 1894

Struck at the Royal Mint with mirror finishes. No known case of issue.

DATE	DENOM.	DESCRIPTION	SP-60	SP-63	SP-65
1890	5¢	Reeded			
1890	10¢	Reeded			
1890	20¢	Reeded			
1890	50¢	Reeded			
1894	1¢	Plain		All Rare - Price Not Established	
1894	5¢	Reeded			
1894	10¢	Reeded			
1894	20¢	Reeded			
1894	50¢	Reeded			

SPECIMEN COINAGE OF 1896 AND 1900

Struck at the Royal Mint with mirror finishes. No known case of issue

DATE	DENOM.	DESCRIPTION	SP-60	SP-63	SP-65
1896	1¢	Plain			
1896	20¢	Large 6, reeded			
1896	50¢	Reeded			
1898	50¢	Reeded			
1899	20¢	Reeded		All Rare - Price Not Established	
1899	50¢	Reeded			
1900	20¢	Reeded			
1900	50¢	Reeded			

SPECIMEN COINAGE OF 1904

Struck at the Heaton Mint with a satiny-mirror finish. No known case of issue.

DATE	DENOM.	DESCRIPTION	SP-60	SP-63	SP-65
1904H	1¢	Plain	1,500.00	6,000.00	12,500.00
1904H	5¢	Reeded	500.00	2,000.00	4,000.00
1904H	10¢	Reeded	750.00	2,500.00	5,000.00
1904H	20¢	Reeded	1,250.00	4,000.00	8,000.00
1904H	50¢	Reeded	2,250.00	7,500.00	17,500.00
1904H	Set	4 coins	6,250.00	20,000.00	45,000.00

SPECIMEN COINS OF 1912

Struck at the Royal Mint in matte finish. No known case of issue.

DATE	DENOM.	DESCRIPTION	SP-60	SP-63	SP-65
1912	5¢	Reeded	400.00	1,500.00	6,000.00
1912	10¢	Reeded	600.00	2,500.00	7,500.00
1912	20¢	Reeded	800.00	3,000.00	10,000.00
1912	Set	3 coins	1,800.00	7,000.00	23,500.00

SPECIMEN COINS OF 1917 AND 1919

Struck at the Royal Canadian Mint in Ottawa, with matte (satin) finishes. No case of issue. The 1917 issue had rim adjustments made by filing at the Mint.

DATE	DENOM.	DESCRIPTION	SP-60	SP-63	SP-65
1917C	1¢	Plain	500.00	1,000.00	3,000.00
1917C	5¢	Reeded	600.00	2,000.00	4,000.00
1917C	10¢	Reeded	600.00	2,000.00	4,000.00
1917C	25¢	Reeded	900.00	3,000.00	6,000.00
1917C	50¢	Reeded	1,500.00	5,000.00	12,500.00
1917C	Set	5 coins	4,200.00	13,500.00	30,000.00
1919C	1¢	Plain	600.00	2,000.00	4,000.00
1919C	5¢	Reeded	600.00	2,000.00	4,000.00
1919C	10¢	Reeded	600.00	2,000.00	4,000.00
1919C	25¢	Reeded	900.00	3,000.00	6,000.00
1919C	50¢	Reeded	1,500.00	5,000.00	12,500.00
1919C	Set	5 coins	4,400.00	14,000.00	31,000.00

SPECIMEN COINAGE OF 1929, 1938 AND 1940

The issues of 1929 and 1938 were struck at the Royal Mint and those of 1940 at the Royal Canadian Mint. All have mirror finishes with no cases of issue.

DATE	DENOM.	DESCRIPTION	SP-60	SP-63	SP-65
1929	1¢	Plain	600.00	1,750.00	4,000.00
1938	1¢	Plain	300.00	900.00	2,500.00
1938	5¢	Reeded	400.00	1,250.00	3,000.00
1938	10¢	Reeded	400.00	1,250.00	3,000.00
1938	Set	3 coins	1,100.00	3,400.00	8,500.00
1940	1¢	Plain	400.00	1,000.00	3,500.00
1940C	5¢	Reeded	1,000.00	2,000.00	4,000.00
1940	10¢	Reeded	1,250.00	2,500.00	4,000.00
1940	Set	3 coins	2,650.00	5,500.00	11,500.00

SPECIMEN COINAGE OF 1941 TO 1947

Struck at the Royal Canadian Mint with mirror finishes. No cases of issue.

DATE	DENOM.	DESCRIPTION	SP-60	SP-63	SP-65
1941	1¢	Plain	Rare - Price Not Established		
1942	1¢	Plain	Rare - Price Not Established		
1943C	1¢	Plain	Rare - Price Not Established		
1943C	5¢	Reeded	Rare - Price Not Established		
1946C	5¢	Reeded	2,000.00	3,500.00	7,000.00
1946C	10¢	Reeded	900.00	2,500.00	4,000.00
1947C	1¢	Plain	600.00	2,000.00	4,000.00

PROVINCE OF PRINCE EDWARD ISLAND

SPECIMEN COINAGE OF 1871

DATE	DENOM.	DESCRIPTION	SP-60	SP-63	SP-65
1871	1¢	Coinage axis	400.00	1,500.00	3,500.00
1871	1¢	Medal axis	400.00	1,500.00	3,500.00

PROVINCE OF NOVA SCOTIA

SPECIMEN COINAGE OF 1861

Struck by the Royal Mint with mirror finishes. Not issued in a case.

DATE	DENOM.	DESCRIPTION	SP-60	SP-63	SP-65
1861	1/2¢		800.00	2,000.00	3,500.00
1861	1¢	Large Rosebud	1000.00	2,500.00	5,000.00

PROVINCE OF NEW BRUNSWICK

SPECIMEN COINAGE OF 1862 AND 1864

Struck by the Royal Mint with mirror finishes.

CHARLTON NUMBER	INTENDED CONTENTS	EXTERIOR COLOUR & DIMENSIONS	INTERIOR COLOURS	PRICE FOR EMPTY CASE
2	New Brunswick, 1862 1¢,5¢,10¢,20¢ 1¢,5¢,10¢,20¢	Details unknown. May be same as case #1.	Unknown	$1,000.00
3	New Brunswick, 1862 1¢,5¢,10¢,20¢	Details unknown.		$600.00

DATE	DENOM.	DESCRIPTION	SP-60	SP-63	SP-65
1861	1/2¢	Plain	1,500.00	3,000.00	6,000.00
1861	1¢	Plain	1,500.00	3,000.00	6,000.00
1862	1¢	Plain	1,500.00	3,000.00	6,000.00
1862	5¢	Plain	2,500.00	5,000.00	10,000.00
1862	10¢	Plain, Normal Date	2,500.00	5,000.00	12,500.00
1862	20¢	Plain	2,000.00	6,000.00	15,000.00
1862	Set	Single, 4 coins	8,500.00	20,000.00	50,000.00
1862	Set	Double, 8 coins	17,000.00	34,000.00	100,000.00
1864	10¢	Plain	3,500.00	7,500.00	15,000.00

PROVINCE OF CANADA

SPECIMEN COINAGE OF 1858 AND 1859

Struck at the Royal Mint for sample coinage and presentation purposes. Coins are mirror specimens.

Case #1 1858

CHARLTON NUMBER	INTENDED CONTENTS	EXTERIOR COLOUR & DIMENSIONS	INTERIOR COLOURS	PRICE FOR EMPTY CASE
1	1858 1¢,5¢,10¢,20¢ 1¢,5¢,10¢,20¢	Black 7.5 X 11.5 cm	u: white l: dark blue	2,000.00

Cases exist for single sets but are not believed to be official. Sets containing the large date five cent will command a premium.

DATE	DENOM.	DESCRIPTION	SP-60	SP-63	SP-65
1858	1¢	Plain	750.00	1,750.00	4,000.00
1858	5¢	Small date, Plain, ↑↑	550.00	1,500.00	4,500.00
1858	5¢	Small date, Reeded	600.00	1,750.00	5,000.00
1858	5¢	Large date, Plain	1,000.00	4,500.00	9,000.00
1858	5¢	Large date, Reeded	1,250.00	5,000.00	10,000.00
1858	10¢	Plain, ↑↓	900.00	2,500.00	7,500.00
1858	10¢	Plain, ↑↑	900.00	2,500.00	7,500.00
1858	10¢	Reeded, ↑↓	1,000.00	3,000.00	8,500.00
1858	20¢	Plain, ↑↓	1,250.00	3,000.00	9,000.00
1858	20¢	Plain, ↑↑	1,250.00	3,000.00	9,000.00
1858	20¢	Reeded, ↑↓	1,500.00	3,500.00	10,000.00
1858	Set	Single, 4 coins, Plain	3,500.00	10,000.00	30,000.00
1858	Set	Double, 8 coins, Plain	7,000.00	20,000.00	60,000.00
1858	Set	Single, 4 coins, Reeded	5,500.00	11,000.00	32,500.00
1858	Set	Double, 8 coins, Reeded	11,000.00	22,000.00	65,000.00
1859	1¢	Plain, bronze	1,500.00	2,500.00	5,000.00
1859/9	1¢	Double punched, N-9	1,750.00	3,000.00	5,500.00

DOMINION OF CANADA

SPECIMEN COINAGE OF 1870

Struck at the Royal Mint in London with mirror finishes.

CHARLTON NUMBER	INTENDED CONTENTS	EXTERIOR COLOUR & DIMENSIONS	INTERIOR COLOURS	PRICE FOR EMPTY CASE
5	1870 5¢,10¢,25¢,50¢	Dark brown 6.5 X 10.5 cm	u: white l: dark blue	$1,000.00

DATE	DENOM.	DESCRIPTION	SP-60	SP-63	SP-65
1870	5¢	Wide rim, plain	750.00	2,000.00	8,000.00
1870	5¢	Narrow rim, plain	750.00	2,000.00	8,000.00
1870	5¢	Wide rim, reeded	750.00	2,000.00	8,000.00
1870	5¢	Narrow rim, reeded	750.00	2,000.00	8,000.00
1870	10¢	Narrow 0, plain	1,250.00	3,000.00	8,500.00
1870	10¢	Narrow 0, reeded	1,250.00	3,000.00	8,500.00
1870	25¢	Plain	2,250.00	4,000.00	10,000.00
1870	25¢	Reeded	2,250.00	4,000.00	10,000.00
1870	50¢	L.C.W., plain	5,500.00	15,000.00	40,000.00
1870	50¢	L.C.W., reeded	5,500.00	15,000.00	40,000.00
1870	50¢	No L.C.W., plain	17,500.00	50,000.00	75,000.00
1870	Set	4 coins, plain edge	10,000.00	24,000.00	65,000.00
1870	Set	4 coins, reeded edge	10,000.00	24,000.00	65,000.00

SPECIMEN COINAGE OF 1871

Struck at the Royal Mint in London with mirror finishes.

DATE	DENOM.	DESCRIPTION	SP-60	SP-63	SP-65
1871	5¢	Reeded			
1871	10¢	Reeded	Rare - Price Not Established		
1871	20¢	Reeded			

SPECIMEN COINAGE OF 1872, 1874 AND 1875

Struck at the Heaton Mint in Birmingham with mirror finishes. No case of issue.

DATE	DENOM.	DESCRIPTION	SP-60	SP-63	SP-65
1872H	5¢	Reeded	1,000.00	5,000.00	12,500.00
1872H	10¢	Reeded	1,750.00	4,500.00	9,000.00
1872H	25¢	Reeded	1,500.00	4,000.00	10,000.00
1872H	50¢	Reeded	5,000.00	20,000.00	40,000.00
1872H	Set	4 coins	9,000.00	33,500.00	70,000.00
1874H	5¢	Crosslet 4, reeded	1,750.00	4,000.00	12,500.00
1875H	5¢	Reeded	4,000.00	12,500.00	30,000.00
1875H	10¢	Reeded	4,500.00	12,500.00	30,000.00
1875H	25¢	Reeded	8,000.00	22,500.00	45,000.00
1875H	Set	3 coins	16,500.00	45,000.00	100,000.00

SPECIMEN COINAGE OF 1876

DATE	DENOM.	DESCRIPTION	SP-60	SP-63	SP-65
1876	1¢	Plain	2,000.00	3,500.00	6,000.00
1876H	1¢	Plain, copper	1,250.00	3,000.00	5,000.00
1876H	1¢	Plain, nickel	2,000.00	4,000.00	7,500.00

SPECIMEN COINAGE OF 1880 AND 1881

Struck at the Heaton Mint with mirror finishes. No case of issue.

DATE	DENOM.	DESCRIPTION	SP-60	SP-63	SP-65
1880H	5¢	Reeded	1,000.00	3,500.00	12,500.00
1880H	10¢	Reeded	1,000.00	3,000.00	12,500.00
1880H	25¢	Wide 0, reeded	2,250.00	7,000.00	20,000.00
1880H	25¢	Narrow 0, reeded	1,750.00	6,000.00	17,500.00
1880H	Set	3 coins, Narrow 0	3,500.00	12,500.00	37,500.00
1881H	1¢	Plain	1,000.00	2,750.00	5,500.00
1881H	5¢	Reeded	1,250.00	4,000.00	12,500.00
1881H	10¢	Reeded	1,250.00	3,000.00	12,500.00
1881H	25¢	Reeded	1,500.00	5,000.00	17,500.00
1881H	50¢	Reeded	5,500.00	15,000.00	35,000.00
1881H	Set	5 coins	11,000.00	30,000.00	85,000.00

SPECIMEN COINAGE OF 1882 and 1883

Struck at the Heaton Mint in Birmingham with mirror finishes.

DATE	DENOM.	DESCRIPTION	SP-60	SP-63	SP-65
1882H	1¢	Plain	1,250.00	2,500.00	6,000.00
1882H	5¢	Reeded	2,000.00	5,000.00	12,500.00
1882H	10¢	Reeded	1,500.00	4,000.00	12,500.00
1882H	25¢	Reeded	2,000.00	5,000.00	17,500.00
1883H	25¢	Reeded	1,500.00	5,000.00	17,500.00

SPECIMEN COINAGE OF 1884 TO 1889

Struck in London by the Royal Mint with mirror finishes.

DATE	DENOM.	DESCRIPTION	SP-60	SP-63	SP-65
1884	1¢	Plain			
1884	5¢	Reeded			
1884	10¢	Reeded			
1885	5¢	Reeded			
1885	10¢	Reeded			
1885	25¢	Reeded			
1886	5¢	Reeded			
1886	10¢	Reeded	All Coins Rare - Price Not Established		
1886	25¢	Reeded			
1887	5¢	Reeded			
1887	10¢	Reeded			
1888	5¢	Reeded			
1888	10¢	Reeded			
1888	25¢	Reeded			
1889	5¢	Reeded			
1889	25¢	Reeded			

SPECIMEN COINAGE OF 1891 AND 1892

Struck at the Royal Mint with mirror finishes. No case of issue.

DATE	DENOM.	DESCRIPTION	SP-60	SP-63	SP-65
1891	5¢	Reeded			
1891	10¢	Reeded			
1891	25¢	Reeded			
1892	5¢	Reeded	All Coins Rare - Price Not Established		
1892	10¢	Reeded			
1892	25¢	Reeded			

SPECIMEN COINAGE OF 1893 TO 1899

Struck at the Royal Mint with mirror finishes. No case of issue.

DATE	DENOM.	DESCRIPTION	SP-60	SP-63	SP-65
1893	1¢	Plain			
1893	5¢	Reeded			
1893	10¢	Reeded			
1894	1¢	Plain			
1894	5¢	Reeded			
1894	10¢	Reeded	All Coins Rare - Price Not Established		
1894	25¢	Reeded			
1899	5¢	Reeded			
1899	10¢	Reeded			
1899	25¢	Reeded			

SPECIMEN COINAGE OF 1900 AND 1901

Struck in London at the Royal Mint with mirror finishes. No case of issue.

DATE	DENOM.	DESCRIPTION	SP-60	SP-63	SP-65
1900	5¢	Oval 0, reeded			
1900	10¢	Reeded			
1900	25¢	Reeded			
1901	5¢	Reeded	All Coins Rare - Price Not Established		
1901	10¢	Reeded			
1901	25¢	Reeded			

SPECIMEN COINAGE OF 1902 AND 1905

Struck at the Heaton Mint with matte (satin) finishes. No case of issue.

DATE	DENOM.	DESCRIPTION	SP-60	SP-63	SP-65
1902H	5¢	Reeded, Large H	1,000.00	2,500.00	6,500.00
1902H	10¢	Reeded	1,200.00	3,000.00	9,000.00
1902H	25¢	Reeded	1,200.00	3,500.00	10,000.00
1902H	Set	3 coins	3,400.00	9,000.00	25,000.00
1903H	10¢	Reeded	3,000.00	7,500.00	12,500.00
1903	25¢	Reeded	3,500.00	10,000.00	15,000.00
1905	5¢	Reeded	1,500.00	3,500.00	7,500.00

SPECIMEN COINAGE OF 1908 TO 1912

Struck to commemorate the opening of the Royal Canadian Mint in Ottawa in 1908. This is the first set of specimen coins offered to the general public. The issue price was $2.00. Coins had a matte finish.

CHARLTON NUMBER	INTENDED CONTENTS	EXTERIOR COLOUR & DIMENSIONS	INTERIOR COLOURS	PRICE FOR EMPTY CASE
6	1908 1¢,5¢,10¢,25¢,50¢	Maroon, 5.3 X 15.5 cm	u:purple,impressed in gold lettering: "First Coinage in Canada/1908/Ottawa" l:purple	$125.00
6a	1908 1¢,5¢,10¢,25¢,50¢	Red, 5.3 X 15.5 cm	u & l:purple	$125.00
6b	1908 1¢,5¢,10¢,25¢,50¢	Red, 5.3 X 15.5 cm top impressed in gold lettering: "First Coinage in Canada/1908/Royal Mint Ottawa"	u & l:purple	$200.00
6c	1908 1¢,5¢,10¢,25¢,50¢	Red, 5.3 X 15.5 cm	u:purple with affixed red leather strip impressed in gold lettering: "First Coinage of Canadian Mint/Ottawa/1908" l:purple	$125.00

The impressed red leather strips were mailed seperately to customers who possibly were initially sent sets housed in box 6a.

DATE	DENOM.	DESCRIPTION	SP-60	SP-63	SP-65
1908	1¢	Plain	100.00	225.00	400.00
1908	5¢	Reeded	200.00	400.00	750.00
1908	10¢	Reeded	275.00	450.00	1,000.00
1908	25¢	Reeded	325.00	900.00	2,000.00
1908	50¢	Reeded	700.00	1,750.00	4,000.00
1908	Set	5 coins	1,500.00	3,700.00	8,000.00
1908	Sovereign	Reeded	4,000.00	5,000.00	10,000.00
1909	Sovereign	Reeded	Rare - Price Not Established		

SPECIMEN COINAGE OF 1911 AND 1912

Struck at the Royal Canadian Mint with matte (satin) finishes. As in 1908 the George V Coronation prompted the Mint to offer this issue to the general public. The original issue prices were:

1911 Set: 5 coins all dated 1911
       1¢, 5¢, 10¢, 25¢, 50¢   Issue Price: $2.00

1911-12 Set: 8 coins, 6 dated 1911,
       1¢, 5¢, 10¢, 25¢, 50¢, £1
       2 dated 1912, $5, $10   Issue Price: $24.00

Case #7a 1911

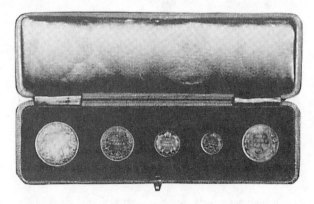

Case #7b 1911

Case #7 1911

CHARLTON NUMBER	INTENDED CONTENTS	EXTERIOR COLOUR & DIMENSIONS	INTERIOR COLOURS	PRICE FOR EMPTY CASE
7	1911 1¢,5¢,10¢,25¢,50¢,$1 £1,$5,$10	Red, 8.9 X 19.7 cm top impressed in gold lettering: "Specimen Coins/Silver and Bronze/ Ottawa Mint/1911"	u & l:purple	$500.00
7a	1911 1¢,5¢,10¢,25¢,50¢,$1 This case for 1911 dated coins.	Red, 5.3 X 19.7 cm top impressed in gold lettering: "Specimen Coins/Silver and Bronze/ Ottawa Mint/1911"	u & l:purple	$200.00
7b	1911 1¢,5¢,10¢,25¢,50¢	As case #7a	As case #7a	$200.00
7c	1911-12 1¢,5¢,10¢,25¢,50¢ 1912 $5,$10 1911 £1 This case for 1911-12 dated coins	Red, 8.9 X 19.7 cm top impressed in gold lettering: "Specimen Coins/Ottawa Mint/ 1911-12"	u & l:purple	$500.00

DATE	DENOM.	DESCRIPTION	SP-60	SP-63	SP-65
1911	1¢	Plain	100.00	250.00	500.00
1911	5¢	Reeded	225.00	500.00	1,000.00
1911	10¢	Reeded	300.00	750.00	1,250.00
1911	25¢	Reeded	500.00	1,250.00	2,500.00
1911	50¢	Reeded	2,250.00	3,750.00	8,000.00
1911	Set	5 coins	3,500.00	6,750.00	14,000.00
1911	Sovereign	Reeded	2,500.00	7,500.00	17,500.00
1912	$5	Reeded	4,500.00	10,000.00	25,000.00
1912	$10.00	Reeded	6,000.00	20,000.00	35,000.00
1911-12	Set	8 coins	16,000.00	45,000.00	100,000.00
1912	1¢	Plain	Rare - Price Not Established		

SPECIMEN COINAGE OF 1913 TO 1920

Struck at the Royal Canadian Mint with a matte finish.

DATE	DENOM.	DESCRIPTION	SP-60	SP-63	SP-65
1913	10¢	Reeded	2,000.00	5,000.00	12,500.00
1920	1¢	Large cent, plain			
1920	1¢	Small cent, plain	All Coins Rare - Price Not Established		
1920	10¢	Reeded			

SPECIMEN COINAGE OF 1921

Struck at the Royal Canadian Mint with a matte (satin) finish. No case of issue.

DATE	DENOM.	DESCRIPTION	SP-60	SP-63	SP-65
1921	1¢	Plain	1,000.00	2,500.00	5,000.00
1921	5¢	Reeded	12,500.00	30,000.00	60,000.00
1921	10¢	Reeded	1,250.00	3,500.00	10,000.00
1921	25¢	Reeded	3,250.00	10,000.00	25,000.00
1921	50¢	Reeded	35,000.00	60,000.00	100,000.00
1921	Set	5 coins	53,000.00	100,000.00	200,000.00

SPECIMEN COINAGE OF 1922 TO 1929

This series 1922 to 1929 was issued by the Royal Canadian Mint in matte finish.

DATE	DENOM.	DESCRIPTION	SP-60	SP-63	SP-65
1922	1¢		400.00	1250.00	3,500.00
1922	5¢		150.00	600.00	1,250.00
1923	1¢		400.00	1,250.00	3,500.00
1923	5¢		700.00	2,000.00	5,000.00
1924	1¢		400.00	1,250.00	3,500.00
1924	5¢		400.00	1,500.00	5,000.00
1925	1¢		700.00	1,500.00	3,500.00
1925	5¢		2,250.00	4,000.00	10,000.00
1926	1¢		400.00	1,250.00	3,500.00
1926N6	5¢		1,250.00	3,000.00	6,000.00
1927	1¢		400.00	1,250.00	3,500.00
1927	5¢		400.00	1,200.00	5,000.00
1927	25¢		Rare - Price not Established		
1928	¢		350.00	1,000.00	3,000.00
1928	5¢		400.00	1,500.00	4,000.00
1928	10¢		700.00	2,000.00	5,000.00
1928	25¢		900.00	3,000.00	7,500.00
1928	Set	4 Coins	2,250.00	7,500.00	19,000.00
1929	1¢		350.00	1,000.00	3,000.00
1929	5¢		400.00	1,500.00	3,500.00
1929	10¢		700.00	2,000.00	5,000.00
1929	25¢		900.00	3,000.00	7,500.00
1929	50¢		2,000.00	7,500.00	15,000.00
1929	Set	5 Coins	4,250.00	15,000.00	34,000.00

SPECIMEN COINAGE OF 1930 TO 1934

This series 1930 to 1934 was issued by the Royal Canadian Mint in a matte finish.

CHARLTON NUMBER		INTENDED CONTENTS	EXTERIOR COLOUR & DIMENSIONS	INTERIOR COLOURS	PRICE FOR EMPTY CASE
8	1931	As case #7a 1¢(small), 5¢(nickel), 10¢,25¢,50¢	As case #7a	As case #7a	$300.00

DATE	DENOM.	DESCRIPTION	SP-60	SP-63	SP-65
1930	1¢		350.00	1,000.00	3,000.00
1930	5¢		700.00	2,000.00	5,000.00
1930	10¢		700.00	1,500.00	6,000.00
1930	25¢		900.00	2,500.00	10,000.00
1930	Set	4 coins	2,700.00	7,000.00	25,000.00
1931	1¢		350.00	1,000.00	3,000.00
1931	5¢		500.00	1,500.00	4,500.00
1931	10¢		700.00	1,500.00	5,000.00
1931	25¢		1,000.00	3,500.00	8,000.00
1931	50¢		2,500.00	6,500.00	15,000.00
1931	Set	5 coins, Case #8	5,000.00	14,000.00	35,000.00
1932	1¢		800.00	2,500.00	5,000.00
1932	5¢		1,750.00	5,000.00	10,000.00
1932	10¢		Rare - Price Not Established		
1932	25¢		Rare - Price Not Established		
1932	50¢		4,000.00	10,000.00	20,000.00
1932	Set	5 coins	Rare - Price Not Established		
1933	1¢		400.00	1,000.00	3,500.00
1933	5¢		1,250.00	3,000.00	6,000.00
1933	10¢		1,250.00	3,000.00	7,000.00
1933	25¢		1,250.00	4,500.00	12,500.00
1933	Set	4 coins	4,000.00	11,000.00	30,000.00
1934	1¢		400.00	1,000.00	3,500.00
1934	5¢		900.00	2,000.00	5,000.00
1934	10¢		700.00	3,000.00	8,500.00
1934	25¢		1,100.00	3,000.00	10,000.00
1934	50¢		3,000.00	7,500.00	20,000.00
1934	Set	5 coins	6,000.00	16,000.00	50,000.00

SPECIMEN COINAGE OF 1935

The silver jubilee of George V in 1935 was also the first year for the introduction of a circulating silver dollar. From this date on this section will list the specimen dollars.

DATE	DENOM.	DESCRIPTION	SP-60	SP-63	SP-65
1935	$1.00		2,000.00	5,000.00	20,000.00
1935	$1.00	2 Coin Case	4,000.00	12,500.00	45,000.00

SPECIMEN COINAGE OF 1936

DATE	DENOM.	DESCRIPTION	SP-60	SP-63	SP-65
1936	1¢		400.00	1,200.00	3,500.00
1936	5¢		700.00	2,000.00	5,000.00
1936	10¢		700.00	2,000.00	5,000.00
1936	25¢		1,500.00	3,500.00	7,500.00
1936	50¢		2,000.00	7,500.00	20,000.00
1936	$1.00		3,000.00	7,500.00	20,000.00
1936	Set	6 coins	8,500.00	24,000.00	60,000.00
1936	1¢	Dot	-	-	75,000.00
1936	10¢	Dot	-	-	75,000.00
1936	25¢	Dot	-	-	20,000.00
1936 Dot	Set	3 coins	-	-	170,000.00

SPECIMEN COINAGE OF 1937 AND 1938

Card Case: Issued - 1295 sets. Original Issue Price: $3.25

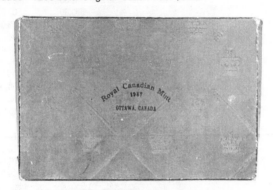

Card Case #9 1937

Case #9a 1937

Case
#9a 1937

Case #9 1937

Case #9b 1937

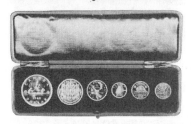

CHARLTON NUMBER	INTENDED CONTENTS	EXTERIOR COLOUR & DIMENSIONS	INTERIOR COLOURS	PRICE FOR EMPTY CASE
9	1937 1¢,5¢,10¢,25¢,50¢,$1	Red cardboard, 10.2 X 15.3 cm, with horizontal ridges, crowns and scepters and in black lettering: "Royal Canadian Mint/ 1937/Ottawa, Canada"	u:coarse white cloth l:royal blue cardboard	$50.00
9a	1937 1¢,5¢,10¢,25¢	As case #7a except date covered by paper Union Jack.	As case #7a	$375.00
9b	1937 1¢,5¢,10¢,25¢,50¢,$1	As case #7a, except the inscription is covered by a blue leather strip upon which is impressed in gold a view of the centre section of the Royal Canadian Mint surrounded on the sides and bottom by a ribbon "1937" is below. On the ribbon is "Royal Canadian Mint"	As case #7a	$250.00

SPECIMEN SETS

DATE	DENOM.	DESCRIPTION	SP-60	SP-63	SP-65
1937	1¢	Matte	20.00	35.00	75.00
1937	5¢	Matte	25.00	60.00	125.00
1937	10¢	Matte	40.00	75.00	150.00
1937	25¢	Matte	60.00	125.00	250.00
1937	50¢	Matte	75.00	175.00	350.00
1937	$1.00	Matte	100.00	250.00	500.00
1937	Set	Case No.9, 6 coins, matte	325.00	700.00	1,500.00
1937	Set	Case No.9b, 6 coins, matte	500.00	900.00	1,700.00
1937	1¢	Mirror	35.00	75.00	150.00
1937	5¢	Mirror	40.00	80.00	150.00
1937	10¢	Mirror	75.00	175.00	350.00
1937	25¢	Mirror	125.00	300.00	650.00
1937	Set	Case No.9a, 4 coins, mirror	300.00	650.00	1,300.00
1937	50¢	Mirror	150.00	450.00	1,000.00
1937	$1.00	Mirror	300.00	1,000.00	2,000.00
1937	Set	Case No.9, 6 coins, mirror	800.00	2,000.00	4,500.00
1937	Set	Case No.9b, 6 coins, mirror	800.00	2,000.00	4,500.00
1938	1¢	Mirror/Matte	250.00	750.00	2,000.00
1938	5¢	Mirror/Matte	1,750.00	5,000.00	10,000.00
1938	10¢	Mirror/Matte	550.00	1,500.00	4,000.00
1938	25¢	Mirror/Matte	700.00	2,000.00	5,000.00
1938	50¢	Mirror/Matte	900.00	2,500.00	7,500.00
1938	$1.00	Mirror/Matte	2,250.00	6,000.00	15,000.00
1938	Set	Case No.9b, 6 coins, mirror	7,000.00	16,000.00	42,000.00

SPECIMEN COINAGE OF 1939

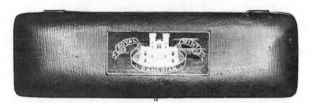

Case #10 1938-1953

Case #11 1939

CHARLTON NUMBER	INTENDED CONTENTS	EXTERIOR COLOUR & DIMENSIONS	INTERIOR COLOURS	PRICE FOR EMPTY CASE
10	1938-1953 1¢,5¢,10¢,25¢,50¢,$1	As case #9b, except for the absence of "1937"	As case #9b	$300.00
11	1939 54 mm medal, $1 54 mm medal	As case #8, except the inscription is covered by an oval blue patch impressed in gold lettering: "Royal Visit/King George VI & Queen Elizabeth/ Commemorative/Medal & Dollar/1939"		$500.00

DATE	DENOM.	DESCRIPTION	SP-60	SP-63	SP-65
1939	10¢	Mirror	400.00	1,500.00	4,000.00
1939	25¢	Mirror	700.00	2,000.00	4,500.00
1939	$1.00	Matte	550.00	1,000.00	1,750.00
1939	$1.00	Mirror	900.00	1,500.00	3,500.00
1939	Set	2 medals, $1, mirror	900.00	1,500.00	3,500.00
1939	Set	10¢, 25¢,$1, mirror	2,000.00	4,500.00	11,000.00

SPECIMEN COINAGE OF 1940 TO 1946

DATE	DENOM.	DESCRIPTION	SP-60	SP-63	SP-65
1941	50¢	Reeded		Rare - Price Not Established	
1942	5¢	Nickel, plain		Rare - Price Not Established	
1942	5¢	Tombac, plain	125.00	350.00	1,200.00
1942	50¢	Reeded		Rare - Price Not Established	
1943	1¢	Plain		Rare - Price Not Established	
1943	5¢	Tombac, plain	75.00	200.00	750.00
1943	10¢	Reeded		Rare - Price Not Established	
1943	25¢	Reeded		Rare - Price Not Established	
1944	1¢		600.00	1,100.00	2,500.00
1944	5¢		90.00	175.00	500.00
1944	10¢		700.00	1,250.00	3,500.00
1944	25¢		900.00	2,250.00	5,000.00
1944	50¢		2,250.00	6,000.00	12,500.00
1944	Set		4,500.00	11,000.00	25,000.00
1945	1¢		90.00	225.00	500.00
1945	5¢		90.00	225.00	500.00
1945	10¢		175.00	350.00	1,000.00
1945	25¢		275.00	450.00	1,250.00
1945	50¢		550.00	1,100.00	2,500.00
1945	$1		1,250.00	2,250.00	5,000.00
1945	Set	Case No. 10	2,500.00	4,500.00	11,000.00
1946	1¢		70.00	110.00	300.00
1946	5¢		90.00	175.00	400.00
1946	10¢		175.00	325.00	750.00
1946	25¢		275.00	450.00	1,250.00
1946	50¢		500.00	1,500.00	3,000.00
1946	$1.00		900.00	2,250.00	4,500.00
1946	Set	Case No.10	2,000.00	5,000.00	10,500.00

SPECIMEN COINAGE OF 1947

DATE	DENOM.	DESCRIPTION	SP-60	SP-63	SP-65
1947	1¢		90.00	175.00	400.00
1947	5¢		100.00	225.00	500.00
1947	10¢		150.00	325.00	850.00
1947	25¢		175.00	450.00	1,250.00
1947	50¢	Straight 7	600.00	1,250.00	3,000.00
1947	50¢	Curved 7	900.00	1,750.00	3,500.00
1947	$1.00	Pointed 7	1,750.00	3,500.00	9,000.00
1947	$1.00	Blunt 7	2,750.00	4,500.00	10,000.00
1947	Set	Pointed Dollar, case No.10	3,500.00	7,000.00	16,000.00
1947	Set	Blunt Dollar, case No.10	5,000.00	8,000.00	17,500.00
1947ML	1¢		60.00	100.00	250.00
1947ML	5¢		90.00	150.00	350.00
1947ML	10¢		90.00	175.00	450.00
1947ML	25¢		125.00	275.00	600.00
1947ML	50¢	Straight 7	900.00	1,750.00	3,500.00
1947ML	50¢	Curved 7	2,250.00	3,000.00	5,000.00
1947ML	$1.00		1,750.00	2,750.00	5,500.00
1947ML	Set	Straight 7	3,000.00	5,250.00	10,000.00
1947ML	Set	Curved 7	4,500.00	7,000.00	11,500.00

SPECIMEN COINAGE OF 1948 AND 1949

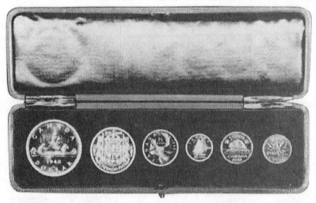

DATE	DENOM.	DESCRIPTION	SP-60	SP-63	SP-65
1948	1¢		70.00	110.00	250.00
1948	5¢		100.00	175.00	350.00
1948	10¢		100.00	200.00	450.00
1948	25¢		175.00	325.00	600.00
1948	50¢	Concave	450.00	650.00	1,500.00
1948	50¢	Convex	450.00	750.00	2,250.00
1948	$1.00		1,500.00	3,000.00	6,000.00
1948	Set	Concave, case No.10	3,000.00	5,000.00	9,000.00
1948	Set	Convex, case No.10	3,000.00	5,500.00	10,000.00
1949	1¢		70.00	125.00	300.00
1949	5¢		90.00	175.00	400.00
1949	10¢		150.00	350.00	750.00

DATE	DENOM.	DESCRIPTION	SP-60	SP-63	SP-65
1949	25¢		275.00	550.00	1,250.00
1949	50¢		450.00	900.00	2,500.00
1949	$1.00	Specimen	125.00	300.00	750.00
1949	$1.00	Proof	1,250.00	3,250.00	7,000.00
1949	Set	Specimen, case No.10	1,250.00	2,750.00	6,000.00
1949	Set	Proof, case No.10	2,500.00	5,000.00	12,500.00

Note: The 1949 business strike dollar was shipped from the Mint in rolls of 20 coins. This method of packaging resulted in high quality dollars reaching collectors. Most of these coins saved by collectors were of proof-like quality. Another striking for sets resulted in specimen coins. Two varieties emerged, a superior specimen coin on full planchets and super strikes with wide square rims. It is said that these examples were prepared by Thomas Shingles, designer of the 1949 dollar.

SPECIMEN COINAGE OF 1950 TO 1952

DATE	DENOM.	DESCRIPTION	SP-60	SP-63	SP-65
1950	1¢		25.00	70.00	200.00
1950	5¢		45.00	100.00	300.00
1950	10¢		50.00	125.00	350.00
1950	25¢		90.00	175.00	450.00
1950	50¢		175.00	350.00	900.00
1950	$1.00	Mirror	400.00	750.00	2,000.00
1950	$1.00	Matte, only one known	-	-	15,000.00
1950ARN	$1.00	Arnprior, mirror	1,250.00	2,500.00	7,500.00
1950	Set	Mirror	900.00	1,750.00	4,500.00
1950	Set	Arnprior	2,750.00	-	8,000.00
1951	1¢		30.00	70.00	200.00
1951	5¢	High relief	2,000.00	3,500.00	6,000.00
1951	5¢	Low relief	40.00	90.00	300.00
1951COMM	5¢	Commemorative	40.00	90.00	300.00
1951	10¢		50.00	125.00	400.00
1951	25¢	High relief	45.00	275.00	600.00
1951	25¢	Low relief	70.00	125.00	300.00
1951	50¢		175.00	400.00	1,000.00
1951	$1.00		400.00	800.00	2,000.00
1951	Set	Low relief, 7 coins	850.00	1,750.00	4,500.00
1951	Set	High relief, 7 coins	2,250.00	4,500.00	9,000.00
1952	1¢		35.00	75.00	200.00
1952	5¢		125.00	175.00	400.00
1952	10¢		70.00	125.00	400.00
1952	25¢	High relief	90.00	175.00	500.00
1952	50¢		175.00	400.00	1,000.00
1952WL	$1.00	Water lines	800.00	1,750.00	4,000.00
1952NWL	$1.00	No water lines	800.00	1,750.00	4,000.00
1952	Set	W.L. dollar, case No.10	1,750.00	3,000.00	7,000.00
1952	Set	N.W.L. dollar, case No.10	1,750.00	3,000.00	7,000.00

SPECIMEN COINAGE OF 1953

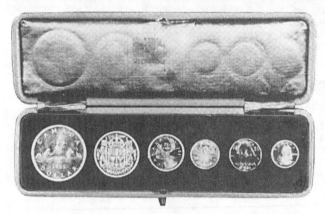

Case #12 1953

CHARLTON NUMBER	INTENDED CONTENTS	EXTERIOR COLOUR & DIMENSIONS	INTERIOR COLOURS	PRICE FOR EMPTY CASE
12	1953 1¢,5¢,10¢,25¢,50¢,$1	Red, top impressed in gold with a view of the centre section of the Royal Canadian Mint surrounded on the sides and bottom by a ribbon bearing "Royal Canadian Mint"	u & l:purple	$300.00

SPECIMEN COINAGE OF 1953

DATE	DENOM.	DESCRIPTION	SP-60	SP-63	SP-65
1953	1¢	N.S.F.	50.00	125.00	275.00
1953	5¢	N.S.F.	50.00	100.00	250.00
1953	10¢	N.S.F.	50.00	100.00	250.00
1953	25¢	N.S.F.	75.00	150.00	350.00
1953	50¢	Small date, N.S.F.	125.00	250.00	650.00
1953	50¢	Large date, N.S.F.	500.00	900.00	2,000.00
1953	$1.00	N.S.F.	400.00	700.00	1,500.00
1953	Set	Small date 50¢, N.S.F., case No.12	900.00	1,500.00	3,500.00
1953	Set	Large date 50¢, N.S.F., case No.12	1,500.00	2,000.00	4,750.00
1953	1¢	S.F.	30.00	45.00	75.00
1953	5¢	S.F.	25.00	40.00	75.00
1953	10¢	S.F.	35.00	70.00	150.00
1953	25¢	S.F.	50.00	80.00	175.00
1953	50¢	Large date, S.F.	90.00	150.00	325.00
1953	$1.00	S.F.	250.00	350.00	750.00
1953	Set	S.F., case No.12	500.00	750.00	1,550.00

SPECIMEN COINAGE OF 1964 TO 1966

DATE	DENOM.	DESCRIPTION	SP-60	SP-63	SP-65
1964	1¢	Plain	20.00	30.00	60.00
1964	5¢	Plain	25.00	50.00	100.00
1964	10¢	Reeded	30.00	65.00	125.00
1964	25¢	Reeded	50.00	100.00	200.00
1964	50¢	Reeded	85.00	175.00	350.00
1964	$1.00	Reeded	150.00	300.00	600.00
1964	Set	6 coins	350.00	750.00	1,500.00
1965	1¢	Plain	20.00	30.00	60.00
1965	5¢	Plain	20.00	35.00	75.00
1965	10¢	Reeded	25.00	50.00	100.00
1965	25¢	Reeded	35.00	75.00	150.00
1965	50¢	Reeded	50.00	100.00	200.00
1965	$1.00	BL-5, reeded	125.00	250.00	500.00
1965	Set	6 coins	300.00	500.00	1,000.00
1966	$1.00	Reeded	150.00	300.00	600.00

Note: This listing of the specimen coins of Canada is not complete. It is our goal to offer the collector a completed list over time, to do this we need your help. If you have any additional information on specimen coinage please write.

CASED SPECIMEN SET 1970

Cased Specimen Set 1970

In 1970 the Royal Canadian Mint considered the possibility of resuming the sale of cased specimen sets to the public on a regular basis. In connection with this and also to provide Prime Minister Pierre Trudeau with special sets for presentation purposes during his trip to China that year, a quantity of specimen sets in narrow cases were made up. After Trudeau's trip, some of these sets were sold to the public for $13.00 each. The total quantity of 1970 specimen sets issued in Canada is believed to be less than 1,000 and the only way 1970 specimen coins were available was in these sets. When the Mint made specimen sets available to the public starting in 1971, they were housed in a larger, eight coin case. These sets are listed under prestige sets 1971-1980 on page 251.

1970 Specimen Set in Black Case $650.00

PATTERNS, TRIAL PIECES & OFFICIAL FABRICATIONS

A PATTERN is a piece submitted as a design sample by engravers when a new coinage is contemplated. If the design is adopted for regular coinage with the same date, the piece ceases to be a pattern. If the design is adopted with a later date, the piece remains a pattern. Patterns are usually struck as proofs.

A TRIAL PIECE or ESSAY is from dies already accepted for regular coinage. It may bear a date or mint mark other than on the coins issued for circulation or it may be in a different metal.

AN OFFICIAL FABRICATION is a piece that was created for some special purpose unconnected with design proposals or experiments on coinage design or metals. For example, the New Brunswick pieces bearing the dates 1870, 1871 and 1875 were obviously not connected with an attempt to revive a separate coinage for that province after Confederation.

The best listing of patterns, trial pieces and official fabrications has been by Fred Bowman in his book *Canadian Patterns*. The present listing is greatly revised compared to Bowman's and new numbers are used. However, Bowman's original numbers are also included for those pieces which were listed in his book.

PROVINCE OF NOVA SCOTIA

PATTERNS

CHARLTON BOWMAN
NS-1

Half cent 1860. Reverse - crown surrounded by wreath of roses; date below wreath. (The illustration is from a matrix. It is uncertain whether patterns bearing this date were actually produced.)

NS-2

One cent 1860. Reverse - crown surrounded by wreath of roses; date below wreath. (The illustration is from a matrix. It is uncertain whether patterns bearing this date were actually produced.)

PATTERNS

CHARLTON   BOWMAN
NS-3   B-11   Half cent 1861, bronze. Proof; dies ↑↓; wt. 2.85g; dia. 20.65mm. Obverse - large bust of
                        Victoria by James Wyon. Reverse - pattern design as on NS-1. (National Currency
                        Collection)

NS-4   B-7   One cent 1861, bronze. Proof; dies ↑↑; wt. 4.69g; dia. 25.4mm. Obverse - large bust of
                        Victoria by James Wyon. Reverse - pattern design as on NS-2. (National Currency
                        Collection)
NS-5   B-13   Half cent 1861, bronze. Proof; dies ↑↓. Obverse - adopted (small bust) design by L.C.
                        Wyon. Reverse - pattern design as NS-3. (National Currency Collection)

NS-6   B-8   One cent 1861, bronze. Not a proof; dies ↑↑; wt. 5.59g; dia. 25.4mm. Obverse - adopted
                        (small bust) design by L.C. Wyon. Reverse - pattern design as NS-4. (National Currency
                        Collection)

NS-7   B-12   Half cent 1861, bronze. Proof; dies ↑↑; wt. 2.78g; dia. 20.65mm. Obverse - pattern design
                        as on NS-3. Reverse - adopted design (crown and date surrounded by a wreath of
                        may-flowers and roses). (New Netherlands Coin Sale 1960)

PATTERNS

CHARLTON BOWMAN
NS-8   B-10   One cent 1861, bronze. Proof; dies ↑↑; wt. 5.65g; dia. 25.4mm and dies ↑↓; wt. 5.74g; dia. 25.4mm. Obverse - pattern design as on NS-4. Reverse - adopted design (1861), large rose bud variety. (National Currency Collection)

NS-8a   B-10   One cent 1861, bronze. Proof; dies ↑↑; wt. 5.80g; dia. 25.4mm. As NS-8, except the reverse is the small rose bud variety (adopted design for 1861-1864).

NS-9   B-14   Half cent 186-, bronze. Proof. As NS-5, except for the incomplete date.

NS-10   B-9   One cent 186-, bronze. Dies ↑↑; wt. 5.78g; dia. 25.4mm. As NS-6, except for the incomplete date.

PROVINCE OF NEW BRUNSWICK

PATTERNS

CHARLTON BOWMAN
NB-1   B-15   One cent 1861, bronze; proof; dies ↑↑; wt. 5.64g; dia. 25.4mm ; obverse - large bust design by James Wyon as on NS-6, etc. reverse - adopted design. (National Currency Collection)

NB-2   B-20   Ten cents 1862, silver; reeded edge; proof; dies ↑↑; wt. 2.34g; dia. 18.0mm; obverse - adopted design; reverse - legend and date surrounded by arabesque design somewhat similar to that used for Newfoundland. The arabesque reverse on this piece was also used for a pattern 10-cent piece for Hong Kong. (National Currency Collection)

TRIAL PIECES

NB-3   One cent 1862, bronze; proof. As adopted design, except for the date. Struck to make the date uniform for the 1862 proof sets.

OFFICIAL FABRICATIONS

NB-4   B-23   Twenty cents 1862, silver.;plain edge; proof; dies ↑↑; wt. 5.6g; dia. 22.0 mm; obverse - plain, except for the legend "G.W. WYON/OBIT/MARCH 27TH 1862/AETAT/26YEARS." Reverse - adopted design. This is an obituary medalet for George W. Wyon, who was resident engraver at the Royal Mint. The fact that this reverse was chosen for the piece suggests that it was engraved by George Wyon. (National Currency Collection)

OFFICIAL FABRICATIONS

The following six pieces (NB-5 to NB-10) obviously have nothing to do with contemplated designs for New Brunswick, since they bear dates after Confederation. It is believed they were struck for exhibition purposes where only the type was considered important.

CHARLTON	BOWMAN	
NB-5	B-18	Five cents 1870, silver; plain edge; proof; dies ↑↑; wt. 1.7g; dia. 15.5 mm; obverse - adopted design; reverse - adopted design for the Dominion of Canada (wire rim variety). (National Currency Collection)

NB-6	B-21	Ten cents 1870, silver; reeded edge; proof; dies ↑↑; wt. 2.3g; dia. 18.03 mm; plain edge; proof; dies ↑↑, wt. 2.32g; dia. 18.03 mm; obverse - adopted design; reverse - adopted design for the Dominion of Canada and New Brunswick. (National Currency Collection, reeded edge; Norweb Collection, plain edge)
NB-7	B-22	Ten cents 1871, silver; reeded edge; proof; dies ↑↑; wt. 2.32g; dia. 18.03 mm; plain edge; wt. 2.3g; dia. 18.03 mm. As NB-6, except for the date. (National Currency Collection)

NB-8	B-24	Twenty cents 1871, silver; reeded edge; proof; dies ↑↑; wt. 5.90g; dia. 22.5mm; plain edge; proof; wt. 4.7g; dia. 23.27 mm. As the adopted design, except for the date. (National Currency Collection)

NB-9	B-19	Five cents 1875, silver; reeded edge; proof; dies ↑↑, wt. 1.16g; dia. 15.5; obverse - adopted design; reverse - adopted design for the Dominion of Canada. (National Currency Collection)
NB-10		Five cents 1875H, silver; reeded edge; proof; dies ↑↑. As NB9, except for the "H" mint mark.

PROVINCE OF NEWFOUNDLAND

PATTERNS

The following five patterns (NF-1 to NF-5) are the result of a directive given by the master of the Royal Mint, Thomas Graham, in which he stated that the designs for the reverses of the Newfoundland coins should be those of New Brunswick. This was later altered.

CHARLTON	BOWMAN	
NF-1		One cent 1864; reverse - similar to the design adopted for the New Brunswick cent. Presently unknown as a struck piece, but may exist.
NF-2	B-28	Five cents 1864, bronze; plain edge; proof; dies ↑↓; wt. 1.40g; dia. 15.5 mm; obverse - adopted design; reverse - crown and wreath design adopted for New Brunswick. (W.W.C. Wilson Sale 1925)
NF-3	B-29	Ten cents 1864, bronze; plain edge; proof; obverse - adopted design; reverse - crown and wreath design adopted for New Brunswick. (British Museum)

NF-4	B-32	Twenty cents 1864, bronze; indented corded edge; proof; dies ↑↓; wt. 6.2g; dia. 22.95 mm; obverse - adopted design; reverse - crown and wreath design adopted for New Brunswick. (National Currency Collection)

NF-5	B-31	Two dollars 1864, bronze; plain edge; proof; dies ↑↓; wt. 2.4g; dia. 17.1 mm; obverse - adopted design; reverse - crown and wreath for New Brunswick. 10 cents with the legend "TWO/DOLLARS/1864" in the centre. (National Currency Collection)

PATTERNS

CHARLTON   BOWMAN
NF-6   B-25   One cent, bronze; not a proof; dies ↑↑; wt. 5.69 grams; dia. 25.4 mm; obverse - similar to adopted design, except the legend reads "VICTORIA QUEEN." Reverse - similar to adopted design, except one leaf is missing from the top of each side of the wreath. (National Currency Collection)

NF-7   B-27   One cent 1865, bronze; proof; dies ↑↓; wt. 5.45 grams; dia. 25.4 mm; obverse - adopted design for Nova Scotia and New Brunswick. Reverse - pattern design as for NF-6, except for the date. (National Currency Collection)

NF-8   Five cents 1865, silver; plain edge; proof; dies ↑↓; wt. 0.9 grams; dia. 15.5 mm; obverse - adopted design; reverse - similar to the adopted design, except the arches are thinner. (National Currency Collection)

NF-9   Ten cents 1865, silver; plain edge; proof; dies ↑↓; obverse - adopted design; reverse - similar to the adopted design, except the arches are much thinner. (National Currency Collection)

PATTERNS

CHARLTON   BOWMAN
NF-10   Twenty cents 1865, silver; plain edge; proof; dies ↑↓; wt. 4.6 grams; dia. 23.19mm;
obverse - adopted design; reverse - similar to the adopted design, except the arches are
much thinner. (National Currency Collection)

NF-11   Five cents 1865, silver; plain edge; proof; dies ↑↓; wt. 1.10 grams; dia. 15.5mm; obverse
- adopted design; reverse - as the adopted design, except the arches and dots have raised
edges. (National Currency Collection)

NF-12   Ten cents 1865, silver; plain edge; proof; dies ↑↓; wt. 2.3 grams; dia. 18.03 mm; obverse
- adopted design; reverse - as the adopted design, except the arches and dots have raised
edges. (National Currency Collection)

NF-13   Twenty cents 1865, silver; plain edge; proof; dies ↑↓; wt. 4.5 grams; dia. 23.19 mm;
obverse - adopted design; reverse - similar to the adopted design, except for some details
of the arches and the presence of a raised line just inside the rim denticles. (National
Currency Collection)

CHARLTON BOWMAN
NF-14   B-33   Two dollars 1865, gold; plain edge; proof; dies ↑↑; wt. 3.3 grams; dia. 17.6 mm;
                      obverse - adopted design; reverse - similar to the adopted design, except the legend
                      and date are in block type. (National Currency Collection)

NF-15   B-34   Two dollars 1865, gold; plain edge; proof; dies ↑↓; wt. 3.36 grams; dia. 17.98 mm;
                      obverse - small bust of Victoria (from the 5 cents) in beaded circle with the legend
                      "VICTORIA D:G REG:/NEWFOUNDLAND." Reverse - pattern design as on NF-14.

NF-16   B-35   Fifty cents 1870, bronze; plain edge; proof; dies ↑↑; wt. 9.4 grams; dia. 29.6 mm;
                      obverse - adopted design; reverse - as the adopted design, except the denticles are
                      longer and touch the device. (National Currency Collection)

NF-17   Two dollars 1870, gold; plain edge; proof; obverse - pattern designs as on NF-15;
                      reverse - adopted design.

TRIAL PIECES

CHARLTON	BOWMAN	
NF-18	B-26	One cent 1864, bronze; proof; dies ↑↑; wt. 5.6 grams; dia. 25.4 mm. As the adopted design, except for the date. This is the piece that is believed to have been included in the specimen sets of 1864-1865. Proofs of the adopted design of the cent dated 1865 seem not to have been produced. (National Currency Collection)

NF-19		Fifty cents 1882, silver; reeded edge; proof. As the adopted design, except for the absence of the "H" mint mark. (British Museum)
NF-20		Ten cents 1945 C, nickel. Struck on a thin blank; not a proof. This piece is rather weakly struck because of the thinness of the blank, suggesting that it is nothing more than a mint error. (National Currency Collection)
NF-21		Twenty cents 1865, bronze; plain edge; proof; dies ↑↑; wt. 5.16g, dia. 23.1 mm as adopted design. (Norweb Collection)

PROVINCE OF BRITISH COLUMBIA

PATTERNS

CHARLTON	BOWMAN	
BC-1	B-37	Ten dollars 1862, silver; dies ↑↓; wt. 11.2g; dia. 27.0mm; obverse - crown and legend; reverse - wreath, denomination and date. (National Currency Collection)
BC-1a	B-37	Ten dollars 1862, silver; reeded edge; dies ↑↑. Design as above. (Brand Sale 1983)

BC-2	B-36	Twenty dollars 1862, silver; dies ↑↓; obverse - crown and legend; reverse - wreath, denomination and date. (Brand Sale 1983).
BC-2a	B-36	Twenty dollars 1862, silver; reeded edge; dies ↑↑; wt. 23.6g; dia. 34.0mm. Design as above. (National Currency Collection)
BC-3	B-37	Ten dollars 1862, gold. Design as BC-1. (B.C. Provincial Archives)
BC-4	B-36	Twenty dollars 1862, gold. Design as BC-2. (B.C. Provincial Archives)

PROVINCE OF CANADA

PATTERNS

CHARLTON BOWMAN
PC-1   B-4   One cent 1858, bronze; not a proof; wt. 5.7g; dia. 23.7mm; uniface - obverse blank; reverse - wreath of maple leaves and seed pods with beaded circle containing "ONE/ CENT/1858." (National Currency Collection)

PC-2   B-4   One cent 1858, bronze; proof; wt. 4.0 - 5.4g; dia. 23.7mm; uniface - obverse blank; reverse - similar to PC-1 except the date is more closely spaced and the device is farther from the inner beaded circle. (National Currency Collection)

PC-3   B-3   One cent 1858, bronze; proof; dies ↑↓; wt. 3.88g; dia. 23.7mm; obverse - adopted legend with diademed bust of Victoria. Reverse - pattern design as on PC-2. (Wayte Raymond Sale 1928)

PC-4   B-6   Twenty cents 1858, silver; plain edge; proof; dies ↑↑; wt. 4.50g; dia. 23.7mm; dies ↑↓; wt. 4.03g; dia. 23.27mm; obverse - adopted design; reverse - adopted design for New Brunswick. (National Currency Collection)

PATTERNS

CHARLTON	BOWMAN	
PC-5	B-5	One cent 1859 (in Roman numerals), bronze; proof; obverse - adopted design; reverse - Britannia reverse for a pattern British halfpenny. (Parsons Collection 1936. The Norweb Collection contains an example struck in copper-nickel; wt. 5.63g; dia. 25.4mm.)

TRIAL PIECES

PC-6	One cent 1858, cupro-nickel; dies ↑↑; wt. 9.11g; dia. 25.4mm. Adopted design; struck from proof dies on an unpolished blank of double thickness. (National Currency Collection)
PC-7	One cent 1858, cupro-nickel; proof; dies ↑↑; wt. 4.42g; dia. 25.4mm. Adopted design; normal thickness. (National Currency Collection)

DOMINION OF CANADA

PATTERNS

CHARLTON   BOWMAN
DC-1   B-38   One cent 1876H, bronze; proof; dies ↑↑; dia. 25.45mm; obverse - adopted laureated head design for the Province of Canada. Reverse - adopted design. The existence of this pattern suggests that the government of the Dominion of Canada initially considered using the Province of Canada laureated obverse for its new cent. (National Currency Collection)

DC-2   Ten cents (no date), bronze; reeded edge; proof; wt. 2.1g; dia. 17.85mm; obverse - adopted design (Haxby Obv. 6); reverse - plain, except for a "B" engraved on the piece after it was struck. Probably unique. (National Currency Collection)

DC-3   Fifty cents 1870, bronze; plain edge; proof; dies ↑↑; wt. 9.2g; dia. 29.72mm; obverse - no "L.C.W." on the truncation, but otherwise very similar to Haxby Obv. 2. Reverse - slight differences in some leaves compared to the adopted design. (National Currency Collection)

DC-4   As DC-3, but silver. Dies ↑↓; wt. 11.2g; dia. 29.72mm.

PATTERNS

CHARLTON   BOWMAN
DC-5

One cent 1911, bronze; dies ↑↑; wt. 5.6g; dia. 25.4mm; specimen. As the adopted design for 1912-1920, except for the date; i.e. the obverse legend has "DEI GRA:." (Royal Mint Collection)

DC-6   B-40

One dollar 1911, silver; reeded edge; specimen; dies ↑↑; obverse - the standard MacKennal design later adopted for the 1936 dollar. Reverse - crown, wreath, legend and date.

In the Dominion of Canada Currency Act of 1910, which received royal assent on May 4, 1910, provision was made for the striking of a Canadian silver dollar. The schedule appended to the act specified a coin of 360 grains weight and a standard fineness of .925 silver. The Dominion Government, having decided to add a silver dollar to the coinage, purchased a new coining-press from Taylor and Challen of Birmingham, England, for the express purpose of striking coins of this size. A pair of dies for the new coin was prepared by the Die and Medal Department of the Royal Mint, London, and at least two specimens were struck. When cases were prepared for the specimen sets of the first Canadian coinage of George V, a space was left for the dollar. Later, however, the Dominion authorities decided against the issue of a silver dollar at that time, although no reason was given for this decision.

Only two specimens of the 1911 silver dollar are known to exist; one is in the National Currency Collection and the other was sold privately in 1979 for $160,000. U.S.

PATTERNS

CHARLTON   BOWMAN

DC-6a   One dollar 1911, lead. As DC-6, except for the metal. Probably unique. This piece was
               only recently discovered by the numismatic world, having been in storage in Ottawa since
               1911. It is believed to be a sample piece struck at the Ottawa mint to be used for gaining
               approval to proceed with the production of coins for circulation. (National Currency
               Collection)

DC-7   B-41   Five dollars 1911, gold; reeded edge specimen; dies ↑↑; dia. 21.6mm. As the adopted
                 design for 1912-1914, except for the date. (Royal Mint Collection)

DC-8   B-42   Ten dollars, 1911, gold; reeded edge specimen; dies ↑↑; dia. 26.9mm. As the adopted
                 design for 1912-1914, except for the date. (Royal Mint Collection)

   In 1926 Dominion notes (the treasury notes issued by the government of the Dominion of Canada) were made
redeemable in gold for the first time since 1914. Since the time of the production of the gold $5 and $10 of 1912-1914,
it had been concluded that the coat-of-arms borne on their reverses was incorrect. Therefore, new reverses were
engraved in the event that a gold coinage would again have to be struck. Bronze patterns were produced to have
samples of the designs. A few of these, probably made for the designer, G.E. Kruger-Gray, have the obverse design
machined off, "SPECIMEN" punched in instead, and the entire piece acid-etched.

PATTERNS

CHARLTON BOWMAN
DC-9

Five dollars 1928, bronze; reeded edge; dies ↑↑; wt. 4.2g; dia. 21.6mm; obverse - as the adopted design for the 1912-1914 issues. Reverse - modified Canadian arms by G.E. Kruger-Gray. (National Currency Collection)

DC-10

Ten dollars 1928, bronze; reeded edge; dies ↑↑; wt. 8.49g; dia. 26.92mm; obverse - as the adopted design for the 1912-1914 issues. Reverse - modified Canadian arms by G.E. Kruger-Gray. (National Currency Collection)

DC-11

Five dollars 1928, bronze; reeded edge; wt. 3.7g; dia. 21.6mm; obverse - planed off flat just inside the denticles after striking; "SPECIMEN" has been punched in by hand. Reverse - pattern design as on DC-9. The entire piece has been acid-etched (officially) giving it a light brown colour. (National Currency Collection)

DC-12

Ten dollars 1928, bronze; reeded edge; wt. 7.2g; dia. 26.92mm; obverse - planed off flat just inside denticles after striking; "SPECIMEN" has been punched in by hand. Reverse - pattern design as on DC-10. The entire piece has been etched as for DC-11. (National Currency Collection)

TRIAL PIECES

CHARLTON   BOWMAN

DC-13   One dollar 1964, tin; plain edge, struck on a thick planchet; not a proof; wt. 26.9g; dia. 35.5mm; obverse - blank, except for small symbol ·┌· Reverse - similar to the adopted design, except for being higher in relief and having thin rounded rim denticles instead of wide square ones. Unique. This unusual piece is a matrix trial. (National Currency Collection)

DC-14   One dollar 1967, silver; reeded edge; not a specimen. Similar to the adopted design, except the fields on both sides are flat instead of concave and the rim beads differ slightly in size and position.

DC-15   Fifty cents (no date), white metal. Trial impression of portrait of Victoria only; as on Haxby Obv.2, 1870-1972. (National Currency Collection)

DC-16   Five cents 1875, silver; reeded edge; proof; dies ↑↓; wt. 1.20g; dia. 15.45mm. As the adopted design, except for the absence of the "H" mint mark. (National Currency Collection)

TRIAL PIECES

CHARLTON   BOWMAN
DC-17

One cent 1876H, cupro-nickel; proof; dies ↑↓; wt. 5.81g; dia. 25.4mm. As the adopted design. These pieces are believed to have been struck for exhibition purposes, without regard to the fact that there was no currency issue corresponding exactly to them. (American Numismatic Society)

DC-18

One cent 1876, bronze; proof; dies ↑↑; wt. 5.6g; dia. 25.4mm. As the adopted design, except for the absence of the "H" mint mark. (National Currency Collection)

The five brass pieces listed below (DC-19 to DC-23) were produced at the Paris mint. It is there that the original matrices for these denominations were engraved as the Royal Mint was too busy producing coins for Great Britain.

DC-19

One cent 1937, brass; specimen; dies ↑↓; wt. 3.1g; dia. 19.05mm. As the adopted design. Slightly thicker than normal. (National Currency Collection)

DC-20

Five cents 1937, brass; specimen; dies ↑↓; wt. 4.98g; dia. 21.5mm. As the adopted design. Slightly thicker than normal. (National Currency Collection)

TRIAL PIECES

CHARLTON   BOWMAN
DC-21   Ten cents 1937, brass; reeded edge; specimen; dies ↑↓; wt. 2.46g; dia. 18.03mm. As the adopted design. Slightly thicker than normal. (National Currency Collection)

DC-22   Twenty-five cents 1937, brass; reeded edge; specimen; dies ↑↓; wt. 6.1g; dia. 23.9mm. As the adopted design. Slightly thicker than normal. (National Currency Collection)

DC-23   Fifty cents 1937, brass; reeded edge; specimen; dies ↑↓; wt. 14.9g; dia. 30.0mm. As the adopted design. Thicker than normal. (National Currency Collection)

DC-24   Twenty-five cents 1937, bronze; reeded edge; dies ↑↑; wt. 5.5g; dia. 23.62mm. As the adopted design. Normal thickness. (National Currency Collection)

TRIAL PIECES

CHARLTON BOWMAN
DC-25

Five cents 1942, nickel; not a specimen; dies ↑↑; wt. 5.5g; dia. 23.62mm. As the 12-sided design adopted for the tombac pieces. (National Currency Collection)

DC-26

One cent 1943, copper-plated steel; not a specimen; dies ↑↑; wt. 3.0g; dia. 19.05mm. As the adopted design. (National Currency Collection)

DC-26a

One cent 1943, steel; not a specimen; dies ↑↑; wt 3.1g; dia. 19.05mm. As the adopted design. (National Currency Collection)

DC-27

Five cents 1943, steel; specimen. As the design adopted for the tombac pieces. (Piece seen, but composition not confirmed.)

DC-28

Five cents 1944, tombac. As the design adopted for the chrome-plated steel pieces. (Piece seen, but composition not confirmed.)

DC-29

Five cents 1951, chrome-plated steel; specimen; dies ↑↑; wt. 4.6g; dia. 21.3mm. As the commemorative design struck in nickel. (National Currency Collection)

TRIAL PIECES

CHARLTON   BOWMAN

DC-30 Five cents 1952, composition unknown; specimen; dies ↑↑; wt. 3.80g; dia. 21.3mm. As the adopted designs. (National Curency Collection)

DC-31 Fifty cents 1959, tin; uniface on thick, oversize blank; obverse - blank except for the engraved inscription (added after the piece was struck) "FIRST TRIAL/Oct 27th/1958." Reverse - as the adopted design, except lacks rim denticles. Unique. (National Currency Collection)

DC-32 One cent 1966, nickel; dies ↑↑; wt. 3.50g; dia. 19.05mm. As the adopted designs.

DC-33 Ten cents 1967, nickel; dies ↑↑; wt. 2.07g; dia. 18.03mm. As the adopted designs.

TRIAL PIECES

CHARLTON BOWMAN
DC-34

Twenty-five cents 1967, nickel; dies ↑↑; wt. 5.07g; dia. 23.62mm. As the adopted designs.

OFFICIAL FABRICATION

DC-50

Twenty cents 1871, silver; reeded edge; proof; dies ↑↓; wt. 4.62g; dia. 23.3mm; plain edge; proof; dies ↑↑; wt. 4.70g; dia. 23.3mm. As the adopted design for the Province of Canada, except for the date. This piece does not represent a proposed 20 cents for the Dominion of Canada. It is believed to have been struck for exhibition to show the Province of Canada 20 cents. Only the type was important; no concern was given to using a date corresponding to the coins actually issued for circulation. (National Currency Collection)

CANADIAN TEST TOKENS

On occasion the mint has produced special tokens for vending-machine testing or other purposes. These tokens are usually the diameter of standard Canadian coins, but they may or may not be of the same composition and other physical properties as the coins to which they correspond.

ONE CENT TEST TOKENS

ROUND COPPER TOKEN; THREE MAPLE LEAVES WITH BEADS; FULL WEIGHT; 1976.

Weight: 3.24grams
Diameter: 19.05 mm
Thickness: 1.42 mm
Edge: Plain
Die Axis: ↑↓

TT-1.1A   English/English legends

ROUND COPPER TOKEN; REDUCED SIZE AND WEIGHT; 1977. The Royal Canadian Mint issued a one-cent test token on December 15, 1977; however, because it was almost identical to those used by the Toronto Transit Commission, it was withdrawn.

Weight: 1.87 grams
Diameter: 16.0 mm
Thickness: 1.35 mm
Edge: Plain
Die Axis: ↑↑

TT-1.2   Obverse and reverse design only

Cat. No.	Date	Description	Price Range
TT-1.1A	1976	Round copper, full weight	100.00-150.00
TT-1.2	1977	Round copper, reduced weight	100.00-150.00

ROUND COPPER TOKEN; THREE MAPLE LEAVES WITH BEADS; REDUCED WEIGHT; 1979. In August 1979 another test token was introduced. This time the weight of the copper planchet was reduced.

Weight: 2.80 grams
Diameter: 19.05 mm
Thickness: 1.38 mm
Edge: Plain
Die Axis: ↑→

TT-1.3A English/English legends "TEST TOKEN ROYAL CANADIAN MINT"

Weight: 2.80 grams
Diameter: 19.05 mm
Thickness: 1.38 mm
Edge: Plain
Die Axis: ↑↑

TT-1.3B French/French legends "EPREUVE MONNAIE ROYALE CANADIENNE"

Weight: 2.80 grams
Diameter: 19.05 mm
Thickness: 1.38 mm
Edge: Plain
Die Axis: ↑↑

TT-1.3C English/French legends "TEST TOKEN ROYAL CANADIAN MINT/
EPREUVE MONNAIE ROYALE CANADIENNE"

Cat. No.	Date	Description	Price Range
TT -1.3A	1979	Beads, English/English	200.00-250.00
TT -1.3B	1979	Beads, French/French	200.00-250.00
TT-1.3C	1979	Beads, English/French	40.00-60.00

CANADIAN TEST TOKENS

ROUND COPPER TOKEN; THREE MAPLE LEAVES WITHOUT BEADS; 1979.

Photograph
Not
Available

Weight: 2.50 grams
Diameter: 19.05 mm
Thickness: 1.38 mm
Edge: Plain
Die Axis: ↑↑

TT-1.4A English/English legends "TEST TOKEN ROYAL CANADIAN MINT"

Weight: 2.50 grams
Diameter: 19.05 mm
Thickness: 1.38 mm
Edge: Plain
Die Axis: ↑↑

TT-1.4B French/French legends "EPREUVE/MONNAIE ROYALE CANADIENNE"

Photograph
Not
Available

Weight: 2.50 grams
Diameter: 19.05 mm
Thickness: 1.38 mm
Edge: Plain
Die Axis: ↑↑

TT-1.4C English/French legends "TEST TOKEN ROYAL CANADIAN MINT/
EPREUVE MONNAIE ROYALE CANADIENNE"

Cat. No.	Date	Description	Price Range
TT-1.4A	1979	Without beads, English/English	Rare
TT-1.4B	1979	Without beads, French/French	200.00-250.00
TT-1.4C	1979	Without beads, English/French	Rare

ROUND COPPER-ZINC TOKEN; 1979.

Weight: 2.70 grams
Diameter: 19.20 mm
Thickness: 1.30 mm
Edge: Plain
Die Axis: ↑↑

TT-1.5A English/English legends "TEST TOKEN ROYAL CANADIAN MINT"

Cat. No.	Date	Description	Price Range
TT-1.5A	1979	English/English	200.00-250.00

12-SIDED COPPER TOKEN; THREE MAPLE LEAVES - SQUARE CORNERS; 1981.

The 12-sided Mark I test token was issued on July 12, 1981, but due to its sharp corners it was replaced by the Mark II test token with rounded corners. This token was accepted, and the new one-cent coin went into production in spring 1982.

Weight: 2.60 grams
Diameter:
    Across corners: 18.95 mm
    Across flat: 18.40 mm
Thickness: 1.50 mm
Edge: Plain
Die Axis: ↑↑

TT-1.6A English/English legends "TEST TOKEN ROYAL CANADIAN MINT"

Technical specifications are the same as TT-1.6A

TT-1.6B French/French legends "EPREUVE/MONNAIE ROYALE CANADIENNE"

Technical specifications are the same as TT-1.6A

TT-1.6C English/French legends "TEST TOKEN ROYAL CANADIAN MINT/
                       EPREUVE MONNAIE ROYALE CANADIENNE

12-SIDED COPPER TOKEN; THREE MAPLE LEAVES -ROUND CORNERS, 1981.

Weight: 2.50 grams
Diameter:
    Across corners: 19.10 mm
    Across flat: 18.80 mm
Thickness: 1.45 mm
Edge: Plain
Die Axis: ↑↑

TT-1.7C English/French legends "TEST TOKEN ROYAL CANADIAN MINT/
                       EPREUVE MONNAIE ROYALE CANADIENNE

Cat. No.	Date	Description	Price Range
TT-1.6A	1981	Square Corners, English/English	200.00-250.00
TT-1.6B	1981	Square Corners, French/French	200.00-250.00
TT-1.6C	1981	Square Corners, English/French	100.00-150.00
TT-1.7A	1981	Round Corners, English/English	200.00-250.00
TT-1.7B	1981	Round Corners, French/French	200.00-250.00
TT-1.7C	1981	Round Corners, English/French	100.00-150.00

FIVE CENT TEST TOKENS

ROUND NICKEL TOKEN; THREE MAPLE LEAVES WITH BEADS; 1976.

Weight: 4.30 grams
Diameter: 21.9 mm
Thickness: 1.71 mm
Edge: Plain
Die Axis: ↑↑

TT-5.1A English/English legends "TEST TOKEN - ROYAL CANADIAN MINT"

Technical specifications are the
same as TT-5.1A

TT-5.1B French/French legends "EPREUVE MONNAIE ROYALE CANADIENNE"

Technical specifications are the
same as TT-5.1A

TT-5.1C English/French legends "TEST TOKEN - ROYAL CANADIAN MINT/
EPREUVE MONNAIE ROYALE CANADIENNE"

Cat. No.	Date	Description	Price Range
TT-5.1A	1976	Beads, English/English	100.00 -150.00
TT-5.1B	1976	Beads, French/French	100.00-150.00
TT-5.1C	1976	Beads, English/French	100.00-150.00

TEN CENT TEST TOKENS

ROUND NICKEL TOKEN; BOUQUET OF FLOWERS AND FLEUR-DE-LIS; 1965.

Weight: 2.09 grams
Diameter: 17.8 mm
Thickness: 1.2 mm
Edge: Reeded
Die Axis: ↑↑

TT-10.1A Legend "R.C.M. TEN TOKENS 1965"

Technical specifications are the same as TT-10.1A

TT-10.1B Legend "TEN TOKENS 1965"

ROUND NICKEL TOKEN; THREE MAPLE LEAVES; 1976.

Weight: 1.75 grams
Diameter: 17.95 mm
Thickness: 1.2 mm
Edge: Reeded
Die Axis: ↑↑

TT-10.2 Legend "TEST TOKEN/ROYAL CANADIAN MINT/EPREUVE/MONNAIE ROYAL CANADIENNE"TWENTY FIVE TOKENS/1965/CANADA"

Cat. No.	Date	Description	Price Range
TT-10.1A	1965	With RCM	50.00-75.00
TT-10.1B	1965	Without RCM	50.00-75.00
TT-10.2	1976	Round, copper	100.00 - 150.00

TWENTY-FIVE CENT TEST TOKENS

ROUND NICKEL TOKEN; THREE CANADA GEESE; 1965. Struck to provide an example of the quality of coins produced by the Royal Canadian Mint and to provide a piece for adjusting vending machines for nickel coins.

Weight: 5.01 grams
Diameter: 23.7 mm
Thickness: 1.6 mm
Edge: Reeded
Die Axis: ↑↑

TT-25.1A Legend "TWENTY FIVE TOKENS/1965/R.C.M"

Technical specifications are the same as TT-25.1A

TT-25.1B Legend " "TWENTY FIVE TOKENS/1965"

ROUND CUPRO-NICKEL TOKEN; CONJOINED BUSTS OF KING GEORGE VI AND QUEEN ELIZABETH/THREE CANADA GEESE; 1965.

Weight:: N/A
Diameter: N/A
Thickness: N/A
Edge: Reeded
Die Axis: ↑↑

TT-25.2A Legend " TWENTY FIVE TOKENS/1965/CANADA"

Weight::
Diameter:
Thickness:
Edge: Reeded
Die Axis: ↑↓

TT-25.2B Legend " TWENTY FIVE TOKENS/1965/CANADA"

Cat. No.	Date	Description	Price Range
TT-25.1A	1965	With RCM	75.00-100.00
TT-25.1B	1965	Without RCM	75.00-100.00
TT-25.2A	1965	Royal Visit Obverse ↑↑	200.00 - 250.00
TT-25.2B	1965	Royal Visit Obverse ↑↓	200.00 - 250.00

FIFTY CENT TEST TOKENS

ROUND BRONZE TOKEN; 1907. Struck to adjust the coining presses prior to the first production of Canadian coins at the new Ottawa branch of the Royal Mint.

Weight: N/A
Diameter: 30.6 mm
Thickness: 2.0 mm
Edge: Reeded
Die Axis: ↑↑

TT-50.1 Legend "OTTAWA MINT/TRIAL RUN/NOVEMBER/1907"

ROUND NICKEL TOKEN; STANDING RAM; 1965. Struck to provide an example of the quality of coins produced at the Royal Canadian Mint.

Weight: N/A
Diameter: N/A
Thickness: N/A
Edge: Reeded
Die Axis: ↑↑

TT-50.2 Legend "50 TOKENS/R.C. MINT/1965"

ROUND BRASS TOKEN; STANDING RAM; 1965.

Weight: N/A
Diameter: N/A
Thickness: N/A
Edge: Reeded
Die Axis: ↑↑

Cat. No.	Date	Description	Price Range
TT-50.1	1907	Round, bronze	1500.00-2000.00
TT-50.2	1965	Round, nickel	500.00-800.00
TT-50.3	1965	Round, brass	500.00-800.00

ONE DOLLAR TEST TOKENS

ROUND NICKEL BONDED STEEL TOKEN; THREE MAPLE LEAVES; 1983.

Weight: 13.0 grams
Diameter: 32.8 mm
Thickness: 2.3 mm
Edge: Plain
Die Axis: ↑↑

TT-100.1 Legend "TEST/ROYAL CANADIAN MINT/N.B.S./EPREUVE/MONNAIE
ROYALE CANADIENNE/N.B.S."

11-SIDED TOKEN (COMPOSITION UNKNOWN); THREE MAPLE LEAVES; 1984.

Weight: 7.0 grams
Diameter: 26.5 mm
Thickness: 1.43 mm
Edge: Plain
Die Axis: ↑↓

TT-100.2 Legend "TEST/ROYAL CANADIAN MINT; EPREUVE/MONNAIE ROYALE
CANADIENNE"

11-SIDED GOLD PLATED ON NICKEL TOKEN; THREE MAPLE LEAVES; 1985. This is
the blank International Nickel submitted to the Royal Canadian Mint upon tendering for the
"Loon" contract.

Weight: 7.09 grams
Diameter: 26.5 mm
Thickness: 1.80 mm
Edge: Plain
Die Axis: ↑↑

TT-100.3 Legend "TEST ROYAL CANADIAN MINT/EPREUVE/MONNAIE ROYALE
CANADIENNE"

11-SIDED BRONZE PLATED ON NICKEL TOKEN; THREE MAPLE LEAVES; 1985. The Sherritt Gordon blank was chosen to produce the 1987 "Loon" dollar.

Weight: 7.09 grams
Diameter: 26.5 mm
Thickness: 1.80 mm
Edge: Plain
Die Axis: ↑↑

TT-100.4 Legend "TEST ROYAL CANADIAN MINT/EPREUVE/MONNAIE ROYALE CANADIENNE"

Cat. No.	Date	Description	Price Range
TT-100.1	1984	Nickel bonded steel	300.00 - 350.00
TT-100.2	1984	Unknown composition, wide rims	100.00 - 150.00
TT-100.3	1985	Gold plated on nickel, narrow rims	100.00 - 150.00
TT-100.4	1985	Nickel brass, narrow rims	100.00 - 150.00

Note: There is no known visual method of distinguishing TT-100.3 and TT-100.4 from each other.

TWO DOLLAR TEST TOKEN

During the conversion period from the two dollar bank note to the two dollar coin, between 1994 and 1995, the Royal Canadian Mint tested many different sizes, shapes and compositions of two dollar blanks. Table One contains a listing of bi-metal planchets, while Table Two lists tri-metal planchets. These test tokens are not priced due to the lack of market activity.

SINGLE METAL TWO DOLLAR TEST TOKENS

Cat.No.	Description	Diameter	Weight	Edge	Composition
TT-200.1	12-sided	22.5mm	4 gms	Scalloped smooth	Copper-zinc
TT-200.2	6-sided	22.5mm	4gms	Scalloped smooth	Copper-zinc
TT-200.3	12-sided	22.5mm	4gms	Scalloped smooth	Stainless steel
TT-200.4	6-sided	22.5mm	4gms	Scalloped smooth	Copper-nickel
TT-200.5	Round	22.5mm	7.5gms	Reeded	Copper-zinc
TT-200.6	Round	22.5mm	10gms	Reeded	Copper-zinc
TT-200.7	7-sided	22.5mm	5.8gms	Plain	Copper-zinc

TT-200.11 English/English legends

BI-METALLIC TWO DOLLAR TEST TOKENS

Cat.No.	Description	Diameter	Weight	Edge	Composition
TT-200.8	Round	22.5mm	5grms	Interrupted reeded	Aluminum-bronze ring Nickel centre
TT-200.9	Round	25.25mm	6.2gms	Interrupted reeded	Nickel ring Copper-tin-zinc Centre
TT-200.10	Round	25.25mm	6.2gms	Interrupted reeded	Nickel ring Aluminum-bronze centre
TT-200.11	Round	27.1mm	7.7gms	Plain	Ring Unknown centre
TT-200.12	7-sided	28mm	7.7gms	Smooth	Copper-nickel ring Aluminum-bronze centre
TT-200.13	8-sided	28mm	8.5gms	Smooth	Copper-nickel ring Aluminum-bronze centre
TT-200.14	9-sided	28mm	8.5gms	Smooth	Copper-nickel ring Aluminum-bronze centre

TRI-METALLIC TWO DOLLAR TEST TOKENS

Cat. No.	Description	Diameter	Weight	Edge	Composition
TT-200.14	11-sided	29mm	9.6gms		Aluminum-bronze outer ring Aluminum-bronze centre Copper-nickel inner ring
TT-200.15	11-sided	29mm	9.6gms		Copper-nickel outer ring Copper-nickel centre Aluminum-bronze inner ring

ROUND BI-METALLIC TOKEN; THREE MAPLE LEAVES; 1996. Bi-metallic test tokens were made available to the public for the first time in 1996.

Weight: 7.30 grams
Diameter: 28 mm
Thickness: 1.7 mm
Edge: Interrupted serration
Die Axis: ↑↑

TT-200.16 Legend "TEST TOKEN/ROYAL CANADIAN MINT/"EPREUVE/MONNAIE ROYALE CANADIENNE"

Cat.No.	Date	Description	Price Range
TT-200.16	1996	Round bi-metallic	100.00 - 125.00

TEST TOKEN SETS

TTS-1 1984: 4 COIN SET

Cat.No.	Date	Description	Price Range
TTS-1	1973	Round one cent	
	1984	12-sided one cent	
	1984	Round dollar	
		11-sided test token	200.00 - 300.00

TTS-2 1986: 3 COIN SET

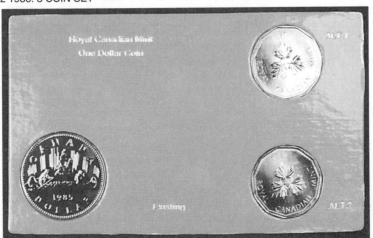

Cat.No.	Date	Description	Price Range
TTS-2	1985	Round dollar	
		Gold plated on nickel test token	
		Bronze plated on nickel test token	200.00 - 300.00

COLLECTOR COINS

INTRODUCTION

From the 19th century onward, mints have often struck small quantities of special coins for collectors in addition to those produced for general circulation. In the Canadian context these collector coins have been of several different qualities and finishes, depending upon the particular period and the mint that produced them. Three terms can be correctly applied to Canadian collectors coins, and it is important for the reader to understand them.

PROOF: The highest quality of collector coins, generally with frosted relief and highly polished mirror fields. The Olympic Proof coins were the first Canadian Proofs produced in this century. The only other 20th century Canadian Proof coins have been the $100 gold pieces and the proof sets of circulating coins which were introduced in 1981.

SPECIMEN: A general term applying to any specially produced collectors coin. Most often it is used in connection with the best quality Canadian collector coins struck between 1858 and 1972. Specimen coins are usually double struck, with very sharp details and square edges, but are not of the same superlative quality as Proofs. Before 1973, the Royal Canadian Mint did not have the equipment sufficient to strike Proof coins.

PROOF-LIKE: A term originated in 1953 by J.E. Charlton to describe special silver dollars and sets that were obviously superior to circulation strikes, but whose surfaces were not as bright as those of other collector coins (Specimens) being struck at that time. It was commonly assumed that Proof-like coins were simply circulation strikes that had been carefully handled to avoid abrasions. This is not the case; these coins are struck using selected dies and blanks and on slower moving presses than for circulation coins. Because of their superior finish, the Proof-like coins are sometimes mistakenly classed as Specimens or Proofs. It should be noted that Proof-like coins are not as sharply struck, and the higher denominations often have a slight roughness at the queen's shoulder as a result. Proofs and Specimens are usually double struck under much greater pressure which results in a flawless surface, sharp wire edge and better detail.

IMPORTANT PRICING NOTE: Proof, Specimen and Proof-like coins were manufactured under special conditions so as to ensure the highest quality product available from the Mint. Unlike ordinary production or business strike coins which are expected to have slight marks, these special coins were intended to be mark free. We have, therefore, shown prices for these coins only in MS-65 condition. Coins or sets that meet the requirements of the MS-65 grade for special strike coins may show very slight hairlines but only detectable after considerable study of the coin. Generally special strike coins that show any visible marks, nicks, or busyness in terms of hairlines (from mishandling or cleaning attempts) will not meet the MS-65 grade and must be priced extremely lower. Those coins that are MS-67 and MS-70 will likely command higher prices from buyers interested in coins of this perfection.

TWENTY-FIVE CENT — NUMISMATIC COINAGE

125TH ANNIVERSARY OF CANADA; SILVER COINAGE; 1992: Issued by the Royal Canadian Mint, in silver, the twelve different designs represent a familiar scene from each of the twelve provinces and territories of Canada. This is the first issue of proof sterling silver twenty-five cent coins since 1919. For illustrations and more information on these issues see page 110 for the companion circulating issue.

Designers and Modellers: See pg. 110
Composition: .925 Silver, .075 Copper
Weight: 6.0 grams
Diameter: 23.88 mm
Thickness: 1.44 mm
Edge: Reeded
Die Axis: ↑↑
Original Issue Price: 25¢ - $9.95,
$1.00 - $19.95
Set - $129.45

Case: (A) Royal Blue Flocked Single Coin Case
(B) Royal Blue Flocked Case, 13 coins. Twelve 25¢ coins and one $1.00 coin.

Date	Description	Quantity Minted	PR65
1992	New Brunswick	Total mintage of all single struck	12.00
1992	Northwest Territories	Silver 25-cent pieces 65,182	12.00
1992	Newfoundland		12.00
1992	Manitoba		12.00
1992	Yukon		12.00
1992	Alberta		12.00
1992	Prince Edward Island		12.00
1992	Ontario		12.00
1992	Nova Scotia		12.00
1992	Quebec		12.00
1992	Saskatchewan		12.00
1992	British Columbia		12.00
1992	Set 13 Coins	84,397	130.00

125TH ANNIVERSARY OF CANADA; NICKEL COINAGE; 1992: Released October 7th, 1992, this collection is mounted in a brilliantly coloured map of Canada, with each different twenty-five cent coin placed in the province or territory commemorated by its design. The Canada Day dollar is the central point of a compass. Each twenty-five cent coin is nickel and specially struck in "Brilliant uncirculated" (proof-like).

Designers and Modellers: See pg. 110
Composition: 1.00 nickel
Weight: 6.0 grams
Diameter: 23.88 mm
Thickness: 1.44 mm
Edge: Reeded
Die Axis: ↑↑

Date	Description	Quantity Minted	Issue Price	PL65
1992	13 Coin Set with "Map" Holder	448,178	17.25	15.00

FIFTY CENT — NUMISMATIC COINAGE

DISCOVERING NATURE, BIRDS OF CANADA; SILVER COINAGE; 1995. Issued to commemorate the birds that are native to Canada. This is the first issue of fifty cent pieces in sterling silver since 1919.

Designers and Modellers:
Obverse: Dora de Pédery-Hunt
Ago Aarand
Reverses: Jean Luc Grondin
Atlantic Puffin: Sheldon Beveridge
Whooping Crane: Stan Whitten
Gray Jay: Sheldon Beveridge
White-tailed Ptarmigans:
Cosme Saffioti
Composition: .925 silver, .075 copper
Weight: 9.30 grams
Diameter: 27.13 mm
Thickness: N/A
Edge: Reeded
Die Axis: ↑↑

Coin No. 1
Atlantic Puffins

Coin No. 2
Whooping Crane

Coin No. 3
Gray Jays

Coin No. 4
White Tailed Ptarmigans

Cases of Issue: Illustrated booklet with protective sleeve.

Date	Description	Issue Price	PR-65
1995	Atlantic Puffin	—	20.00
1995	Whooping Crane, 2 coin set	29.95	20.00
1995	Gray Jay	—	20.00
1995	White-tailed Ptarmigans, 2 coin set	29.95	20.00
1995	As above, 4 coin set	56.95	60.00

DISCOVERING WILDLIFE, LITTLE WILD ONES; SILVER COINAGE, 1996. Issued to commemorate the young wildlife of Canada in their natural habitat..

Designers and Modellers:
Obverse: Dora de Pédery-Hunt,
Ago Aarand
Reverses:Dwayne Harty
Moose Calf: Ago Aarand
Wood Duck: Sheldon Beveridge
Cougar Kitten: Stan Whitten
Black Bear Cub: Sheldon Beveridge
Composition: .925 silver, .075 copper
Weight: 9.30 grams
Diameter: 27.13 mm
Thickness: N/A
Edge: Reeded
Die Axis: ↑↑

Coin No.1
Moose Calf

Coin No. 2
Wood Ducklings

Coin No. 3
Cougar Kittens

Coin No. 4
Black Bear Cubs

Cases of Issue: Illustrated booklet with protective sleeve.

Date	Description	Issue Price	PR-65
1996	Moose Calf	—	20.00
1996	Wood Duck, 2 coin set	29.95	20.00
1996	Cougar Kittens	—	20.00
1996	Black Bear, 2 coin set	29.95	20.00
1996	As above, 4 coin set	56.95	60.00

ONE DOLLAR — NUMISMATIC COINAGE

PROOF-LIKE SILVER DOLLARS 1954 - 1967

In 1954 the Royal Canadian Mint began a program of selling specially struck coins to collectors; one such coin was the silver dollar. These proof-like dollars were packaged in cellophane envelopes between the years 1954 and 1961, and from 1962 to 1964 in pliofilm envelopes. Because of the unofficial issues and the long standing popularity of this series we have continued the listings to 1967, the last year of the circulating silver dollar.

Date and Description	Issue Price	Mintage	PL-65
1954	1.25	5,300	175.00
1955 Normal Water Lines	1.25	7,950	135.00
1955 Arnprior	1.25	Incl. above	200.00
1956	1.25	10,212	80.00
1957	1.25	16,241	40.00
1958	1.25	33,237	35.00
1959	1.25	13,583	14.00
1960	1.25	18,631	12.00
1961	1.25	22,555	10.00
1962	1.25	47,591	10.00
1963	1.25	290,529	10.00
1964	1.25	1,209,279	10.00
1965 Variety 1	Issued only in sets	N/A	10.00
1965 Variety 2	Issued only in sets	N/A	10.00
1965 Variety 3	Unofficial issue	N/A	150.00
1965 Variety 4	Unofficial issue	N/A	150.00
1966 Small Beads Obverse	Unofficial issue	364	2,500.00
1966 Large Beads Obverse	Issued only in sets	N/A	10.00
1967	Issued only in sets	N/A	12.00

PROOF-LIKE NICKEL DOLLARS 1968 - 1969

Proof-like nickel dollars were issued for collectors in 1968 and 1969. They were packaged by the Royal Canadian Mint in pliofilm strips of five coins per strip. This method of packaging was discontinued in 1970.

Date and Description	Issue Price	Proof-like Nickel Dollars	
		Mintage	PL-65
1968 Voyageur	1.25	885,124	2.00
1969 Voyageur	1.25	211,112	2.00

COMMEMORATIVE DOLLARS 1968 TO DATE

The following pages list the silver, nickel and nickel bronze dollars issued by the numismatic department of the Royal Canadian Mint over the past years. The characteristics of these issues are itemized below.

COMMEMORATIVE DOLLAR SPECIFICATIONS

Specifications	Specimen Nickel Dollars 1968-1976 1982, 1984	Specimen Proof Silver Dollars 1971-1991	Proof Nickel/ Bronze Dollars 1987-date	Proof Silver Dollars 1992-date
Composition:	1.00 Nickel	.500 Silver .500 Copper	Nickel Plated with Bronze	.925 Silver .075 Copper
Weight (grams)	15.62	23.30	7.00	25.175
Diameter (mm)	32.13	36.07	26.50	36.07
Edge:	Reeded	Reeded	11-Side Plain	Reeded
Die axis:	↑↑	↑↑	↑↑	↑↑

VOYAGEUR NICKEL DOLLAR 1968 AND 1969: A cased 1968 and 1969 nickel dollar was available from the numismatic department of the Mint during 1968-69. The department did not aggressively market this product until 1970. Thus the years 1968 and 1969 saw the development of the "cased dollar" line with the evolution of a "clam" style case.

Obverse:	Designer:Arnold Machin
	Modeller: Patrick Brindley
Reverse:	Designer: Raymond Taylor
	Modeller: Walter Ott
Case:	Square, black leatherette with gold side trim. Gilt Royal Mint Building as crest. Blue inside with black insert and gilt Coat of Arms of Canada

Date	Description	Issue Price	Mintage	SP-65
1968	Nickel	N/A	N/A	3.00
1969	Nickel	N/A	N/A	3.00

MANITOBA CENTENNIAL NICKEL DOLLAR 1970. The year 1970 saw Canada's first commemorative nickel dollar, with a special reverse featuring a prairie crocus in recognition of the centenary of Manitoba's entry into Confederation.

Obverse: Designer: Arnold Machin   **Reverse:**   Designer: Raymond Taylor
             Modeller: Patrick Brindley   Modeller: Walter Ott

Case: (A) Square, black leatherette, gilt RCM crest, blue insert
         (B) Rectangular, maroon leatherette case, gold stamped crest of Canada, red inside with black insert
         (C) Rectangular, black leatherette case, gold stamped with the Japanese characters Maple Leaf, Canada. Red inside with black insert. Card insert. (Sold at the Canada pavillion in Japan, during 1970.)

Date	Description	Issue Price	Mintage	SP-65
1970	Nickel, Case A	2.00	349,120	3.00
1970	Nickel, Case B	N/A	Incl. above	5.00
1970	Nickel, Case C	N/A	Incl. above	5.00

BRITISH COLUMBIA CENTENNIAL NICKEL DOLLAR 1971. The nickel dollar for 1971 commemorates the entry in 1871 of British Columbia into Confederation. Its design is based on the arms of the province, with a shield at the bottom and dagwood blossoms at the top. The design of the specimen nickel dollar is identical to the circulating issue. See page No. 139.

Obverse:	Designer: Arnold Machin	**Reverse:**	Designer: Thomas Shingles
	Modeller: Patrick Brindley		Modeller: Thomas Shingles
Case:	Rectangular blue leatherette case, coat of arms of Canada stamped in silver, blue and black insert		

Date	Description	Issue Price	Mintage	SP-65
1971	Nickel	2.00	181,091	3.00

BRITISH COLUMBIA CENTENNIAL SILVER DOLLAR 1971. The first non-circulating silver dollar was issued to the public in 1971. It was a commemorative for the entry of British Columbia into Confederation in 1871. Its design is based upon the provincial arms. The obverse features a modification of the Machin portrait in which the portrait of the Queen was reduced slightly and her hair extensively redone.

Obverse:	Designer: Arnold Machin	**Reverse:**	Designer: Patrick Brindley
	Modeller: Patrick Brindley		Modeller: Patrick Brindley
Case:	(A) Rectangular black leatherette, coat of arms, maroon and black insert		
	(B) Rectangular black leatherette, coat of arms, white and black insert.		

Date	Description	Issue Price	Mintage	SP-65
1971	Silver	3.00	585,217	12.00

VOYAGEUR NICKEL DOLLAR 1972. The numismatic department of the Royal Canadian Mint issued a specimen nickel dollar of the same design as the circulating dollar.

Obverse:	Designer: Arnold Machin	**Reverse:**	Designer: E. Hahn
	Modeller: Patrick Brindley		Modeller: Terry Smith
Case:	Rectangular blue leatherette case, blue and black insert		

Date	Description	Issue Price	Mintage	SP-65
1972	Nickel	2.00	143,392	3.00

VOYAGEUR SILVER DOLLAR 1972. The reverse of the 1972 silver dollar is the voyageur design somewhat modified from its last use on the 1966 silver dollar. One of the most noticeable differences is the substitution of beads for denticles at the rim.

Designers and modellers are as for the nickel issue.
Case: Rectangular black leatherette case, maroon and black insert

Date	Description	Issue Price	Mintage	SP-65
1972	Silver	3.00	341,581	6.50

PRINCE EDWARD ISLAND CENTENNIAL NICKEL DOLLAR 1973. The 100th anniversary of the entry of Prince Edward Island into Confederation was commemorated with the reverse design depicting the provincial legislature building in Charlottetown.

Obverse: Designer: Arnold Machin **Reverse:** Designer: Terry Manning
Modeller: Patrick Brindley Modeller: Walter Ott
Case: Rectangular blue leatherette case, coat of arms, blue and black insert.

Date	Description	Issue Price	Mintage	SP-65
1973	Nickel	2.00	466,881	3.00

ROYAL CANADIAN MOUNTED POLICE CENTENNIAL SILVER DOLLAR 1973. In 1973 the reverse of the silver dollar recognized the founding of the North West Mounted Police which later became the Royal Canadian Mounted Police.

Obverse: Designer: Arnold Machin **Reverse:** Designer: Paul Cedarberg
Modeller: Patrick Brindley Modeller: Patrick Brindley
Case: (A) Rectangular black leatherette case, coat of arms, maroon and black insert
(B) Rectangular blue leatherette case, gilt RCMP crest, maroon and black insert.

Date	Description	Issue Price	Mintage	SP-65
1973	Silver, Case A	3.00	904,723	8.00
1973	Silver, Case B	3.00	Incl. Above	8.00

WINNIPEG CENTENNIAL NICKEL DOLLAR 1974. The 1974 cased specimen nickel dollar carried the same design as the circulating dollar. See page 141.

Obverse:	Designer: Arnold Machin	Reverse:	Designer: Paul Pederson
	Modeller: Patrick Brindley		Modeller: Patrick Brindley
Case:	Rectangular blue leatherette case, coat of arms, blue and black plastic insert.		

Date	Description	Issue Price	Mintage	SP-65
1974	Nickel	2.00	363,786	3.00

WINNIPEG CENTENNIAL SILVER DOLLAR 1974. The 100th anniversary of the establishment of Winnipeg, Manitoba, as a city was marked by the reverse of the 1974 silver dollar. The design is identical to that of the nickel dollar.

Obverse:	Designer: Arnold Machin	Reverse:	Designer: Paul Pederson
	Modeller: Patrick Brindley		Modeller: Patrick Brindley
Case:	Rectangular black leatherette case, coat of arms, maroon and black plastic insert.		

Date	Description	Issue Price	Mintage	SP-65
1974	Silver	3.50	628,183	8.00

VOYAGEUR NICKEL DOLLAR 1975. Issued by the numismatic department of the Royal Canadian Mint as a specimen quality example of the circulating nickel dollar.

Obverse:	Designer: Arnold Machin	Reverse:	Designer: E. Hahn
	Modeller: Patrick Brindley		Modeller: Terry Smith
Case:	Rectangular blue leatherette case, coat of arms, blue and black insert.		

Date	Description	Issue Price	Mintage	SP-65
1975	Nickel	2.50	88,102	3.00

CALGARY CENTENNIAL SILVER DOLLAR 1975. For the centenary of the founding of Calgary, Alberta, the silver dollar of 1975 bore a special reverse showing a cowboy atop a bucking bronco. Oil wells and the modern city skyline appear in the background.

Obverse:	Designer: Arnold Machin	Reverse:	Designer: D. D. Paterson
	Modeller: Patrick Brindley		Modeller: Patrick Brindley
Case:	Rectangular black leatherette case, coat of arms, maroon and black insert.		

Date	Description	Issue Price	Mintage	SP-65
1975	Silver	3.50	833,095	7.00

VOYAGEUR NICKEL DOLLAR 1976. Issued by the numismatic department of the Royal Canadian Mint in specimen quality. This was the last year of issue for a single voyageur nickel dollar.

Obverse:	Designer: Arnold Machin	Reverse:	Designer: E. Hahn
	Modeller: Patrick Brindley		Modeller: Terry Smith
Case:	Rectangular blue leatherette case, coat of arms, blue and black insert.		

Date	Description	Issue Price	Mintage	SP-65
1976	Nickel	2.50	74,209	3.00

LIBRARY OF PARLIAMENT CENTENNIAL SILVER DOLLAR 1976. The reverse of the 1976 silver dollar was employed to commemorate the 100th anniversary of the completion of the Library of Parliament. This attractive building was the only part of the original centre block of the Parliament Buildings that was saved during the disastrous fire of 1916. It is still in use and is a popular tourist attraction in Ottawa.

Obverse:	Designer: Arnold Machin	Reverse:	Designers: Walter Ott,
	Modeller: Patrick Brindley		Patrick Brindley
			Modeller: Walter Ott
Case:	(A) Rectangular black leatherette case, coat of arms, maroon and black insert.		
	(B) Rectangular blue leatherette case, coat of arms, light blue insert with purple satin cloth printed "Library of Parliament - Bibliotheque du Parlement 1876-1976."		

Date	Description	Issue Price	Mintage	SP-65
1976	Silver Case A	4.00	483,722	10.00
1976	Silver Case B	4.00	Incl above	10.00

QUEEN ELIZABETH II SILVER JUBILEE SILVER DOLLAR 1977. During 1977 the Queen celebrated the 25th anniversary of her accession to the throne. Many countries, including Canada, recognized the event with a special commemorative coin. The design on the reverse depicts the throne of the Senate of Canada, which is used by the Queen or the Governor General for ceremonial occasions.

The obverse was specifically designed for this coin and bears a special legend and the dates 1952-1977.

Obverse:	Designer: Arnold Machin Modeller: Royal Mint Staff	**Reverse:**	Designer: Raymond Lee Modeller: Ago Aarand

Case: (A) Rectangular black leatherette case, coat of arms, maroon and black plastic insert.

            (B) Rectangular maroon leatherette case, coat of arms, maroon and black plastic insert.

            (C) Rectangular maroon velveteen case, coat of arms, maroon velveteen insert.

Date	Description	Issue Price	Mintage	SP-65
1977	Silver, Case A	4.25	744,848	8.00
1977	Silver, Case B	4.25	Incl. above	8.00
1977	Silver, Case C	4.25	Inc. above	8.00

COMMONWEALTH GAMES SILVER DOLLAR 1978. The 1978 silver dollar commemorated the 11th Commonwealth Games, held in Edmonton, Alberta, August 3-12 of that year. The reverse design features the symbol of the Games in the centre, and the official symbols of the ten sports which comprise the Games along the perimeter.
The obverse was made specifically for this issue.

Obverse:	Designer: Arnold Machin	**Reverse:** Designer: Raymond Taylor
	Modeller: Royal Mint Staff	Modeller: Victor Coté
Case:	Rectangular black leatherette case, coat of arms, maroon and black plastic insert.	

Date	Description	Issue Price	Mintage	SP-65
1978	Silver	4.50	640,000	8.00

GRIFFON TRICENTENNIAL SILVER DOLLAR 1979. The 300th anniversary of the first voyage by a commercial ship on the Great Lakes was commemorated on the reverse of the 1979 silver dollar.

Obverse:	Designer: Arnold Machin	**Reverse:** Designer: Walter Schluep
	Modeller: Patrick Brindley	Modeller: Terry Smith
Case:	Square black leatherette, maroon insert, capsule.	

Date	Description	Issue Price	Mintage	SP-65
1979	Silver	5.50	688,671	18.00

ARCTIC TERRITORIES CENTENNIAL SILVER DOLLAR 1980. The 1980 commemorative silver dollar marked the centenary of the transfer of the Arctic islands from the British Government to the government of the Dominion of Canada.

Obverse:	Designer: Arnold Machin	Reverse:	Designer: D. D. Paterson
	Modeller: Patrick Brindley		Modeller: Walter Ott
Case:	Square black leatherette, maroon insert, capsule.		

Date	Description	Issue Price	Mintage	SP-65
1980	Silver	22.00	389,564	35.00

TRANS-CANADA RAILWAY CENTENNIAL SILVER DOLLAR 1981. The 1981 silver dollar commemorates the 100th anniversary of the approval by the Canadian government to build the Trans-Canada Railway. This is the first year of issue by the Mint of two different qualities of silver dollars.

Obverse:	Designer: Arnold Machin	Reverse:	Designer: Christopher Gorey
	Modeller: Patrick Brindley		Modeller: Walter Ott
Case:	Proof - Square black leatherette, maroon insert, capsule		
	Uncirculated - Clear plastic, black insert.		

Date	Description	Issue Price	Mintage	Price
1981	Silver, Proof (PR65)	18.00	353,742	25.00
1981	Silver, UNC (MS65)	14.00	148,647	22.50

CONSTITUTION NICKEL DOLLAR 1982. The reverse features a faithful reproduction of the celebrated painting of the Fathers of Confederation. This nickel dollar commemorates the Constitution with the inscription "1867 CONFEDERATION" above the painting and "CONSTITUTION 1982" beneath it. The condition of this dollar is "select uncirculated" as offered by the Mint.

Obverse:	Designer: Arnold Machin	**Reverse:**	Designer: Ago Aarand
	Modeller: Royal Mint Staff		Modeller: Royal Mint Staff
Case:	Maroon case with maple leaf logo, maroon insert, capsule.		

Date	Description	Issue Price	Mintage	MS-65
1982	Nickel	9.75	107,353	4.50

REGINA CENTENNIAL SILVER DOLLAR 1982. Issued to commemorate the centennial of the founding of Regina in 1882.

Obverse:	Designer: Arnold Machin	**Reverse:**	Designer: Huntley Brown
	Modeller: Patrick Brindley		Modeller: Walter Ott
Case:	Proof - Square black leatherette case, maroon insert, capsule.		
	Uncirculated - Clear plastic case, black insert		

Date	Description	Issue Price	Mintage	Price
1982	Silver, Proof (PR 65)	15.25	577,959	7.00
1982	Silver, Unc (MS 65)	10.95	144,989	22.50

WORLD UNIVERSITY GAMES SILVER DOLLAR 1983. Issued to commemorate the World University Games held in Edmonton, Alberta, during July of that year.

Obverse: Designer: Arnold Machin
          Modeller: Patrick Brindley
Reverse: Designer: Carola Tietz
          Modeller: Walter Ott
Case: Proof - Square black leatherette case, maroon insert, capsule
       Uncirculated - Clear plastic case, black insert.

Date	Description	Issue Price	Mintage	Price
1983	Silver, Proof (PR 65)	16.15	340,068	11.00
1983	Silver, Unc (MS 65)	10.95	159,450	15.00

JACQUES CARTIER NICKEL DOLLAR 1984. The 450th year of Jacques Cartier's landing at Gaspe, Quebec was honoured on July 24, 1984, by the issuing of a commemorative nickel dollar.

Obverse: Designer: Arnold Machin
          Modeller: Royal Mint Staff
Reverse: Designer: Hector Greville
          Modeller: Victor Coté
Case: Rectangular green velvet case, green insert, capsule.

Date	Description	Issue Price	Mintage	PR-65
1984	Nickel	9.75	87,776	8.00

TORONTO SESQUICENTENNIAL SILVER DOLLAR 1984. Issued to commemorate the 150th anniversary of the incorporation of the City of Toronto in 1834.

Obverse: Designer: Arnold Machin   **Reverse:** Designer: David Craig
Modeller: Patrick Brindley   Modeller: Walter Ott
Case: Proof - Square black leatherette case, maroon insert, capsule.
Uncirculated - Clear plastic case, black insert

Date	Description	Issue Price	Mintage	Price
1984	Silver, Proof (PR65)	17.50	571,079	6.50
1984	Silver, Unc (MS65)	11.40	133,563	27.50

NATIONAL PARKS CENTENNIAL SILVER DOLLAR 1985. The 1985 silver dollar commemorates the 100th anniversary of one of Canada's important heritages, the National Parks.

Obverse: Designer: Arnold Machin   **Reverse:** Designer: Karel Ruhlicek
Modeller: Patrick Brindley   Modeller: Walter Ott
Case: Proof - Square black leatherette case, maroon insert, capsule.
Uncirculated - Clear plastic case, black insert

Date	Description	Issue Price	Mintage	Price
1985	Silver, Proof (PR65)	17.50	537,297	8.50
1985	Silver, Unc (MS65)	12.00	162,873	20.00

VANCOUVER CENTENNIAL SILVER DOLLAR; 1986. Issued to commemorate the 100th anniversary of the founding of Vancouver and the arrival of the first trans-Canada train in Vancouver. Canadian Pacific Engine No. 371 was the first to arrive in 1886.

Obverse: Designer: Arnold Machin
          Modeller: Patrick Brindley

Reverse: Designer: Elliott John Morrison
          Modeller: Ago Aarand
                     Victor Coté

Case: Proof: Square black leatherette case, maroon insert, capsule.
           Uncirculated: Clear plastic case, black insert

Date	Description	Issue Price	Mintage	Price
1986	Silver, Proof (PR65)	18.00	496,418	11.00
1986	Silver, Unc (MS65)	12.25	124,574	32.50

THE LOON NICKEL/BRONZE DOLLAR; 1987. A proof striking of the loon dollar was issued by the numismatic department of the Royal Canadian Mint in 1987.

Obverse: Designer: Arnold Machin
          Modeller: Patrick Brindley

Reverse: Designer: R. R. Carmichael
          Modeller: Terry Smith

Case: Blue velvet case, blue velvet insert, capsule.

Date	Description	Issue Price	Mintage	PR-65
1987	Nickel/Bronze	13.50	178,120	12.00

JOHN DAVIS SILVER DOLLAR 1987. The 400th anniversary of John Davis' historic expedition in search of the North West Passage is commemorated on the 1987 silver dollar.

Obverse: Designer: Arnold Machin
Modeller: Patrick Brindley

Reverse: Designer: Christopher Gorey
Modeller: Ago Aarand, Victor Coté

Case: Proof: Square black leatherette case, maroon insert, capsule
Uncirculated: Clear plastic black insert

Date	Description	Issue Price	Mintage	Price
1987	Silver, Proof (PR65)	19.00	405,688	15.00
1987	Silver, Unc (MS65)	14.00	118,722	25.00

SAINT-MAURICE IRONWORKS SILVER DOLLAR, 1988. The 250th anniversary of the Saint-Maurice Ironworks, Canada's first heavy industry, is commemorated on the 1988 silver dollar.

Obverse: Designer: Arnold Machin
Modeller: Patrick Brindley

Reverse: Designer: R. R. Carmichael
Modeller: Sheldon Beveridge

Case: Proof: Square, black leatherette case, maroon insert, capsule.
Uncirculated: Clear plastic case, black insert

Date	Description	Issue Price	Mintage	Price
1988	Silver, Proof (PR65)	20.00	259,230	35.00
1988	Silver, Unc (MS65)	15.00	106,702	40.00

MACKENZIE RIVER BICENTENNIAL SILVER DOLLAR 1989. The bicentennial of the first full length voyage of the Mackenzie River by Alexander Mackenzie and his European crew. This expedition of the Mackenzie River, all the way to the Arctic Ocean, is commemorated on the 1989 silver dollar.

Obverse: Designer: Arnold Machin **Reverse:** Designer: John Mardon
Modeller: Patrick Brindley Modeller: Sheldon Beveridge
Case: Proof: Square black leatherette case, maroon insert, capsule
Uncirculated: Clear plastic black insert

Date	Description	Issue Price	Mintage	Price
1989	Silver, Proof (PR65)	21.75	272,319	37.50
1989	Silver, Unc (MS65)	16.25	110,650	25.00

HENRY KELSEY TRICENTENNIAL SILVER DOLLAR. The 300th anniversary of Henry Kelsey's ventures into the Canadian West is commemorated on the 1990 silver dollar.

Obverse: Designer: Dora de Pédery-Hunt **Reverse:** Designer: D. J. Craig
Modeller: Dora de Pédery-Hunt Modeller: Ago Aarand
Case: Proof - Square black leatherette case, maroon insert, capsule
Uncirculated - Clear plastic case, black insert

Date	Description	Issue Price	Mintage	Price
1990	Silver, Proof (PR65)	22.95	222,983	22.50
1990	Silver, Unc (MS65)	16.75	85,763	18.00

FRONTENAC SILVER DOLLAR 1991. Commemorates the 175th anniversary of the first steamship to sail on the Great Lakes. Built by a partnership of Kingston merchants in 1815, the *Frontenac* established a regular passenger and freight route between Prescott and Burlington by 1817, thus becoming the first Canadian built steamship to operate on Lake Ontario.

Obverse: Designer: Dora de Pédery-Hunt   **Reverse:** Designer: David J. Craig
         Modeller: Dora de Pédery-Hunt   Modeller: Sheldon Beveridge
Case: Proof - Square black leatherette case, maroon insert, capsule
       Uncirculated - Clear plastic case, black insert

Date	Description	Issue Price	Mintage	Price
1991	Silver, Proof (PR65)	22.95	222,892	25.00
1991	Silver, Unc (MS65)	16.75	82,642	20.00

125TH ANNIVERSARY OF CANADA NICKEL/BRONZE DOLLAR, 1992. Issued as part of the "125" coin program by the numismatic department of the Mint. This proof coin is the companion piece to the circulating issue of the same design. For more information on this coin see page 144.

Obverse: Designer: Dora de Pédery-Hunt   **Reverse:** Designer: Rita Swanson
         Modeller: Dora de Pédery-Hunt   Modeller: Ago Aarand
Case: Royal blue flocked case, blue insert, capsule

Date	Description	Issue Price	Mintage	PR65
1992	Nickel-bronze, proof	19.95	24,227	17.50

KINGSTON TO YORK STAGECOACH SILVER DOLLAR 1992. Commemorating the 175th anniversary of the first stage coach service between Kingston and York in January 1817. Samuel Purdy was only able to maintain regular service during the winter months, hence the sleigh with runners. This is the first issue of a dollar coin in sterling silver since the pattern dollar was struck in London by the Royal Mint in 1911.

Obverse: Designer: Dora de Pédery-Hunt
Modeller: Dora de Pédery-Hunt
Reverse: Designer: Karsten Smith
Modeller: Susan Taylor
Case: Proof - Square black leatherette case, maroon insert, capsule.
Uncirculated - Clear plastic case, black insert

Date	Description	Issue Price	Mintage	Price
1992	Silver, Proof (PR65)	23.95	187,612	25.00
1992	Silver, Unc (MS65)	17.50	78,160	18.00

STANLEY CUP SILVER DOLLAR 1893 - 1993: Commemorating the 100th anniversary of the Stanley Cup, first presented during the 1892 - 1893 season to the Montreal Amateur Athletic Association team by Lord Stanley.

Obverse: Designer: Dora de Pédery-Hunt
Modeller: Dora de Pédery-Hunt
Reverse: Designer: Stewart Sherwood
Modeller: Sheldon Beveridge
Case: Proof - Square black leatherette case, maroon insert, capsule.
Uncirculated - Clear plastic case, black insert

Date	Description	Issue Price	Mintage	Price
1993	Silver, Proof (PR65)	23.95	294,314	22.50
1993	Silver, Unc (MS65)	17.50	88,150	18.00

RCMP NORTHERN DOG TEAM PATROL SILVER DOLLAR 1994. Issued to commemorate the 25th anniversary of the last RCMP Northern Dog Team Patrol.

Obverse: Designer: Dora de Pédery-Hunt
 Modeller: Dora de Pédery-Hunt
Case: Proof - Square black leatherette case, maroon insert, capsule.
 Uncirculated - Clear plastic case, black insert

Reverse: Designer: Ian D. Sparkes
 Modeller: Ago Aarand

Date	Description	Issue Price	Mintage	Price
1994	Silver, Proof (PR65)	24.50	178,485	25.00
1994	Silver, Unc (MS65)	17.95	65,295	18.00

REMEMBRANCE NICKEL/BRONZE DOLLAR 1994. The war memorial was first built to commemorate the participation of all Canadians in the First World War. The memorial was rededicated in 1982 to include veterans of the Second World War and the Korean War. For circulating issue please see page 145.

Obverse: Designer: Dora de Pédery-Hunt
 Modeller: Dora de Pédery-Hunt
Case: Royal blue flocked case, blue insert, capsule.

Reverse: Designer: R.C.M. Staff
 Modeller: T. Smith,
 Ago Aarand

Date	Description	Issue Price	Mintage	Price
1994	Nickel-bronze, proof (PR65)	16.95	54,524	17.50

325TH ANNIVERSARY OF THE FOUNDING OF THE HUDSON'S BAY COMPANY, SILVER DOLLAR, 1995.

From 1670 to the current day the history of the Hudson's Bay Company has been intertwined with that of Canada.

Obverse: Designer: Dora de Pédery-Hunt
Modeller: Dora de Pédery-Hunt

Reverse: Designer: Vincent McIndoe
Modeller: Susan Taylor

Case: Proof - Square black leatherette case, maroon insert, capsule
Uncirculated - Clear plastic case, black insert

Date	Description	Issue Price	Mintage	Price
1995	Silver, proof (PR65)	24.50	157,818	25.00
1995	Silver, unc (MS65)	17.95	58,812	18.00

PEACEKEEPING IN CONJUNCTION WITH THE 50TH ANNIVERSARY OF THE UNITED NATIONS, NICKEL/BRONZE, 1995.

Issued to commemorate Canada's role in the United Nations peacekeeping forces. For circulating issue see page 145.

Obverse: Designer: Dora de Pédery-Hunt
Modeller: Dora de Pédery-Hunt

Reverse: Designer: J.K. Harman,
R. G. Henriguez,
C. H. Oberlander
Modeller: Susan Taylor
Ago Aarland

Case: Royal blue frocked display case, blue insert, capsule

Date	Description	Issue Price	Mintage	PR-65
1995	Nickel-bronze, proof	17.95	N/A	17.50

200TH ANNIVERSARY OF JOHN MCINTOSH, SILVER DOLLAR, 1996. John McIntosh arrived in Canada in 1796 and settled in Ontario. Issued to pay tribute to the originator of Canada's most important commercial apple.

Obverse: Designer: Dora de Pédery-Hunt   **Reverse:** Designer: Roger Hill
         Modeller: Dora de Pédery-Hunt   Modeller: Sheldon Beveridge
Case: Proof - Black with red flock
         Uncirculated - Plastic capsule with silver coloured sleeve

Date	Description	Issue Price	Mintage	Price
1996	Silver, proof (PR65)	29.95	N/A	30.00
1996	Silver, unc (MS65)	19.95	N/A	20.00

TWO DOLLAR — NUMISMATIC COINAGE

POLAR BEAR REVERSE; GOLD TWO DOLLAR; 1996. This is the first two dollar gold coin struck in Canada by the Royal Canadian Mint.

Designers and Modellers: See page 146
Composition:
	Inner Core — .9167 Au, .041 Ag, .0423 Cu
	Outer Core — .172 Au, .776 Ag, .052 Cu
Weight:	11.40 grams
Diameter:	28 mm
Thickness:	1.80 mm
Edge:	Interrupted serration
Die Axis:	↑↑
Case:	Blue ultrasuede, certificate of authenticity, encapsulated.

Date	Description	Issue Price	Mintage	Price
1996	Gold	299.95	5,000	475.00

POLAR BEAR REVERSE; BI-METALLIC TWO DOLLAR; 1996. Issued by the numismatic department of the Royal Canadian Mint during 1996 to commemorate the introduction of the two dollar coin.

Specifications: see page 146
Cases: Proof - Black with a blue flock and sleeve
Uncirculated - Presentation folder with polar bears

Date	Description	Issue Price	Mintage	Price
1996	Proof (PR65)	24.95	N/A	25.00
1996	Unc (MS65)	10.95	N/A	11.00

OLYMPIC FIVE AND TEN DOLLAR COINS 1973 - 1976

In 1976, Montreal, Quebec, hosted the XXI Olympiad. To commemorate and help finance Canada's first Olympics, the federal government agreed to produce a series of twenty-eight silver and two gold coins (see section following for the $100 gold coins). There are seven series of silver coins. Each series has two $5 and two $10 coins, making a total of fourteen coins of each denomination. Each series depicts different Olympic themes on the reverse and has a common design (except for the date) on the obverse. The date on the coins is usually the year of minting. Orders for the Olympic coins were accepted up to the end of December 1976, so a small unit continued to function into 1977 on the Olympic Coin Program. Mintage by series was never recorded, but the annual reports of the Royal Canadian Mint give the following figures by year: 1973 - 537,898 $10, 543,098 $5; 1974 - 3,949,878 $10, 3,981,140 $5; 1975 - 4,952,433 $10, 3,970,000 $5; 1976 - 3,970,514 $10, 3,775,259 $5. These figures do not necessarily coincide with the actual post office sales figures for the coins.

The Olympic coins were offered to the collector in two conditions, uncirculated and proof. The uncirculated issues were packaged and offered for sale in four different formats: (1) encapsulated (single coins only in styrene crystal capsules); (2) one-coin "standard" case (single coins in black case with red interior); (3) four-coin "custom" set (two $5 and two $10 coins by series in black case with gold trim and red insert); and (4) four-coin "prestige" set (two $5 and two $10 coins by series in matte black leatherette case with blue insert).

The proof coins were only offered in sets, and the "deluxe" case of issue was made of Canadian white birch with a specially tanned steer hide cover and black insert.

Due to the fluctuating price of silver during the years of the program (1973 to 1976), the original issue prices varied somewhat from series to series.

Original Issue Prices

PACKAGE TYPE	SERIES I	SERIES II	SERIES III-VII
$5 Encapsulated	6.00	7.50	8.00
$10 Encapsulated	12.00	15.00	15.75
Set of 4 Encapsulated	36.00	45.00	47.50
$5 in Standard Case	7.50	9.00	9.00
$10 in Standard Case	14.00	17.00	17.00
Set of 4 in Standard Case	43.00	52.00	52.00
Custom Set	45.00	55.00	55.00
Prestige Set	50.00	60.00	60.00
Deluxe Proof Set	72.50	82.50	82.50

$5 COIN
Composition: .925 silver, .075 copper
Weight: 24.30 grams
Diameter: 38.00 mm
Edge: Reeded
Die Axis: ↑↑

$10 COIN
Composition: .925 silver, .075 copper
Weight: 48.60 grams
Diameter: 45.00 mm
Edge: Reeded
Die Axis: ↑↑

SERIES I

Coin No. 1
World Map

Coin No. 2
Map of North America

Coin No. 3
Montreal Skyline

Coin No. 4
Kingston and Sailboats

Theme: Geographic
Official Release Date:

December 13, 1973. (The Series I issuing period began in late 1973
and was carried over into 1974. During the last half of the period a 1974 dated
obverse die - possibly made in advance for the Series II coins - was mated
inadvertently with a Series I reverse die of the Map of the World resulting in the
production and release of a Series I mule dated 1974.)

Designer of Reverse:

Georges Huel, worked by invitation.

Modellers:

Coin No. 1 ($10 Map of the World): design was photochemically etched
Coin No. 2 ($5 Map of North America): design was photochemically etched
Coin No. 3 ($10 Montreal Skyline): Ago Aarand
Coin No. 4 ($5 Kingston and Sailboats): Terrence Smith

Date	$5 Coin	$10 Coin	Custom Set	Prestige Set	Proof Set
1973	6.00	12.00	32.00	32.00	40.00
1974 Mule	-	300.00	-	-	-

SERIES II

Coin No. 5
Head of Zeus

Coin No. 6
Athlete with Torch

Coin No. 7
Temple of Zeus

Coin No. 8
Olympic Rings and Wreath

Theme: Olympic Motifs
Official Release Date: September 16, 1974
Designer of Reverse: Anthony Mann, winner of an invitational competition.
Modellers: Coin No. 5 ($10 Head of Zeus): Patrick Brindley
Coin No. 6 ($5 Athlete with Torch): Patrick Brindley
Coin No. 7 ($10 Temple of Zeus): Walter Ott
Coin No. 8 ($5 Olympic Rings and Wreath): Walter Ott

Date	$5 Coin	$10 Coin	Custom Set	Prestige Set	Proof Set
1974	6.00	12.00	32.00	32.00	40.00

SERIES III

Coin No. 9
Lacrosse

Coin No. 10
Canoeing

Coin No. 11
Cycling

Coin No. 12
Rowing

Theme: Early Canadian Sports
Official Release Date: April 16, 1975
Designer of Reverse: Ken Danby, winner of an invitational competition.
Modellers: Coin No. 9 ($10 Lacrosse): Walter Ott
        Coin No. 10 ($5 Canoeing): Patrick Brindley
        Coin No. 11 ($10 Cycling): Ago Aarand
        Coin No. 12 ($5 Rowing): Terrence Smith

Date	$5 Coin	$10 Coin	Custom Set	Prestige Set	Proof Set
1974	6.00	12.00	32.00	32.00	40.00

SERIES IV

Coin No. 13
Men's Hurdles

Coin No. 14
Marathon

Coin No. 15
Women's Shot Put

Coin No. 16
Women's Javelin

Theme: Olympic Track and Field Sports
Official Release Date: August 12, 1975
Designer of Reverse: Leo Yerxa, winner of an invitational competition.
Modellers: Coin No. 13 ($10 Men's Hurdles): Patrick Brindley
Coin No. 14 ($5 Marathon): Walter Ott
Coin No. 15 ($10 Women's Shot Put): Patrick Brindley
Coin No. 16 ($5 Women's Javelin): Walter Ott

Date	$5 Coin	$10 Coin	Custom Set	Prestige Set	Proof Set
1975	6.00	12.00	32.00	32.00	40.00

SERIES V

Coin No. 17
Paddling

Coin No. 18
Diving

Coin No. 19
Sailing

Coin No. 20
Swimming

Theme: Olympic Summer Sports
Official Release Date: December 1, 1975
Designer of Reverse: Lynda Cooper, winner of an open national competition.
Modellers: Coin No. 17 ($10 Paddling): design was photochemically etched
Coin No. 18 ($5 Diving): design was photochemically etched
Coin No. 19 ($10 Sailing): design was photochemically etched
Coin No. 20 ($5 Swimming): design was photochemically etched

Date	$5 Coin	$10 Coin	Custom Set	Prestige Set	Proof Set
1975	6.00	12.00	32.00	32.00	40.00

SERIES VI

Coin No. 21
Field Hockey

Coin No. 22
Fencing

Coin No. 23
Soccer

Coin No. 24
Boxing

Theme: Olympic Team and Body Contact Sports
Official Release Date: March 1, 1976
Designer of Reverse: Shigeo Fukada, winner of an open international competition.
Modellers: Coin No. 21 ($10 Field Hockey): design was photochemically etched
Coin No. 22 ($5 Fencing): design was photochemically etched
Coin No. 23 ($10 Soccer): design was photochemically etched
Coin No. 24 ($5 Boxing): design was photochemically etched

Date	$5 Coin	$10 Coin	Custom Set	Prestige Set	Proof Set
1976	6.00	12.00	32.00	32.00	40.00

SERIES VII

Coin No. 25
Olympic Stadium

Coin No. 26
Olympic Village

Coin No. 27
Olympic Velodrome

Coin No. 28
Olympic Flame

Theme: Olympic Games Souvenir Designs
Official Release Date: June 1, 1976
Designer of Reverse: Elliott John Morrison, winner of an invitational competition.
Modellers: Coin No. 25 ($10 Olympic Stadium): Ago Aarand
Coin No. 26 ($5 Olympic Village): Sheldon Beveridge
Coin No. 27 ($10 Olympic Velodrome): Terrence Smith
Coin No. 28 ($5 Olympic Flame): Walter Ott

Date	$5 Coin	$10 Coin	Custom Set	Prestige Set	Proof Set
1976	6.00	12.00	32.00	32.00	40.00

OLYMPIC FIFTEEN DOLLAR COINS

OLYMPIC CENTENNIAL COINS
SERIES 1 - THE OLYMPIC VISION

The International Olympic Committee initiated a commemorative coin programme to mark the centennial of the modern Olympic movement in 1996. Five mints, Canada, Australia, France, Austria and Greece will participate by issuing one gold and two silver coins over a five year period. The total collection will comprise five gold and ten silver coins.

The Royal Canadian Mint issued the first three coins in 1992. The silver fifteen dollar coins are listed here, the gold on page No. 265.

The standard catalogue will list only the coins issued by RCM.

Designer: Dora de Pédery-Hunt
Composition: .925 silver, .075 copper
Thickness: 3.1 mm
Weight: 33.63 gms
Edge: Lettering: Citius, Altius, Fortius
Diameter: 40.0 mm
Die Axis: ↑↑

Coin A
Speed Skater, Pole Vaulter, Gymnast

Coin B
The Spirit Of The Generations

Reverse Designers: Coin A: David Craig, Coin B: Stewart Sherwood
Sculpture Engravers: Coin A: Sheldon Beveridge, Coin B: Terry Smith
Boxes: Single coin — Burgundy leatherette case
Set: Wooden display
Issue Price: Single Coin: $46.95 - Set (10 coins): $469.50

Date	Description	Mintage	Proof
1992	Skater	105,645	60.00
1992	Spirit	Incl. Above	60.00

OLYMPIC TWENTY DOLLAR COINS 1985 - 1988

In 1988, Calgary, Alberta, hosted the XV Olympic Winter Games. To commemorate and assist in the financing, the Federal Government, through the Royal Canadian Mint, agreed to produce a series of ten sterling silver coins and one gold coin. The silver coins were issued in sets of two $20.00 coins over the period September 1985 through September 1987. Unlike the 1976 Olympic coins, the Calgary Winter Olympic coins were issued in proof quality only.

The date on the coins (obverse) is the year of minting while the reverse carries the date 1988, the year of the games. Mintage is limited to a total of 5,000,000 coins, resulting if minted in equal numbers, of 500,000 complete sets of the ten coins series.

The first offering of the coins for sale by the Royal Mint was based on 350,000 complete sets at $370.00 per set, by the fifth series the complete set was being offered at $420.00.

Edge lettering was used for the first time on Canadian silver coins. "XV OLYMPIC WINTER GAMES - JEUX OLYMPIQUES D'HIVER" appeared on all ten silver coins. There are existing varieties that have missed the edge lettering process.

Designer: Arnold Machin
Composition: .925 silver, .075 copper
Weight: 34.07 grams
Diameter: 40 mm
Edge: Lettered
Die Axis:

FIRST SERIES

Coin No. 1
Downhill Skiing

Coin No. 2
Speed Skating

Official Release Date: September 16, 1985
Official Issue Price: $37.00 per coin, $74.00 per series
Reverse Designers: Coin No. 1 — Ian Stewart, Coin No. 2 — Friedrich Peter
Sculpture Engravers: Coin No. 1 — Terrence Smith, Coin No. 2 — Ago Aarand
Case: Green Velvet, Olympic Logo, one or two coin display.

Date	Description	Quantity Minted	Proof-Single	Proof-Set
1985	Downhill Skiing	406,360	22.00	-
1985	Speed Skating	354,222	22.00	44.00
1985	Speed Skating, no edge lettering	Incl. Above	150.00	-

SECOND SERIES

Coin No. 3
Hockey

Coin No. 4
Biathlon

Official Release Date: February 25, 1986
Official Issue Price: $37.00 per coin, $74.00 per series
Reverse Designers: Coin No. 3 — Ian Stewart, Coin No. 4 — John Mardon
Sculpture Engravers: Coin No. 3 — Victor Coté, Coin No. 4 — Sheldon Beveridge
Case: Green Velvet, Olympic Logo, one or two coin display.

Date	Description	Quantity Minted	Proof-Single	Proof-Set
1986	Hockey	396,602	22.00	-
1986	Hockey, no edge lettering	Incl. Above	150.00	-
1986	Biathlon	308,086	22.00	44.00
1986	Biathlon, no edge lettering	Incl. Above	150.00	-

THIRD SERIES

Coin No. 5
Cross-Country Skiing

Coin No. 6
Free-Style Skiing

Official Release Date: August 18, 1986
Official Issue Price: $39.50 per coin, $79.00 per series
Reverse Designers: Coin No. 5 — Ian Stewart, Coin No. 6 — Walter Ott
Sculpture Engravers: Coin No. 5 — Terrence Smith, Coin No. 6 — Walter Ott
Case: Green Velvet, Olympic Logo, one or two coin display.

Date	Description	Quantity Minted	Proof-Single	Proof-Set
1986	Cross-Country Skiing	303,199	22.00	-
1986	Free-Style Skiing	294,322	22.00	44.00
1986	Free-Style Skiing, no edge lettering	Incl. Above	150.00	-

FOURTH SERIES

Coin No. 7
Figure Skating

Coin No. 8
Curling

Official Release Date: March 14, 1987
Official Issue Price: $39.50 per coin, $79.00 per series
Reverse Designers: Coin No. 7 — Raymond Taylor, Coin No. 8 — Ian Stewart
Sculpture Engravers: Coin No. 7 — Walter Ott, Coin No. 8 — Sheldon Beveridge
Case: Green Velvet, Olympic Logo, one or two coin display.

Date	Description	Quantity Minted	Proof-Single	Proof-Set
1987	Figure Skating	334,875	22.00	-
1987	Curling	286,457	22.00	44.00

FIFTH SERIES

Coin No. 9
Ski-Jumping

Coin No. 10
Bobsleigh

Official Release Date: August 11, 1987
Official Issue Price: $42.00 per coin, $84.00 per series
Reverse Designers: Coin No. 9 — Raymond Taylor, Coin No. 10 — John Mardon
Sculpture Engravers: Coin No. 9 — David Kierans, Coin No. 10 — Victor Coté
Case: Green Velvet, Olympic Logo, one or two coin display.

Date	Description	Quantity Minted	Proof-Single	Proof-Set
1987	Ski-Jumping	290,954	22.00	-
1987	Bobsleigh	274,326	22.00	44.00

AVIATION TWENTY DOLLAR COINS 1990 - 1997

FIRST SERIES

Canada's aviation heroes and achievements are commemorated on this series of twenty dollar sterling silver coins. The series was be made up of ten coins issued two per year over five years. For the first time each coin design contains a 24 karat gold covered oval cameo portrait of the aviation hero commemorated. All coins were issued in proof condition and a maximum of 50,000 of each coin was offered for sale during the program.

Specifications common to the whole series are:

Obverse:
Designer — Dora de Pédery-Hunt
Modeller — Dora de Pédery-Hunt
Composition: .925 silver, .075 copper
with 24 karat gold cameo
Weight: 31.103 grams
Diameter: 38 mm
Edge: Interrupted serration
Die Axis: ↑↓

The issue price of the ten coin case was $37.00

Case: Aluminum, in the shape of a wing, two and ten coin display cases.

Coin No. 1
Avro Anson and the North American Harvard,
Robert Leckie

Official Release Date: September 15, 1990
Reverse Designers: No. 1: R.R. Carmichael
No. 2: Geoff Bennett
Portrait Designers: No. 1: Terrence Smith
No. 2: Sheldon Beveridge

Coin No. 2
Avro Lancaster,
J. E. Fauquier

Engravers: No.1: Sheldon Beveridge
No. 2: Ago Aarand

Date	Description	Issue Price	Quantity Minted	PR-65
1990	Anson and Harvard, Leckie	55.50	41,844	55.00
1990	Lancaster, Fauquier	55.50	43,596	250.00

Coin No. 3
A.E.A. Silver Dart;
F.W. Baldwin & John A.D. McCurdy

Official Release Date: May 16, 1991
Reverse Designers: No. 3: George Velinger
No. 4: Peter Mossman
Portrait Designers: No. 3: Terrence Smith
No. 4: William Woodruff

Coin No. 4
de Havilland Beaver;
Phillip C. Garratt

Engravers: No. 3: Sheldon Beveridge
No. 4: Ago Aarand

Date	Description	Issue Price	Quantity Minted	PR-65
1991	Silver Dart, Baldwin, McCurdy	55.50	35,202	55.00
1991	Beaver, Garratt	55.50	36,197	55.00

Coin No. 5
Curtiss JN-4 (Canuck);
Sir Frank Wilton Baillie

Official Release Date: August 13, 1992
Reverse Designers: No. 5: George Velinger
No. 6: John Mardon
Portrait Designers: No. 5: Terry Smith
No. 6: Susan Taylor

Coin No. 6
de Havilland Gipsy Moth;
Murton A. Seymour

Official Issue Price: $54.35
Engravers: No. 5: Sheldon Beveridge
No. 6: Ago Aarand

Date	Description	Issue Price	Quantity Minted	PR-65
1992	Curtiss, Baillie	55.50	33,105	55.00
1992	Gipsy Moth, Seymour	55.50	32,537	55.00

Coin No. 7
The Fairchild 71c/
James A Richardson

Official Release Date: May 3, 1993
Reverse Designers: No. 7: Robert R. Carmichael
No. 8: Robert R. Carmichael
Portrait Designers: No. 7: Susan Taylor
No. 8: Sheldon Beveridge

Coin No. 8
Lockheed 14 Super Electra/
Zebulon Lewis Leigh

Engravers: No. 7: Susan Taylor
No. 8: Sheldon Beveridge

Date	Description	Issue Price	Quantity Minted	PR-65
1993	Fairchild, Richardson	55.50	32,199	55.00
1993	Lockheed, Leigh	55.50	32,550	55.00

Coin No. 9
The Curtiss HS-2L
Stuart Graham

Official Release Date:
Reverse Designers: No. 9: John Mardon
No. 10: W.T. Ried
Portrait Designers: No. 9: Susan Taylor
No. 10: Sheldon Beveridge

Coin No. 10
The Canadian Vickers Vedette
Wilfred T.Reid

Engravers: No. 9: Sheldon Beveridge
No. 10: Sheldon Beveridge

Date	Description	Issue Price	Quantity Minted	PR-65
1994	Curtiss, Graham	55.50	31,242	55.00
1994	Vedette, Reid	55.50	30,880	55.00

SECOND SERIES

This is the second series of the aviation cameo coins of Canada. The theme of this series is "Powered Flight in Canada —Beyond World War II."

Coin No. 1
The Fleet 80 Canuck
J.Omer (Bob) Noury

Official Release Date:
Reverse Designers:
    No. 1 — N/A
    No. 2 — N/A
Portrait Designer:
    No. 1 — Cosme Saffioti
    No. 2 — Ago Aarand

Coin No. 2
DHC-1 Chipmunk
W/C Russell Bannock

Engravers:
    No. 1 — Cosme Saffioti
    No. 2 — William Woodruff

Date	Description	Issue Price	Quantity Minted	PR-65
1995	The Fleet 80 Canuck	57.95	10,849	60.00
1995	DHC-1 Chipmunk	57.95	10,674	60.00

Coin No. 3
The Avro Canada CF-100 Canuck
Janus Zurakowski

Official Release Date:
Reverse Designers
    No. 3 — N/A
    No. 4 — N/A
Portrait Designer:
    No. 3 — Cosme Saffioti
    No. 4 — Sheldon Beveridge

Coin No. 4
The Avro Canada CF-105 Arrow
James A. Chamberlin

Engravers
    No. 3 — Stan Whitten
    No. 4 — William Woodruff

Date	Description	Issue Price	Quantity Minted	PR-65
1996	CF- 1OO Canuck	57.95	N/A	58.00
1996	CF-105 Arrow	57.95	N/A	58.00

GOLD 20 DOLLAR COINS

CENTENNIAL OF CONFEDERATION COMMEMORATIVE 1967. The highlight of the coins issued in 1967 to mark the centenary of Canadian Confederaton was a $20 gold coin. It was issued only as part of a $40.00 specimen set in a black leather-covered case (see section on specimen sets), but many were later removed from the sets for separate trading. The reverse design is an adaption of the Canadian coat of arms, as on the 50-cent piece of 1960-1966. It is the only coin in the Centennial set that bears the single date 1967 instead of 1867-1967.

Designer: Portrait — Arnold Machin
Reverse — RCM staff
Modeller: Obverse — Myron Cook, using the Machin portrait model
Reverse — Myron Cook, using the Thomas Shingles model of the Canadian coat-of-arms
Composition: .900 gold, .100 copper
Weight: 18.27 grams
Diameter: 27.05 mm
Edge: Reeded
Die Axis: ↑↑

Date	Description	Quantity Minted	PR-65
1967	Confederation Commemorative	334,288	285.00

GOLD 100 DOLLAR COINS

OLYMPIC COMMEMORATIVES 1976. As part of the series of collectors coins struck to commemorate and help finance the XXI Olympiad, two separate $100 gold coins were issued in 1976. The reverse design for each shows an ancient Grecian athlete being crowned with laurel by the goddess Pallas Athena. The uncirculated edition (uniformly shiny surface) is 14k gold and has rim denticles. The proof edition (mirror fields and matte devices and legends) is 22k gold, slightly smaller, and lacks rim denticles.

Designer: Portrait — Arnold Machin
Reverse — Dora de Pédery-Hunt
Modeller: Obverse — Walter Ott, using the Machin portrait model
Reverse — Dora de Pédery-Hunt and Walter Ott
Composition: .583 gold, .417 copper alloy
Weight: 13.338 grams
Diameter: 27.00 mm
Edge: Reeded
Die Axis: ↑↑
Original Issue Price: $105.00

Date	Description	Quantity Minted	MS-65
1976	14k Uncirculated Olympic Commemorative	650,000	135.00

Designer & Modeller: as previous
Composition: .917 gold, .083 copper alloy
Weight: 16.966 grams
Diameter: 25.00 mm
Edge: Reeded
Die Axis: ↑↑
Original Issue Price: $150.00

Date	Description	Quantity Minted	PR-65
1976	22k Proof Olympic Commemorative	350,000	265.00

ELIZABETH II SILVER JUBILEE COMMEMORATIVE 1977. Following the sales success of the Olympic $100 coins, the government decided to embark upon a program to issue a $100 coin every year. The 1977 coin formed part of a two-coin set, the other coin was the silver dollar, issued in recognition of the Queen's Silver Jubilee. The special reverse shows a bouquet of flowers made up of the official flowers of the provinces and territories. All of the issue was of proof quality, with mirror fields and matte devices and legends.

Designer: Obverse — Arnold Machin
Reverse — Raymond Lee
Modeller: Reverse - Walter Ott
Composition: .917 gold, .083 silver
Weight: 16.965 grams
Diameter: 27.00 mm
Edge: Reeded
Die Axis: ↑↑
Original Issue Price: $140.00

Date	Description	Quantity Minted	PR-65
1977	Silver Jubilee Commemorative	180,396	265.00

CANADIAN UNITY COIN 1978. The reverse of the proof $100 gold coin for 1978 depicts twelve Canada geese flying in formation. The image represents the ten provinces and two territories, and so promotes Canadian unity.

Designer: Obverse — Arnold Machin
Reverse — Roger Savage
Modeller: Obverse — Royal Canadian
Mint staff, using the Machin model
Reverse — Ago Aarand
Composition: .917 gold, .083 silver
Weight: 16.965 grams
Diameter: 27.00 mm
Edge: Reeded
Die Axis: ↑↑
Original Issue Price: $150.00

Date	Description	Quantity Minted	PR-65
1978	Unity Coin	200,000	265.00

INTERNATIONAL YEAR OF THE CHILD COMMEMORATIVE 1979. Children playing hand in hand beside a globe adorns the reverse of the 1979 $100 gold coin struck in honour of the International Year of the Child.

Designer: Obverse — Arnold Machin
Reverse — Carola Tietz
Modeller: Obverse — Royal Canadian Mint staff, using the Machin portrait model
Reverse — Victor Coté
Original Issue Price: $185.00

The physical and chemical specifications are as for the 1978 issue.

Date	Description	Quantity Minted	PR-65
1979	International Year of the Child Commemorative	250,000	265.00

ARCTIC TERRITORIES COMMEMORATIVE 1980. The gold $100 coin for 1980 is a commemorative marking the 100th anniversary of the transfer of the Arctic Islands from the British government to the government of the Dominion of Canada. Its reverse shows an Inuk paddling a kayak near a small iceberg and has no lettering or date. The obverse features the Machin bust of Queen Elizabeth, with the legend and date.

Designer: Obverse — Arnold Machin
Reverse — Arnaldo Marchetti
Modeller: Reverse — Sheldon Beveridge
Original Issue Price: $430.00

The physical and chemical specifications are as for the 1978 issue.

Date	Description	Quantity Minted	PR-65
1980	Arctic Territories Commemorative	130,000	265.00

"O CANADA" COMMEMORATIVE 1981. The $100 gold coin for 1981 marks the decision of the Canadian Parliament, on July 1, 1980, to adopt the song "O Canada" as our national anthem.

Designer: Obverse — Arnold Machin
Reverse — Roger Savage
Modeller: Reverse — Walter Ott
Original Issue Price: $300.00

The physical and chemical specifications are as for the 1978 issue.

Date	Description	Quantity Minted	PR-65
1981	"O Canada" Commemorative	100,950	265.00

PATRIATION OF THE CANADIAN CONSTITUTION 1982. The $100 gold coin for 1982 commemorates the patriation of the Constitution of Canada. The reverse of the coin portrays this historical event by a page turning in an open book bearing the coat of arms of Canada and a maple leaf. The obverse of this coin, the seventh in the 22 karat $100 series, depicts Arnold Machin's effigy of Her Majesty Elizabeth II and the legend "100 Dollars" and "Elizabeth II."

Designer: Obverse — Arnold Machin
Reverse — Friedrich Peter
Modeller: Reverse — Walter Ott
Original Issue Price: $290.00

The physical and chemical specifications are as for the 1978 issue.

Date	Description	Quantity Minted	PR-65
1982	Canadian Constitution	121,706	265.00

SIR HUMPHREY GILBERT'S LANDING IN NEWFOUNDLAND 1983. The $100 gold coin for 1983 commemorates Gilbert's landing in Newfoundland to proclaim it as Britain's first overseas colony. The word "CANADA" appears on the edge for the first time in Canadian coinage.

Designer: Obverse — Arnold Machin
Reverse — John Jaciw
Modeller: Reverse — Walter Ott
Edge: Lettered, Reeded
Original Issue Price: $310.00

The physical and chemical specifications are as for the 1978 issue.

Date	Description	Quantity Minted	PR-65
1983	Sir Humphrey Gilbert's Landing	83,128	265.00

JACQUES CARTIER'S VOYAGE OF DISCOVERY 1984. The $100 gold coin for 1984 commemorates Cartier's landing at Gaspe, Bonaventure in 1534. The reverse portrays a profile of Jacques Cartier and a ship of his era. Arnold Machins effigy of Her Majesty Queen Elizabeth II is continued. The edge security lettering of 1983 was not continued in 1984.

Designer: Obverse — Arnold Machin
Reverse — Carola Tietz
Modeller: Reverse — Walter Ott
Original Issue Price: $325.00

The physical and chemical specifications are as for the 1978 issue.

Date	Description	Quantity Minted	PR-65
1984	Jacques Cartier Voyage	67,662	265.00

NATIONAL PARKS CENTENARY 1985. The $100 gold coin of 1985 commemorates the centennial of one of Canada's most important heritages, the National Parks. The reverse of the coin portrays a bighorn sheep poised on a cliff in the Canadian Rockies.

Designer: Obverse — Arnold Machin
Reverse — Hector Greville
Modeller: Reverse — Walter Ott
Original Issue Price: $325.00

The physical and chemical specifications are as for the 1978 issue.

Date	Description	Quantity Minted	PR-65
1985	National Parks Centenary	58,520	265.00

INTERNATIONAL YEAR OF PEACE 1986. The $100 gold coin for 1986 signifies Canada's support for world peace. The reverse depicts a branch of maple leaves intertwined with a branch of olive leaves, symbols of Canada and Peace coming together. The words "Peace-Paix" forming a circle are superimposed on the design.

Designer: Obverse — Arnold Machin
Reverse — Dora de Pédery-Hunt
Modeller: Obverse — RCM staff
Reverse — Dora de Pédery-Hunt
Original Issue Price: $325.00

The physical and chemical specifications are as for the 1978 issue.

Date	Description	Quantity Minted	PR-65
1986	International Year of Peace	76,255	265.00

XV OLYMPIC WINTER GAMES 1987. The $100 gold coin for 1987 commemorates the XV Olympic Winter Games held in Calgary in 1988. The reverse portrays a hand holding the Olympic Torch with a stylized flame forming an image of the Canadian Rocky Mountains. This is the second $100 gold coin to have a lettered edge. The inscription reads "XV Olympic Winter Games - XVes Jeux Olympiques D'Hiver."

Designer: Obverse — Arnold Machin
Reverse — Friedrich Peter
(FP below flame)
Sculptor Engraver: Reverse -
Ago Aarand
Composition: .583 gold, .417 silver
Weight: 13.338 grams
Diameter: 27 mm
Edge: Lettered
Die Axis: ↑ ↑
Original Issue Price: $255.00

Date	Description	Quantity Minted	PR-65
1987	XV Olympic Winter Games	145,175	135.00

COLLECTOR COINS

THE BOWHEAD WHALE (BALAENA MYSTICETUS) 1988. The $100 gold coin for 1988 celebrates a precious national treasure. The reverse portrays a bowhead whale and her calf surrounded by a circle.

Designer: Obverse — Arnold Machin
Reverse — Robert Ralph
Carmichael
(RRC above tail)
Modeller: Ago Aarand
Edge: Reeded
Original Issue Price: $255.00

The physical and chemical specifications are as for the 1987 issue

Date	Description	Quantity Minted	PR-65
1988	Bowhead Whale	52,239	150.00

SAINTE-MARIE 1639-1989. In 1639 the French Jesuits founded a fortified mission village near Midland, Ontario, which they named Sainte-Marie among the Hurons. 1989 was the 350th anniversary of this first self-sufficient settlement in Ontario, where one-fifth of the European population of Canada lived.

Designer: Obverse — Arnold Machin
Reverse — David J. Craig
(DJC below church)
Modeller: Obverse — Patrick Brindley
Reverse — Ago Aarand
Edge: Reeded
Original Issue Price: $245.00

The physical and chemical specifications are as for the 1987 issue.

Date	Description	Quantity Minted	PR-65
1989	Sainte-Marie	63,881	135.00

INTERNATIONAL LITERACY YEAR 1990. The General Assembly of the United Nations declared 1990 as the International Year of Literacy, setting the stage to eradicate illiteracy around the world by the year 2000.

Designer: Obverse — Dora de Pédery-Hunt
Reverse — John Mardon
(JM below child)
Modeller: Obverse — Dora de Pédery-Hunt
Reverse — Ago Aarand and
Susan Taylor
Edge: Reeded
Original Issue Price: $245.00

The physical and chemical specifications are as for the 1987 issue

Date	Description	Quantity Minted	PR-65
1990	International Literacy	49,940	140.00

EMPRESS OF INDIA 1991. Commemorating the 100th anniversary of the *Empress of India*'s first arrival in Vancouver from Yokohama, Japan. The Canadian Pacific's trans-Pacific Empress ships were among the world's first cruise ships.

Designer: Obverse — Dora de Pédery-Hunt
Reverse — Karsten Smith
Modeller: Obverse — Dora de Pédery-Hunt
Reverse — Sheldon Beveridge
Edge: Reeded
Original Issue Price: $245.00

The physical and chemical specifications are as for the 1987 issue

Date	Description	Quantity Minted	PR-65
1991	Empress of India	36,595	170.00

CITY OF MONTREAL, 350TH ANNIVERSARY, 1642-1992. On May 17, 1642, three vessels arrived from France landing Maisonneuve and his men on an island in the St. Lawrence River. They called the island Ville-Marie which was renamed Montreal in the early 1700's.

Designer: Obverse — Dora de Pédery-Hunt
Reverse — Stewart Sherwood
Modeller: Obverse — Dora de Pédery-Hunt
Reverse — Ago Aarand and
Cosme Saffioti
Edge: Reeded
Original Issue Price: $239.85

The physical and chemical specifications are as for the 1987 issue.

Date	Description	Quantity Minted	PR-65
1992	Montreal	28,162	170.00

1893 THE ERA OF THE HORSELESS CARRIAGE, 1993. The five vehicles pictured on the reverse of the 1993 gold coin are, clockwise from the left, the French Panhard-Levassor's Daimler, the American Duryea, the German Benz Victoria, the Simmonds Steam Carriage and, in the centre, the first Canadian built electric car, the Featherstonhaugh

Designer: Obverse — Dora de Pédery-Hunt
Reverse — John Mardon
Modeller: Obverse — Dora de Pédery-Hunt
Reverse — Ago Aarand and
William Woodruff
Edge: Reeded
Original Issue Price: $239.85

The physical and chemical specifications are as for the 1987 issue.

Date	Description	Quantity Minted	PR-65
1993	Horseless Carriage	25,971	180.00

COLLECTOR COINS

THE HOME FRONT 1994. This coin is part of the Remembrance & Peace Issue. The design was taken from a 1945 painting by P. Clark, entitled "Maintenance Jobs in the Hangar."

Designer: Obverse — Dora de Pédery-Hunt
Reverse — Paraskeva Clark
Modeller: Obverse — Dora de Pédery-Hunt
Reverse — Susan Taylor
Ago Aarand
Edge: Reeded
Original Issue Price: $249.95

The physical and chemical specifications are as for the 1987 issue.

Date	Description	Quantity Minted	PR-65
1994	Home Front	17,603	225.00

275TH ANNIVERSARY OF THE FOUNDING OF LOUISBOURG, 1995. Louisbourg, built in 1720 as a strategic centre for the French military in North America, is commemorated on the $100.00 gold coin of 1995.

Designer: Obverse — Dora de Pédery-Hunt
Reverse — Lewis Parker
Modeller: Obverse — Dora de Pédery-Hunt
Reverse — Sheldon Beveridge
Edge: Reeded
Original Issue Price: $249.95

The physical and chemical specifications are as for the 1987 issue.

Date	Description	Quantity Minted	PR-65
1995	Louisbourg	16,916	225.00

100TH ANNIVERSARY OF THE FIRST MAJOR GOLD DISCOVERY IN THE KLONDIKE, 1996. In 1896 the Gold Rush began when George and Kate Carmack, Skookum Jim and Dawson Charlie made the Klondike's first major gold find.

Designer: Obverse — Dora de Pédery-Hunt
Reverse — John Mantha
Modeller: Obverse — Dora de Pédery-Hunt
Reverse — Cosme Saffioti
Edge: Reeded
Original Issue Price: $259.95

The physical and chemical specifications are as for the 1987 issue.

Date	Description	Quantity Minted	PR-65
1996	Klondike Gold Rush	35,000	260.00

GOLD 175 DOLLAR COINS

OLYMPIC CENTENNIAL COINS
SERIES 1 THE OLYMPIC VISION

Commemorating the 100th anniversary of the Olympic movement in 1996, Canada and four other countries, Australia, France, Austria and Greece, issued a three coin set, one gold and two silver coins. They were issued each year beginning with Canada in 1992. See page no. 249 for the Royal Canadian Mint silver issues. Only the Royal Canadian Mint issued coins are listed in the Standard Catalogue.

Designer: Obverse — Dora de Pédery-Hunt
Reverse — Stewart Sherwood
Modeller: Obverse — Dora de Pédery-Hunt
Reverse — Ago Aarand
Composition: .916 Gold
.084 Copper
Weight: 16.97g
Diameter: 28.00 mm
Thickness: 2.00 mm
Edge: Lettering - Citius, altius, fortius
Die Axis: ↑↑
Issue Price: Single gold coin - $429.75
Set (5) - one from each
mint $2,148.75

Date	Description	Mintage	PR-65
1992	Flame	22,092	500.00

GOLD 200 DOLLAR COINS

CANADA FLAG SILVER JUBILEE 1990. Issued to commemorate the 25th anniversary of the proclamation approving Canada's flag.

Designer:
    Obverse — Dora de Pédery-Hunt
    Reverse — Stewart Sherwood
Modeller:
    Obverse — Dora de Pédery-Hunt
    Reverse — Ago Aarand
Composition: .916 gold, .083 silver
Weight: 17.106 grams
Diameter: 29 mm
Edge: Reeded
Die Axis: ↑↑
Original Issue Price: $395.00
Case: Woven Jacquard case, certificate encapsulated

Date	Description	Quantity Minted	PR-65
1990	Canada Flag	20,980	280.00

A NATIONAL PASSION 1991. The 1991 two hundred dollar proof gold coin was issued as a tribute to the spirit and vitality of Canadian youth and the national game of hockey.

Designer:
    Obverse — Dora de Pédery-Hunt
    Reverse — Stewart Sherwood
Modeller:
    Obverse — Dora de Pédery-Hunt
    Reverse — Susan Taylor
Original Issue Price: $425.00

The physical and chemical specifications are as for the 1990 issue.

Date	Description	Quantity Minted	PR-65
1991	A National Passion	10,215	345.00

NIAGARA FALLS 1992. The 1992 two hundred dollar gold coin was issued as a tribute to the beauty and majesty of Niagara Falls. The coin features two children playing near the falls.

Designer: Obverse — Dora de Pédery-Hunt
Reverse — John Mardon
Modeller: Obverse — Dora de Pédery-Hunt
Reverse — Susan Taylor
Original Issue Price: $389.65

The physical and chemical specifications are as for the 1990 issue.

Date	Description	Quantity Minted	PR-65
1992	Niagara Falls	9,465	345.00

ROYAL CANADIAN MOUNTED POLICE 1993: The 1993 issue of the two hundred dollar gold coin pays tribute to the unique contribution of the R.C.M.P. to Canadian history.

Designer: Obverse — Dora de Pédery-Hunt
Reverse — Stewart Sherwood
Modeller: Obverse — Dora de Pédery-Hunt
Reverse — Susan Taylor
Original Issue Price: $389.65

The physical and chemical specifications are as for the 1990 issue.

Date	Description	Quantity Minted	PR-65
1993	R.C.M.P.	10,807	315.00

ANNE OF GREEN GABLES 1994: Issued as a tribute to the famous character in the novel by Canadian writer Lucy Maud Montgomery, this is the last coin in the youth and heritage series.

Designer: Obverse — Dora de Pédery-Hunt
Reverse — Pheobe Gilman
Modeller: Obverse — Dora de Pédery-Hunt
Reverse — Susan Taylor
Original Issue Price: $399.99

The physical and chemical specifications are as for the 1990 issue.

Date	Description	Quantity Minted	PR-65
1994	Anne of Green Gables	10,655	375.00

COLLECTOR COINS

THE SUGAR BUSH, 1995. Commemorating the time honored rite of spring, known in Canada as "sugaring off."

Designer: Obverse — Dora de Pédery-Hunt
Reverse — J.D. Mantha
Modeller: Obverse — Dora de Pédery-Hunt
Reverse — Sheldon Beveridge
Original Issue Price: $399.95

The physical and chemical specifications are as for the 1990 issue.

Date	Description	Quantity Minted	PR-65
1995	Sugar Bush	7,621	375.00

TRANSCONTINENTAL LANDSCAPE, 1996. Issued to commerate the railway, a central symbol of national life.

Designer: Obverse — Dora de Pédery-Hunt
Reverse — Suzanne Duranceau
Modeller: Obverse — Dora de Pédery-Hunt
Reverse — Cosme Saffioti
Composition: .916 gold, .083 silver
Weight: 17.135 grams
Diameter: 29 mm
Edge: Reeded
Die Axis: ↑↑
Original Issue Price: $414.95
Case: Woven Jacquard case, certificate encapsulated

Date	Description	Quantity Minted	PR-65
1996	Transcontinental Landscape	25,000	415.00

COLLECTOR SETS

SILVER PROOF-LIKE SETS 1953 - 1967

Although some silver dollars of proof-like quality were issued prior to 1953, it has not been confirmed that any entire sets were issued. Certainly some minor coins in the sets of 1950-1952 are proof-like, but either the few proof-likes made were mixed up with circulation strikes in making up the sets, or certain denominations were not made as proof-likes to begin with. In any event, the majority of the coins in the sets sold to the public by the Mint in 1950-1953 were no more than circulation strikes that had not gone through mint bags. Beginning in 1954 and continuing through 1969, all mint sets that the Royal Canadian Mint sold to the public were Proof-like. The quality was somewhat inferior in 1965 due to greatly increased production, and in 1968-1969 due to the inexperience of the Mint in producing larger proof-like coins in nickel.

During the period 1953 to 1970, specimen sets were also produced in some years. This generally does not pose a difficulty because the specimen coins were either issued in special packaging or were markedly better quality than the corresponding proof-like coins.

Proof-like sets issued from 1953 to 1960 came in flat white cardboard holders housed in cellophane envelopes. The black stamp, "ROYAL CANADIAN MINT / OTTAWA, CANADA," appears on some 1960 holders. From 1961 the proof-like sets were issued in a sealed pliofilm pack embossed with "ROYAL CANADIAN MINT" in the gutters between the coins.

Proof-like Sets as Issued 1953-1960

Date	Issue Price	Mintage	PL-65
1953 No Shoulder Fold (in case #12)	2.20	1,200	1,500.00
1953 Shoulder Fold	2.20	Included	1,200.00
1954 Shoulder Fold	2.50	3,000	260.00
1954 No Shoulder Fold	2.50	Included	585.00
1955 Normal Water Lines Dollar	2.50	6,300	185.00
1955 Arnprior Dollar	2.50	Included	195.00
1956	2.50	6,500	100.00
1957	2.50	11,862	55.00
1958	2.50	18,259	50.00
1959	3.00	31,577	25.00
1960	3.00	64,097	15.00
1961*	3.00	98,373	14.00
1962	3.00	200,950	10.00
1963	3.00	673,006	8.00
1964	3.00	1,653,162	8.00
1965 Variety 1 Dollar	4.00	2,904,352	8.00
1965 Variety 2 Dollar	4.00	Included	8.00
1966 Large Beads Dollar	4.00	672,514	8.00
1967	4.00	963,714	14.00

*From 1961 onward, sets were no longer issued in cardboard holders but in Pliofilm packs. See photo overleaf. 1961 set will have spotted or toned cents.

NICKEL PROOF-LIKE SETS 1968-1980

This was a continuation of the set offered previously. It contained one of each denomination (for a total of six coins) packaged in a flat pliofilm pouch. From 1971 to 1976 the quality of the coins was proof-like; since that time it has been specimen.

Date	Issue Price	Mintage	PL-65
1968	4.00	521,641	3.00
1968 Small Island $1	4.00	Included	15.00
1969	4.00	326,203	3.00
1970	4.00	349,120	4.50
1971	4.00	253,311	3.50
1972	4.00	224,275	3.50
1973 Large Bust 25¢	4.00	243,695	150.00
1973 Small Bust 25¢	4.00	Included	4.00
1974	5.00	213,589	3.50
1975	5.00	197,372	5.00
1976	5.15	171,737	5.00
1977	5.15	225,307	4.50
1978 Square Jewels	5.25	260,000	3.50
1978 Round Jewels	4.00	Included	13.00
1979	6.25	187,624	4.50
1980	8.00	169,390	6.75

UNCIRCULATED SETS 1981 TO DATE

The uncirculated set contains six coins from the 1-cent to the nickel dollar. The coins in this set are among the best struck for circulation and they are available sealed in an envelope of polyester film, similar to the proof-like sets of previous years.

Date	Dollar Coin	Issue Price	Mintage	PL-65
1981	Nickel/Voyager	5.00	186,250	5.00
1982	Nickel/Voyager	5.00	203,287	4.50
1983	Nickel/ Voyager	5.00	190,838	10.00
1984	Nickel/Voyager	5.00	181,415	8.50
1985	Nickel/Voyager	6.95	173,924	9.00
1986	Nickel/Voyager	6.95	167,338	11.50
1987	Nickel/ bronze Loon	6.95	212,136	8.00
1988	Nickel/bronze Loon	6.95	182,048	8.00
1989	Nickel/bronze Loon	7.70	158,636	14.00
1990	Nickel/bronze Loon	7.70	170,791	14.00
1991	Nickel/bronze Loon	8.50	147,814	37.50
1992	Nickel/bronze Loon	9.50	217,597	18.50
1993	Nickel/bronze Loon	9.50	171,680	9.00
1994	Nickel/bronze Loon	9.75	141,676	9.25
1995	Nickel/bronze Loon	9.75	138,322	9.75
1996	Nickel/bronze Loon	9.75	N/A	9.75
1997	Nickel/bronze Loon	9.75	N/A	9.75

"BABY" UNCIRCULATED SET, 1995 TO DATE. First issued in 1995, this six-coin uncirculated, one-cent-to-the-dollar set was specially packaged for the gift market.

Date	Dollar Coin	Issue Price	Mintage	PL65
1995	Nickel/bronze Loon	19.95	30,108	17.00
1996	Nickel/bronze Loon	19.95	N/A	20.00
1997	Nickel/bronze Loon	19.95	N/A	20.00

"OH CANADA" UNCIRCULATED SET, 1994 TO DATE. First issued in 1994, this six-coin set included the nickel-bronze dollar (commemorative) current to the year of issue. Packaged with it is an illustrated booklet.

Date	Dollar Coin	Issue Price	Mintage	PL65
1994	Nickel/bronze Remembrance	16.95	18,794	16.00
1995	Nickel/bronze Peacekeeping	16.95	48,334	15.00
1996	Nickel/bronze Loon	16.95	N/A	20.00
1997	Nickel/bronze Loon	19.95	N/A	20.00

SPECIMEN SETS 1971-1980

The custom set contained one of each denomination, with an extra cent to show the obverse. It was housed in a square vinyl-covered case. From 1971 to 1976 the quality of the coins was proof-like; since that time it has been specimen.

Cases: **1971**: Coins in black vinyl-covered case with Canada's coat of arms and the word "CANADA" stamped in gold on the top.

1972-1973: as 1971, except the vinyl is red.

1974-1978: as 1971, except the vinyl is maroon.

1979-1980: as 1971-1978, except a gold maple leaf replaces the coat of arms and "CANADA"

1981-1987: Blue leatherette, booklet type (103 mm x 141 mm), inside a hinged blue plastic frame housing, six encapsulated coins. All enclosed in a silver box.

1988 to Date: Blue leatherette, wallet type, (96 mm x 153 mm) silver stamped mint crest, inside clear plastic frame with blue plastic insert. All enclosed in a silver sleeve.

Date	Dollar Coin	Issue Price	Mintage	SP-65
1971	Nickel/B.C.	6.50	33,517	5.00
1972	Nickel/Voyageur	6.50	38,198	5.00
1973 Large Bust 25¢	Nickel/P.E.I.	6.50	49,376	150.00
1973 Small Bust 25¢	Nickel/P.E.I.	6.50	Included	5.00
1974	Nickel/Voyageur	8.00	44,296	5.00
1975	Nickel Voyageur	8.00	36,851	5.00
1976	Nickel/Voyageur	8.15	28,162	5.00
1977	Nickel/Voyageur	8.15	44, 198	5.00
1978	Nickel/Voyageur	8.75	41,000	5.00
1979	Nickel/Voyageur	10.75	31,174	5.00
1980	Nickel/Voyageur	12.50	41,447	5.00
1981	Nickel/Voyageur	10.00	71,300	7.00
1982	Nickel/Voyageur	11.50	62,298	7.00
1983	Nickel/Voyageur	12.75	60,329	7.00
1984	Nickel/Voyageur	12.95	60,030	7.00
1985	Nickel/Voyageur	12.95	61,533	7.50
1986	Nickel/Voyageur	12.95	67,152	8.00
1987	Nickel/Bronze Loon	14.00	74,441	8.00
1988	Nickel/Bronze Loon	14.00	70,205	9.00
1989	Nickel/Bronze Loon	16.95	66,855	14.00
1990	Nickel/Bronze Loon	17.95	76,611	14.00
1991	Nickel/Bronze Loon	17.95	68,552	40.00
1992	Nickel/Bronze Loon	18.95	78,328	22.50
1993	Nickel/Bronze Loon	18.95	77,351	18.00
1994	Nickel/Bronze Loon	19.25	75,973	18.00
1995	Nickel/Bronze Loon	19.25	N/A	18.00
1996	Nickel/Bronze Loon	19.25	N/A	25.00
1997	Nickel/Bronze Loon	19.25	N/A	25.00

PRESTIGE SETS 1971-1995
(Double Dollar Sets)

When it was first introduced in 1971, the prestige set had two nickel dollars (and no silver dollar), with the second nickel dollar used to show the obverse. This was also true for 1972, but from 1973 on the second nickel dollar was replaced with a silver dollar. The quality of the coins in the prestige set has been specimen until 1990 and proof until 1995.

Cases: **1971-1973:** Crest of Canada; black leather, book type with clasp. Red satin inside red flocked 7-hole stationary display - coloured flocked jackets.

1974-1978: Crest of Canada; black leather, book type with clasp. Red satin inside, hinge black plastic 7-hole display - coloured flocked jackets.

1979-1985: Maple Leaf; black cardboard box, book type with clasp. Red satin inside, hinge black plastic 7-hole display - coloured flocked jackets.

1986-1996: Maple Leaf; black plastic box, wallet type. Red satin inside, hinge black plastic 7-hole display - coloured flacked jacket.

SPECIMEN COINS 1971 TO 1980

Date	Dollar Coins	Issue Price	Mintage	SP-65
1971	B.C./B.C.	12.00	66,860	14.00
1972	Voyageur/Voyageur	12.00	36,349	25.00
1973 Large Bust 25¢	P.E.I./RCMP	12.00	119,891	150.00
1973 Small Bust 25¢	P.E.I./RCMP	12.00	Included	15.00
1974	Winnipeg/Winnipeg	15.00	85,230	15.00
1975	Voyageur/Calgary	15.00	97,263	15.00
1976	Voyageur/Parliament	16.00	87,744	17.00
1977	Voyageur/Jubilee	16.00	142,577	15.00
1978	Voyageur/Edmonton	16.50	147,000	15.00
1979	Voyageur/Griffon	18.50	155,698	20.00
1980	Voyageur/Polar Bear	36.00	162,875	40.00

PROOF COINS 1981 TO 1985

Date	Dollar Coins	Issue Price	Mintage	SP-65
1981	Voyageur/Train	36.00	199,000	30.00
1982	Voyageur/Bison	36.00	180,908	16.00
1983	Voyageur/Games	36.00	166,779	17.00
1984	Voyageur/Toronto	40.00	161,602	17.00
1985	Voyageur/Parks	40.00	153,950	20.00
1986	Voyageur/Vancouver	40.00	176,224	17.00
1987	Loon/Davis Strait	43.00	175,686	20.00
1988	Loon/Ironworks	43.00	175,259	45.00
1989	Loon/MacKenzie	46.95	66,855	45.00
1990	Loon/Kelsey	48.00	158,068	45.00
1991	Loon/Empress	48.00	131,888	110.00
1992	Loon/Stagecoach	49.75	147,061	55.00
1993	Loon/Hockey	49.75	143,065	45.00
1994	Loon/Dogsled Team	50.75	104,485	50.00
1995	Loon/Hudson's Bay	50.75	94,662	50.00

PRESTIGE SET 1996 TO DATE
(Double Dollar Set)

Beginning in 1996 the five cent, ten cent, twenty-five cent and fifty cent coins were struck in sterling silver (92.5% Ag and 7.5% Cu). The dollar and one cent coins remain the same as previous years.

Date	Dollar Coin	Issue Price	Mintage	PR-65
1996	Loon/Hudson's Bay	66.25	N/A	70.00
1997	Loon/MacKenzie	66.95	N/A	70.00

SILVER MEDALLION AND GOLD PRESENTATION SETS 1967

In 1967 the Royal Canadian Mint produced two special cased coins sets to mark the 100th anniversary of Confederation. The silver medallion set in the red leather-covered case contained one each of the 1¢ to $1 (proof-like quality) and a sterling silver medallion designed and modelled by Thomas Shingles. The gold presentation set contained a $20 gold coin and one each of the 1¢ to $1, all of specimen quality. The coins were housed in a black leather-covered case.

Date	Issue Price	Mintage	PL-65
1967 (Silver Medallion)	12.00	72,463	20.00
1967 (Gold Presentation)	40.00	337,687	300.00

LIMITED EDITION PROOF SETS 1994 - 1995

First issued in 1994 these proof sets were limited to 50,000. They contained the silver dollar commemorative, along with the bronze/nickel commemorative of the year. The other five coins are the same as contained in the prestige set of that year.

Case: Burgundy display case, wallet type, dated on spine with year of issue. Inside white satin with brown plastic display frame - burgundy plastic box.

Date	Dollar Coins	Issue Price	Mintage	PR-65
1994	Remembrance/Dogsled Team	59.50	49,222	50.00
1995	Peacekeeping/Hudson's Bay	66.95	49,259	65.00

MAPLE LEAF PROOF BULLION ISSUES 1989

To commemorate the 10th anniversary of the maple leaf bullion coin program the Royal Canadian Mint in 1989 issued a series of proof condition silver, gold and platinum coins individually and in sets. The single coins and sets were packaged in solid maple wood presentation cases with brown velvet liners.

Composition	Description	Mintage	Issue Price	Market Price
Gold	Gold Coin 1 ounce maple	6,817	795.00	600.00
	Gold Coin Set, 4 coins 1, 1/2, 1/4, 1/10 ounce maple	6,998	1,395.00	1,250.00
Platinum	Platinum Coin Set, 4 coins 1, 1/2, 1/4, 1/10 ounce maple	1,999	1,995.00	1,250.00
Silver	Silver Coin 1 ounce maple	29,999	39.00	65.00
Silver, Gold and Platinum	1 ounce Coin Set, 3 coins 1 ounce maples of silver, gold and platinum	3,966	1,795.00	1,250.00
	Precious Metal Set, 3 coins 1 ounce silver and 1/10 ounce maples of gold and platinum	10,000	195.00	150.00

TWO DOLLAR COIN AND BANK NOTE SETS

To inaugurate the launch of Canada's new two dollar coin the Royal Canadian Mint issued a proof and uncirculated version of the coin in conjunction with a two dollar bank note. The proof coin is accompanied by an uncirculated X numbered note and the uncirculated coin is accompanied by one of the last $2 bank notes printed.

Cases: Proof : Blue presentation box
Unc: Presentation folder illustrated with polar bears.

Date	Description	Mintage	Issue Price	Market Price
1996	Proof Set	30,000	79.95	79.95
1996	Unc Set	unlimited	29.95	29.95

PROOF PLATINUM ISSUES

1990 POLAR BEARS PROOF PLATINUM SET

In 1990 the Royal Canadian Mint entered the luxury market for high quality collector coins. Canada's "Monarch of the North" has been transferred from the sparkling Arctic environment by Robert Bateman to the gleaming surface of pure platinum coins.

Designer:
    Obverse — Dora de Pédery-Hunt
    Reverse — Robert Bateman
Original Issue Price: $1,990.00

Modellers:
    Obverse — Dora de Pédery-Hunt
    Reverse — $300 - Terry Smith
              $150 - William Woodruff
              $75 - Ago Aarand
              $30 - Sheldon Beveridge

Case of Issue: Walnut case with a black suede four hole insert, encapsulated.
Physical and chemical specifications:
    Denomination: $300 $150 $75 $30
    Weight: (oz)   1.000 .500 .250 .100
    Diameter: (mm) 30.0 25.0 20.0 16.0
    Composition: .9995 platinum
    Edge: Reeded
    Die Axis: ↑ ↑

Date	Description	Quantity Minted	PF-65
1990	Polar Bears; 4 coins; 300, 150, 75, 30 Dollars	2,629	1,450.00

1991 - SNOWY OWLS PROOF PLATINUM SET

This is the second set in the series of proof platinum coins dedicated to Canadian wildlife.

Designer:
Obverse — Dora de Pédery-Hunt;
Reverse — Glen Loates
Original Issue Price: $1,990.00
Physical and chemical specifications: Same as 1990 issues
Case of Issue:
Walnut case with a black suede,
four hole insert, encapsulated.

Modellers:
Obverse — Dora de Pédery-Hunt
Reverse — $300 - Sheldon Beveridge
$150 - Ago Aarand
$75 - Terry Smith
$30 - William Woodruff

Date	Description	Quantity Minted	PR-65
1991	Snowy Owls; 4 coins; 300, 150, 75, 30 Dollars	1,164	1,600.00

1992 - COUGARS PROOF PLATINUM SET

This is the third set in the series of proof platinum coins dedicated to Canadian wildlife.

Designer:
Obverse — Dora de Pédery-Hunt
Reverse — George McLean
Original Issue Price: $1,955.00
Physical and chemical specifications: Same as 1990 issues
Case of Issue:
Walnut case with a black suede,
four hole insert, encapsulated

Modellers:
Obverse — Dora de Pédery-Hunt
Reverse — $300 - Ago Aarand and
Cosme Saffioti
$150 - Susan Taylor
$75 - Sheldon Beveridge
$30 - Ago Aarand

Date	Description	Quantity Minted	PR-65
1992	Cougars; 4 coins; 300, 150, 75, 30 Dollars	1,081	1,575.00

1993 - ARCTIC FOXES PROOF PLATINUM SET

This is the fourth set in the series of proof platinum coins dedicated to Canadian wildlife.

Designer:
    Obverse — Dora de Pédery-Hunt;
    Reverse — Claude D'Angelo
Original Issue Price: $1,955.00
Physical and chemical specifications: Same as 1990 issues
Case of Issue: Walnut case with black suede,
                 four hole insert, encapsulated.

Modellers:
    Obverse — Dora de Pédery-Hunt
    Reverse — $300 - Susan Taylor
              $150 - Sheldon Beveridge
              $75 - Ago Aarand
              $30 - Ago Aarand

Date	Description	Quantity Minted	PR-65
1993	Arctic Foxes, 4 coins; 300, 150, 75, 30 Dollars	1,033	1,600.00

1994 - SEA OTTERS PROOF PLATINUM SET

This is the fifth set in the series of proof platinum coins dedicated to Canadian wildlife.

Designer:
    Obverse — Dora de Pédery-Hunt;
    Reverse — Ron S. Parker
Original Issue Price: $1,995.00
Physical and chemical specifications: Same as 1990 issues
Case of Issue: Walnut case with burgundy flocked,
                 four hole insert, encapsulated

Modellers:
    Obverse — Dora de Pédery-Hunt
    Reverse — $300 - Sheldon Beveridge
              $150 - William Woodruff
              $75 - Terry Smith
              $30 - Susan Taylor

Date	Description	Quantity Minted	PR-65
1994	Sea Otters, 4 coins; 300, 150, 75, 30 Dollars	766	1,650.00

SERIES II

1995 CANADA LYNX PROOF PLATINUM COINS

This is the first set in the 2nd series of platinum coins.

Designer:
  Obverse — Dora de Pédery-Hunt
  Reverse — Michael Dumas
Original Issue Price: $1,950.00
  4 coin set
  $150.00 coin
  $ 30.00 coin

Modellers:
  Obverse — Dora de Pédery-Hunt
  Reverse — $300 - Susan Taylor
  $150 - Cosme Saffioti
  $75 - S. Whitten
  $30 - Ago Aarand

Physical and chemical specifications: Same as 1990 issues
Case of Issue:
  1/10 oz coin — leather display case, encapsulated coin
  1/2 oz coin — mahogany case, encapsulated coin
  Set, 4 coins — mahogany case, inside green satin, coins individually encapsulated

Date	Description	Quantity Minted	PR-65
1995	Lynx, 30 Dollars	249	160.00
1995	Lynx, 150 Dollars	65	600.00
1995	Lynx, 4 coins; 300, 150, 75, 30 Dollars	312	2,100.00

1996 PEREGRINE FALCON PROOF PLATINUM COINS

This is the second set in the 2nd series of platinum coins.

Designer:
  Obverse — Dora de Pédery-Hunt
  Reverse — Dwayne Harty
Original Issue Price: $2,095.95
Physical and chemical specifications: Same as 1990 issues
Case of Issue: N/A

Modellers:
  Obverse — Dora de Pédery-Hunt
  Reverse — $300 - Sheldon Beveridge
  $150 - Stan Whitten
  $75 - Cosme Saffioti
  $30 - Ago Aarand

Date	Description	Quantity Minted	PR-65
1996	Peregrine Falcon, 30 Dollars	N/A	160.00
1996	Peregrine Falcon, 150 Dollars	N/A	600.00
1996	Falcons, 4 coins; 300, 150, 75, 30 Dollars	1,500	2,100.00

APPENDICES

GOLD CONTENT OF CANADIAN GOLD COINS

Date and Denom.	Mint Mark	Gross Weight (Grams)	Fineness	Gold Content Grams	Troy Oz.
		NEWFOUNDLAND			
$2	1865-1888	3.33	.917	3.05	.100
		CANADA			
£1	1908C-1910C	7.99	.917	7.32	.236
£1	1911C-1919C	7.99	.917	7.32	.236
$1 ML	1982 to date	1.55	.9999	1.55	.050
$2 ML	1982 to date	2.07	.9999	2.07	.067
$5	1912-1914	8.36	.900	7.52	.242
$5 ML	1982 to Date	3.131	.9999	3.131	.101
$10	1912-1914	16.72	.900	15.05	.484
$10 ML	1982 to Date	7.797	.9999	.797	.251
$20	1967	18.27	.900	16.45	.529
$20 ML	1986 to Date	15.575	.9999	15.575	.500
$50 ML	1979 to Date	31.150	.9999	31.150	1.000
$100	1976 (Unc.)	13.33	.583	7.78	.250
$100	1976 (Proof)	16.96	.917	15.55	.500
$100	1977-1986	16.96	.917	15.55	.500
$100	1987 to Date	13.338	.583	7.78	.250
$175	1992	16.97	.916	15.54	.500
$200	1990 to Date	17.106	.916	15.67	.500

SILVER CONTENT OF CANADIAN SILVER COINS

Denom.	Date	Fineness	Silver Content Grams	Troy Oz.
$20	1985-1988	.925	31.549	1.000
$10	1973-1976	.925	44.955	1.445
$5	1973-1976	.925	22.477	.723
$5 ML	1988 to Date	.9999	31.035	1.000
$1	1935-1967	.800	18.661	.600
$1	1971 to Date	.500	11.662	.375
50¢	1870-1919	.925	10.792	.347
50¢	1920-1967	.800	9.330	.300
50¢	1995	.925	8.60	.280
25¢	1870-1919	.925	5.370	.173
25¢	1920-1967	.800	4.665	.150
25¢	1967-1968	.500	2.923	.094
25¢	1992	.925	5.550	.180
10¢	1858-1919	.925	2.146	.069
10¢	1920-1967	.800	1.866	.060
10¢	1967-1968	.500	1.170	.038
5¢	1858-1919	.925	1.080	.034
5¢	1920-1921	.800	.933	.030

BULLION VALUES OF CANADIAN SILVER COINS
(Computed from $10/ounce to $70/ounce in increments of $5 Canadian)

Denom.	Fineness	$5	$10	$15	$20	$25	$30	$35	$40	$45	$50	$55	$60	$65	$70
$1	.800	3.00	6.00	9.00	12.00	15.00	18.00	21.00	24.00	27.00	30.00	33.00	36.00	39.00	42.00
$1	.500	1.88	3.75	5.63	7.50	9.37	11.25	13.12	15.00	16.87	18.75	20.62	22.50	24.37	26.25
50¢	.925	1.74	3.47	5.20	6.94	8.67	10.41	12.14	13.88	15.61	17.35	19.08	20.82	22.55	24.29
50¢	.800	1.50	3.00	4.50	6.00	7.50	9.00	10.50	12.00	13.50	15.00	16.50	18.00	19.50	21.00
25¢	.925	.87	1.73	2.60	3.46	4.32	5.19	6.05	6.92	7.78	8.65	9.51	10.38	11.24	12.11
25¢	.800	.75	1.50	2.25	3.00	3.75	4.50	5.25	6.00	6.75	7.50	8.25	9.00	9.75	10.50
25¢	.500	.47	.94	1.40	1.88	2.35	2.82	3.29	3.76	4.23	4.70	5.17	5.64	6.11	6.58
10¢	.925	.35	.69	1.04	1.38	1.72	2.07	2.41	2.76	3.10	3.45	3.79	4.14	4.48	4.83
10¢	.800	.30	.60	.90	1.20	1.50	1.80	2.10	2.40	2.70	3.00	3.30	3.60	3.90	4.20
10¢	.500	.19	.38	.56	.76	.95	1.14	1.33	1.52	1.71	1.90	2.09	2.28	2.47	2.66
5¢	.925	.17	.34	.51	.68	.85	1.02	1.19	1.36	1.53	1.70	1.87	2.04	2.21	2.38
5¢	.800	.15	.30	.45	.60	.75	.90	1.05	1.20	1.35	1.50	1.65	1.80	1.95	2.10

GLOSSARY

ASSAY: Analytical test to determine the purity and weight of metal.

BAG MARK: Slight scratches and nicks acquired by coins in contact with others in a mint bag. Most common on large and heavy silver and gold coins.

BLANK: See Planchet.

BROCKAGE: A coin with the same design raised on one side and incused on the other, caused by a previously struck coin sticking in the die and striking another blank.

BULLION: Uncoined gold or silver in the form of bars, ingots and plates. Bullion value is a term used in reference to value of metal content in common and mutilated gold and silver coins.

BUSINESS STRIKE: Any coin struck with the intention of circulating as money.

CABINET FRICTION: The friction on uncirculated coins attributed to their storage in a collection.

CAMEO-EFFECT: A description of the appearance of certain gold and silver proof coins that have frosty devices on highly polished fields.

CLASHED DIES: Damaged dies caused by the absence of a planchet at the time of striking. Each die retains a portion of its opposite's design, in addition to its own. The resulting coins show a partial impression of the reverse design on the obverse and/or vice versa. Such marks are referred to as clash marks.

CLEANED: A general term referring to cleaning a coin by any method. This often reduces the value and is not recommended.

COIN: A piece of metal with a distinctive design, fixed value, and specific weight and diameter, that was issued by a government as money.

COLLAR: The part of the die which affixes to the edge of the planchet to prevent movement during striking. Reeded edge coins are made by having the collar grooved; 12-sided 5-cent pieces are made by having regular round blanks struck in a 12-sided collar.

COMMEMORATIVE: A coin issued to commemorate a special event or honour an outstanding person.

DEBASEMENT: Debasement of a coin takes place when the issuing authority reduces the purity of the metal, lowering the intrinsic value of the coin but circulating it at par with the previous coins of the originial purity. This happened in Canada in 1968 when the silver content of coins for circulation was replaced entirely with nickel.

DENTICLES: Tooth-like projections running inside the rim of a coin. Used to discourage counterfeiters.

DEVICE: Any design feature appearing on the obverse, reverse or edge of a coin.

DIADEMED: A coin where the portrait head has a headband or fillet as a sign of royalty.

DIE: Engraved metal stamp used to strike the design of a coin, medal or token.

DIE BULGE: A roundish, raised area on a coin caused by the swelling of a die.

DIE CRACK: A raised line appearing on a coin caused by a broken die.

DIE STRIATION: A series of fine, raised and nearly parallel lines resulting from extreme pressure used in the striking of a coin. Occasionally seen on well-struck gem business strikes.

ESSAY: A trial piece from dies already accepted for regular coinage. It may bear a date or mint mark other than on the coins issued for circulation or it may be a different metal.

EXERGUE: The lower part of a coin or medal which is usually divided from the field by a line under which is contained the date, place of minting or engraver's initials.

FIELD: The open areas on either side of a coin not occupied by the portrait, design or inscription.

FIRST-STRIKE: A coin struck from new dies. Usually fully struck and frequently proof-like.

FLAN: See Planchet.

HIGH POINTS: The highest points on the design of a coin. The first points to show wear.

IMPAIRED PROOF: A coin struck as a proof but no longer in mint state.

INCUSE: Coins with either obverse or reverse design sunk below the coin's surface. A design raised above the surface is in relief.

INGOT: A piece of precious metal shaped in a mould. Much of the gold reserves of various nations are stored in ingots and bars.

INTRINSIC: The intrinsic value of a coin is the actual metal value of the coin. Canadian silver coins before 1968 are worth more intrinsically than their face value, while the nickel 10¢, 25¢, 50¢ and $1 coins from 1968 to date are worth less intrinsically than their face value.

IRIDESCENT: A multi-coloured blending or toning, frequently found in older uncirculated coins.

KARAT: The degree of fineness of gold. Pure gold is 24 karats and most gold coins have a fineness of 22 karats

LEGEND: The principal inscription on a coin.

MATTE PROOF: A proof coin for which the planchet is treated in a manner other than polishing. A dull and frosted finish is achieved.

MEDAL: A piece of metal struck to commemorate an historical event or as an award for merit or achievement. Not money.

MINT ERROR: A mis-struck or defective coin produced by a mint.

MINT MARK: A symbol, usually a small letter, used to indicate the mint at which a coin was struck.

MULE: A coin struck from dies not designed to be used together.

OBVERSE: The "face-up" side of the coin, regarded as more important than the reverse side and usually bearing the head or principal design.

OVERDATE: The date made by an engraver at the mint punching one or more numbers on a previously dated die.

OVERSTRIKE: A design impressed with new dies on a previously struck coin already bearing a design.

PATINA: A green or brown surface film frequently found on ancient copper and bronze coins caused by oxidation over a long period of time, also by moisture and certain soils.

PATTERN: Trial piece or proposed design for a coin, generally of a new design, denomination or metal. If the design is adopted for regular coinage with the same date, the piece ceases to be a pattern.

PLANCHET: The blank piece of metal on which the coin design is impressed. Also called a blank, disc or flan.

PLANCHET DEFECT: The general term for any of several types of imperfections on a planchet.

PLANCHET FLAKE: A geometrically shaped depressed area of a coin that occurred in preparation of the planchet.

PRESENTATION PIECE: A coin that was struck for a purpose other than to circulate or to sell to the public; similar to a proof.

PROOF: The highest quality of coins struck for collectors and using specially polished or otherwise prepared dies.

PROOF-LIKE: Quality of choice coins obviously superior to circulation strikes, but whose surfaces are not as bright as those of other specimen coins. Struck using selected dies and planchets and on slower moving presses than for circulation coins.

REEDING: Grooved or serrated lines running vertically around the edge of a coin.

RELIEF: A relief design is one where the lettering and design is raised above the surface of the coin. The opposite of incuse.

RESTRIKE: Any coin struck later than the date appearing on the coin, but from the original dies.

REVERSE: The back or "tails" side of a coin. Opposite from obverse.

RIM: The raised portion around the perimeter of a coin that protects the design from wear.

ROTATED DIE: Dies are positioned and locked on a coining press by means of a key. When these keys come loose, rotation can occur resulting in the next coin being struck with the obverse and reverse dies rotated. Coins struck from rotated dies are errors.

SPECIMEN: A general term applying to any specially produced collectors coin.

TOKEN: Usually a piece of durable material unofficially issued for monetary, advertising, services or other purposes.

TRIAL PIECE: A piece struck at any stage in the preparation of regular dies up to the point of their being put to use for the striking of actual coins.

TYPE: A coin's basic distinguishing design.

UNCIRCULATED: A piece in new condition as issued by a mint.

GLOSSARY

VARIETY: Any alteration in the design of a coin. A major variety is a coin of the same date, mint mark and denomination as another, but struck from another pair of dies and having at least the major device added, removed or redesigned. A minor variety is one with all major devices the same as another, but with some easily recognizable variation.

WIRE EDGE: A sharp rim caused by excessive striking pressure.

NOTES

NOTES

NOTES

Other Titles from our Numismatic Library

The Charlton Standard Catalogue of Canadian Colonial Tokens, *3rd Edition*

A complete guide to the tokens used in Canada between 1794 and 1867. The tokens of Upper Canada, Lower Canada, Prince Edward Island, Nova Scotia, New Brunswick and Newfoundland are all listed and illustrated here, including Canadian blacksmith tokens. Each token is priced and described, including its composition, measurements, date and reference numbers.

272 pages; 5 1/2" x 8 1/2"; softcover; $24.95

The Charlton Standard Catalogue of Canadian Government Paper Money, *9th Edition*

Over 300 years of Canadian paper money. This new edition illustrates and prices all Canadian government paper money from the French colonial issues of 1685 to the current Bank of Canada notes. Army bills, provincial issues, municipal notes, Province of Canada bills, Dominion of Canada issues, special serial numbers and paper money errors are all included.

320 pages; 5 1/2" x 8 1/2"; softcover; $19.95

The Charlton Standard Catalogue of Canadian Bank Notes, *3rd Edition*

More information than in any other book of Canadian bank notes. All the bank notes produced in Canada since the 1700s are in this one easy-to-use, illustrated reference. For this edition a team of numismatic experts has expanded the data and updated the prices.

464 pages; 8 1/2" x 11"; softcover; $59.95

The Charlton Standard Catalogue of Canadian Tire Cash Bonus Coupons, *2nd Edition, by Ross Irwin*

The latest in collectables. Two hundred gas bar and store coupons produced by Canadian Tire since 1958 are described, illustrated and priced in three grades. This catalogue also includes a history of the Canadian Tire Corporation and information on the printing and grading of coupons.

72 pages; 5 1/2" x 8 1/2"; softcover; $14.95

The Charlton Standard Catalogue of Canadian Communion Tokens, *First Edition*

Over 130 years of Canadian communion tokens. From 1770 to the early 1900s, all tokens from Canada West, Canada East and the Maritimes are described, illustrated and priced in this handy catalogue. Also included are communion tokens from Canadian churches in the Caribbean and stock tokens. An introduction provides a history of the use of communion tokens.

288 pages; 5 1/2" x 8 1/2"; softcover; $19.95